T0386107

THE ECOLOGY OF
THE SPOKEN WORD

MICHAEL A. UZENDOSKI AND
EDITH FELICIA CALAPUCHA-TAPUY

THE ECOLOGY OF
THE SPOKEN WORD

Amazonian Storytelling and
Shamanism among the Napo Runa

University of Illinois Press
URBANA, CHICAGO, AND SPRINGFIELD

Acknowledgments for the use of previously published
material appear on page xiv, which constitutes an extension
of the copyright page.

Manufactured in the United States of America
C 5 4 3 2 1
♾ This book is printed on acid-free paper.

Library of Congress Cataloging-in-Publication Data
Uzendoski, Michael, 1968–
The ecology of the spoken word : Amazonian storytelling
and shamanism among the Napo Runa /
Michael A. Uzendoski and Edith Felicia Calapucha-Tapuy.
pages   cm
Includes translations from Quechua.
Includes bibliographical references and index.
ISBN 978-0-252-03656-9 (cloth)
1. Quechua mythology—Napo River Valley (Ecuador and
Peru). 2. Quechua Indians—Napo River Valley (Ecuador
and Peru)—Songs and music. 3. Storytelling—Napo River
Valley (Ecuador and Peru). 4. Shamanism—Napo River Valley
(Ecuador and Peru). I. Calapucha-Tapuy, Edith Felicia.
II. Title.
GR133.E22N378   2012
398.208998'323—dc23   2011047446
ISBN 978-0-252-09360-9 (ebook)

For Donald and Linda Uzendoski
and María Teresa (Beatriz) Tapuy and
Venancio Calapucha, our parents

CONTENTS

PREFACE

Today, the Western pattern of life has brought us on the verge of destroying the planet through climate change and environmental destruction, results of a long historical pattern of dominating, controlling, and abusing "nature." The concept itself of "nature," an ontological category cut off from human culture, reveals the Western insensitivity to the way plants, trees, animals, rocks, mountains, and a myriad of other ecological beings can enrich human life when they are viewed as social partners rather than mere objects for crude exploitation. As this book shows, Amazonian peoples have developed philosophies of life and communicative systems that are not only ecologically sustainable but also intellectually, spiritually, and aesthetically enriching. These systems, which are unappreciated by modern scientists, philosophers, politicians, and development agents, have continued to define life in indigenous Amazonian communities for millennia, despite the historical intrusions of the Europeans: the conquests of the 16th century, systematic colonial oppression and patronage, and more recently the modernization and globalization of the world-system.

The "West"—which brought the current world-system into dominance—is no longer just a geographical region. It is a particular cultural structure of values, norms, symbols, technology, and social relations that has become the dominant pattern of the world order. In our view the West is not an identity and not external to South America or to Ecuador's rainforest region. As a set of values and structures imposed and meant to be imitated (usually though the concept of "development"), there are few cultures in the world that can reproduce themselves without incorporating at least some or many aspects of the Western pattern.

At the end of the world, what Quichua speakers refer to as *izhu punzha* (see chapter 2), will the story of the West, Ecuador, and the rest of the global world-system be one of the rise and fall of a dominating, arrogant system of world destruction? Is it possible for moderns to lose their bigheaded view that they are destined to domineer and abuse all living and existing things without seeing other possible social and communicative possibilities? And will Amazonian peoples and cultures also be destroyed by the Western machine, which, in its drive to extract petroleum, minerals, lumber, and other valuables, is irreversibly altering some of the world's most diverse and sensitive ecological regions?

We do not know the answers to these questions. But if people are looking for other ways of thinking and relating to the world, speakers of the world's dominating languages can indeed learn much from the wisdom and social philosophies of life embedded in Amazonian storytelling and poetic practices. Compared to the industrial world's ideology of machine-driven "naturalism," which sees the world as a vast storehouse of resources and living things meant to be extracted and converted into things and money, the Amazonian way of life discussed in this book defines the human condition through a greater sensitivity and aesthetic sense of our relatedness to all things, including death and its relationship to new life. This humility, this interconnectedness, this grounding, and the liberation it provides to the soul, is the secret wisdom embedded in the stories and songs that follow.

ACKNOWLEDGMENTS

We would not have been able to complete this project without the help of many individuals and institutions. First of all we must thank the National Science Foundation and the "Documenting Endangered Languages" Program, which provided funding for both fieldwork and data analysis associated with this project (Award 0755628, "Documenting and Archiving Napo *Quichua* Verbal Art"). We also thank Florida State University for a timely and necessary sabbatical period, without which this book would have never been finished. We thank the FSU Libraries and International Programs, the Fulbright Program, and the Facultad Latinoamericano de Ciencias Sociales (FLACSO) of Ecuador.

We are most indebted to the storytellers and musicians in this book, who, through some connection of blood, marriage, or residence, are part of our *ayllu*, our family or extended family. We name all of them here: Lucas Tapuy (deceased), Fermin Shiguango, Federico Calapucha, Verna Grefa, Camilo Tapuy, Gerardo Bolivar Andi, Gervacio Cerda, Jacinta Andi, Serafina Shiguango and Vicente Calapucha (both deceased), Anibal Andy (el Ductur), and our compadre Carlos Alvarado as well as his musical group, "Los Yumbos Chawamangos." We thank the families and communities of these amazing people and are grateful for their permission to make their talents public.

This book is only part of a larger effort to archive and circulate Quichua stories as well as create more awareness about storytelling and Amazonian Quichua verbal arts. In Ecuador we were able to create a digital archive of stories and songs for Quichua students, and we must thank Blas Chimbo of the

Dirección Intercultural Bilingüe de Napo and Nancy Andi, the director of the Intercultural Bilingual School Venancio Calapucha of Pano, for their support in this endeavor. We thank all of the professors at the school in Pano, all of whom provided lots of help and assistance with this project, especially Natalia Tapuy, who transcribed many of the speech acts and stories. For almost two years, this humble and underfunded school was the social and logistic center of the project and our personal lives. Not only did our daughter attend this school for first grade and half of second grade, but in addition Michael was given the opportunity to share all of the stories in this book with the students during the 2009–2010 school year in the capacity of a volunteer instructor. This opportunity provided numerous insights into the social dynamics of stories and their role in the lives of children. In this vein, we must thank all of the children who contributed illustrations of their mythology for the website and for sharing with us their enthusiasm and energy for storytelling and life in general. Also, the Ecuadorian side of our project has been helped by Joel Sherzer and Heidi Johnson of the Archive of Indigenous Languages of Latin America (AILLA). They assisted in the creation of the Napo Quichua collection of AILLA, which contains dozens of Napo Quichua stories and songs that will be accessible to future generations of Quichua speakers after we are gone.

Our intellectual debts are too many and run too deep for us to really be able to do them justice, but we will try. First, we thank Dell and Virginia Hymes, who introduced Michael to verse analysis at the University of Virginia and who helped us work through our first attempt at translating Napo Quichua narrative. We also thank Dennis Tedlock, who inspired us to use our ears, and Edith Turner, who inspired us to use our bodies and to feel the reality and power of the storytelling and spirit worlds. Juan Carlos Galeano has been a faithful Amazonian *hermano* over the years and has helped us to see that poetry is more than words on a page: a way of life, a mode of perception. Joel Sherzer has always been a presence in our work as well as Greg Urban, Jonathan Hill, Michael Jackson, and Alex King. We thank Eduardo Viveiros de Castro for perspectivism and Neil Whitehead for his work on indigenous historicity. The philosopher Edward Casey's notion of "place" and other work on place theory has been influential. We thank Janis Nuckolls for helping Michael to realize this book was about communication rather than language and for her incredible work on ideophone and "evidentials" in Amazonian Quichua. Norman Whitten has provided enduring support and continues to produce insightful publications for us to draw on. We also thank Dorothea Whitten for her work with ceramics and Amazonian Quichua aesthetics. Ethnomusicology has also been a big influence, and our good friend Dale

Olsen, as well as legions of his students who have taken Michael's classes, have all done much to help us to appreciate and understand music in relation to storytelling. In this regard, we must thank Mark Hertica, who had the original breakthrough of the Iluku complex and who provides the audio recording of the bird's song for the website. Denise Arnold and Juan de Dios Yapita were major figures in our thinking; they helped us to see textuality in a whole new way and to understand the regimes of power that define writing. We are also inspired by the creative "lines" approach of Timothy Ingold, Eduardo Kohn's "anthropology of life," and Roy Wagner's use of figure-ground reversals. Our thinking has been shaped by Frederick Damon's course on economic anthropology and Marshall Sahlin's work on culture—these ideas are at the root of our thinking about forms, systems, and value. We both thank George Mentore at Virginia for his constant encouragement and intellectual energy. We thank Carmen Martínez of FLACSO for her insightful work on inter-cultural bilingual education and her help with many other things. We also thank Fernando García, Eduardo Kingman, Fernando Hinojosa, Luz Maria de la Torre, Carmen Chuquín, Julie Williams, Sharimiat Shiguango, Joseph Hellweg, Robinson Herrera, Syed Ali, Nelson Chimbo, Tod Swanson, and Steven Rubenstein.

We are especially grateful to our family in Sapo Rumi and to Federico, Esteban, Lydia, Salomne, Galo, Faviola, Gerarado and María Teresa, María, Klever, Tío Gobierno, Kiricha, Tía Carmela, Comadre Clemencia, and Tim-belo, as well as to all of the children, our nieces and nephews who are the future of the place. We thank Estuardo (Pájaro Loco), Jaime Calapucha, and the Shiguango family from Campo-Cocha, who hosted Michael when he first came to Ecuador. We remain indebted to Edith's father Venancio Santiago Calapucha, Carola, and many other people in Pano. We also thank Michael's parents, Don and Linda, for their support and understanding throughout these years of research, travel, and study, and for making the effort to become part of our world in Ecuador. We also thank Kerry and Kathy, Michael's sisters, for their support.

There are countless other Quichua people who have assisted us in acts of kindness or who provided details and information about Quichua culture and storytelling. We are sorry for not mentioning your individual names, but we are grateful for your help. *Ashka pagarachu runakuna.*

We are grateful to Dr. Alfredo Jijón of Hospital Metropolitano of Quito, who delivered our son, and for the help of many others in Ecuador who at-tended to our health problems and needs.

We must lastly acknowledge our debt to Joan Catapano of the University of Illinois Press, who helped move the book along from a proposal into a manuscript, and who kept our work moving when we needed it most. We also thank Daniel Nasset for picking up the project and for helping it along in the final stages, as well as Malcom Shackelford, who designed the companion website. We are very grateful to Jane Curran's eye for detail and for the amazing job she did with the text, but any mistakes you will find must be attributed to us.

Sources

An earlier version of chapter 1 appeared as "Somatic Poetry in Amazonian Ecuador" in *Anthropology and Humanism* 33(1/2):12–29, 2008. Used by permission of the American Anthropological Association.

An earlier version of chapter 2 appeared as "The Primordial Flood of *Izhu*: An Amazonian Quichua Myth-Narrative" in *Latin American Indian Literatures Journal* 21 (1):1–20, 2005. Used with permission.

An earlier version of chapter 3 was presented at the American Anthropological Association Meetings in San Francisco (2008) for the session "Symbolic Affinities, Pragmatic Engagements: Shaping Latin American Ethnology through the Collaborative Work of Norman and Dorothea Scott Whitten."

An earlier version of chapter 4 appeared as "The Phenomenology of Perspectivism: Aesthetics, Sound, and Power in Women's Songs from Amazonian Ecuador," by Michael A. Uzendoski, Mark Hertica, and Edith Calapucha-Tapuy, in *Current Anthropology* 46(4):656–662, 2005. Used with permission.

An earlier version of chapter 5 appeared as Michael A. Uzendoski, "Twins and Becoming Jaguars: Verse Analysis of a Napo Quichua Myth Narrative" in *Anthropological Linguistics* 41(4):431–461, 1999. Used with permission.

THE ECOLOGY OF
THE SPOKEN WORD

WHAT IS STORYTELLING?

I n this book, which takes advantage of digital technology in addition to the printed word, we present a theoretical and experiential translation of Napo Runa mythology and music.[1] One of our goals is to translate myths and songs so that readers can get a better appreciation for the beauty and complexity of Amazonian Quichua poetic expressions. While artful translation is one of our primary tasks, we are equally committed to articulating Napo Runa performative practices in terms of more complex issues related to what storytelling can teach us about language, communication, culture, and experience. As the reader will see, for the people who are the subject of this book, life is conceptualized as a journey in which experience and mythological realities converge. Experience, as we will argue, is the lifeblood of the storytelling world.

What is storytelling? We define storytelling as the complex whole of telling stories, artful descriptions of and about life that involve past, present, and future happenings, happenings that also including mythological transformations and experiences. Storytelling, as we discuss, involves multiple genres and musical and ritual performances, as well as narratives about the past, present, and future. But what really defines storytelling is that stories are conveyed in gatherings, in communities of people that share in a social tradition and culturally defined way of perceiving the world. Stories, as we show, entail moments of epiphany and communitas as people achieve the feeling of mythological truths becoming one with the destiny of the community.

Storytelling is a facet of human existence that, when explored deeply and socially, tells us significant things about the pragmatics of daily life, including experiential realities. Values, social assumptions about life and death, language and communication, traces and inscriptions of the past, perceptions of time and space, and memory and history are all congealed within the stories that people tell to themselves and to others. Stories are not just static representations of beliefs or cultural ideas. Stories, as we show, are central to the processes by which culture itself is created and practiced.

The stories in this book provide insight into Native Amazonian ways of thinking and being in the world, but, as we illustrate, translating the stories of any cultures is difficult, perhaps impossible to do only through words.[2] Indeed, one of our main arguments is that the words, especially those captured through recordings or transcriptions, are only a small part of a total storytelling reality. Storytelling is a complex aesthetic and social whole that is constituted through experience, the senses, imagery, music, and implicit social and ecological knowledge, as well as words.

Like many other indigenous peoples, Quichua speakers create meanings through language and other practices that do not correspond to the communicative or social assumptions of Western culture. For Quichua speakers, plants, animals, and the landscape are part of a much wider communicative landscape where messages circulate among all living—including plants, trees, and animals—and some nonliving beings. Language itself is but part of a larger, more diverse communicative world that includes the sentient sociality and subjectivities of the vegetable and animal worlds as well as the landscape. The communicative field, in other words, is much wider and more diverse than just the human domain. Stories, as we will demonstrate, provide rich material that can help one make sense of how such relations are conceptualized and created in the living reality of experience.

There are serious theoretical implications to this work because storytelling, as we demonstrate, informs current discussions about the nature of language—including current debates about writing versus orality—and their relationship to culture. Following the work of Paul Friedrich (1989, 1996, 2001, 2006), Dell Hymes (2003), Virginia Hymes (1992), Dennis Tedlock (1983, 1985), Dennis Tedlock and Bruce Mannheim (1995), Jerome Rothenberg (1968, 1994), Michael Jackson (1989, 1995, 1996, 1998), Ruth Finnegan (2007), Janis Nuckolls (2010), Greg Urban (1991), Richard Bauman and Charles Briggs (1990), Joel Sherzer (1983, 2003), Bruce Mannheim (1991, 1998), John Miles Foley (2002), Stephen Feld and Aaron Fox (1994)—and numerous others—we position ourselves within the field of ethnopoetics, a multicultural, interdisciplinary approach that takes narratives, music, and other diverse forms of poetic forms of expression as its main subject and inspiration. The "ethno" refers to "humanity" in its broadest possible sense, while "poetics" refers to the complex forms of beauty that define poetry, oral narratives, musical performances, and storytelling among the world's diverse cultures. Ethnopoetics also includes ethnographic poetry, poetry inspired by the cultural or historical beauty of distant places and peoples (Friedrich 2006; Galeano 2000), as well as overlaps with ethnomusicology. In ethnopoetics no artistic tradition is considered superior or more advanced than any other. Appreciating the poetic traditions of many of the world's cultures requires rethinking fundamental Western assumptions about language and communication in general.

For example, we approach the semiotic complexities of storytelling as performative practices that engender a different conceptualization of communication, and also language, where the distinction between writing and orality becomes muddled. As we show, Quichua storytellers use words and language, but also other semiotic modes (gestures, ideophones, musicality), to create multidimensional works of art whereby a telling is simultaneously a reading of already inscribed meanings found within the landscape and one's experience of the Amazonian world.

Our research also provides compelling examples of the intimacy among language, culture, and aesthetics among Native Amazonian peoples (Nuckolls 2010:3). Culture and aesthetics are usually regarded as tangential to the core areas of language study (phonetics, phonology, morphology, syntax, and semantics), but Amazonian Quichua people consider artful expression a necessary ingredient for quality living. Much of the poetry of Amazonian Quichua storytelling derives from culturally patterned aesthetic practices, practices that include multiple modes of expression. Here we must go beyond language and imagine the full richness of Amazonian communication and its relation to experience. Amazonian communicative practices are a complex whole that includes music, gestures, imagery, bodily kinesthetics, mimesis, ecological perceptions, and ideophones. These expressive modes are not tangential to discourse but rather are part of a more complex communicative competency that allows speakers to enrich speech through complex image-forms (Nuckolls 1996, 2000, 2010). As we show, these diverse ways of creating imagery are central to Amazonian Quichua communicative practices and a defining feature of storytelling and musical performances.

For example, a book by Brian Rotman (2008:21) has discussed how the dominant theories of communication have viewed gesticulatory activity as an "unnecessary addendum to utterance," a trivial mode of expression. Rotman challenges this assumption to show that gestures achieve semiotic tasks that define many communicative acts by working in relation to words, but how gestures work together with language (and other communicative modes) is not much studied. Of the many gestures discussed by Rotman (2008:21–22) are the (1) iconographic, (2) kinetographic or miming, (3) beat gestures, (4) contrastive pairs, and (5) experiential gestures. There are also "gestures of the voice," the "audible body movements which operate inside speech: gestures which constitute the voice itself" (23). In Rotman's view, the communicative world is grounded in the body and its multiple capacities for expressiveness. Language, as demonstrated, is not supracorporeal but only one part of a larger multimodal whole of bodily communication.

Rotman's arguments build upon a larger body of anthropological linguistic research dealing with gestures. Such scholars as Duranti and Goodwin (1992), Goodwin (2007), Enfield (2001), Haviland (2000, 2004), Kendon (1972, 1980, 1997, 2004), Farnell (1999), and McNeill (1992, 2000, 2005) have brought attention to the complex ways that the expressive body is integral rather than superficial to language in communicative acts. In *Hand and Mind* (1992) McNeill demonstrates that gestures occur "in exact synchrony with the spoken words they relate to" (Rotman 2002:95), revealing the common origins of somatic and mental expressiveness. As McNeill (1992:2) specifies, "gestures are an integral part of language, as much as are words, phrases, and sentences—gesture and language are one system." We can see, thus, that the dominant view of language, one that views gestures and the body as superficial to language, already limits our understanding of the body's communicative potency (Cassell and McNeill 1991).[3]

Among modernized, dominant language–speaking populations, as in the English-speaking world, there is a lack of appreciation for how communication is organized and practiced in other cultures where gestures and various semiotic modes of expression are not left in the ideological wake of alphabetic writing and a narrow view of language.[4] Today, even the West's "lettered self" is changing in response to people redefining themselves through digital technologies and virtual networks rather than traditional texts and their monolithic incantations (Abram 1996:273–274; Rotman 2008; Wesch 2009). Despite the changes, it remains to be seen how far digital technologies and their associated practices will go in transforming Western philosophical and social assumptions about communication and language. Certainly some will use technology to serve the ends of the lettered empire rather than liberate and explore other forms and practices of textuality.

A recurrent theme in the literature on gesture discusses the role of the body in drawing "lines" of connectedness within space and the local environment, "lines' that are interwoven with the complex meanings created by speech (Haviland 2000; Goodwin 2007). Joining these scholars' concerns with the self's embeddedness in spatiotextual networks, we invite readers to consider a whole new approach for communication, one in which experience, poetics, language, and textuality are rethought and freshly considered from the communicative potency of the body. As we show, in Native Amazonian cultures, the body has an amazing capacity to create communicative worlds that are complex, poetic, and emotionally fulfilling to the humans that create and live in them.

Following these lines of thought, we set out to demonstrate that storytelling, an oral medium of expression, is not without its own forms of textuality (Arnold and Yapita 2006; Derrida 1967; Hanks 1989; Finnegan 2007; Clifford 1986:117). As we detail, Amazonian textuality is rooted in practices by which people inscribe meanings using a variety of substrates and threads that go through and are linked to the body's social and cosmic qualities, qualities by which people embody the realities of the storytelling world (Ingold 2007). This emphasis on the body's power and capacities, which has been described in detail in many studies about the Amazonian world (Vilaça 2005, 2009; Viveiros de Castro 1998, 2001; T. Turner 1995), is the vital energy that moves storytelling, music, and many other daily practices. Because of this emphasis on the body's capacity for aesthetic expression, we theorize Amazonian Quichua storytelling generally as a somatic poetry, an ethnopoetics of the body and its expressiveness in the world.

As we illustrate, Amazonian somatic poetry derives from the power of the human voice and the body's presence, both of which have a social and phenomenological power that surpasses the efficacy ascribed to the body's presence in modern Western cultures, cultures in which print and mechanical reproduction are dominant communicative modes (Ingold 2007). In Amazonia, the body and its presence have multiple capacities to elicit imaginative and social relations with people as well as with the larger ecological and spiritual world. Stories are social acts that explore the aesthetics of bodily experiences and potentialities, potentialities that are grounded in a rich communicative and sentient landscape of people, plants, rivers, trees, animals, insects, and other socialities.

In addition to their imaginative and relational power, stories also cultivate feelings and emotional qualities that draw people out of themselves and into a circularity of relations with others and the landscape they inhabit. Storytelling is how Amazonian Quichua people create, define, and feel—as well as think—the social, ecological, and spiritual realities of their world, the community of social and cosmological relations that defines them. And all of these expressions and performative modes are socially recognized as culturally salient processes of production, ways of creating relations and experiencing spiritual realities that are just as real as material things to the people that live them.

Communicative Hegemony, Orality, and Textuality

As Finnegan (2007) has noted, the storytelling practices of many cultures have been studied and analyzed by Western scholars in ways that repeatedly mark their "primitiveness" in contrast to the more "civilized" practices of the West. In this, our study of storytelling, we follow Finnegan in insisting on the need for a more nuanced appreciation of the communicative realities of other cultures, one that strives to erase "the difference between savagery and civilization by applying the same methods and conceptual language to both" (Rubenstein 2007:359; Latour 1993:100–103). Part of the problem is that tropes of primitiveness and savagery are often implied or elicited through the very categories of English assumptions about communication that are used to describe and frame the communicative realities of other cultures. Many studies about "orality," for example, do not even address the issue of language or communicative differences and proceed to define the communicative realties of others as if the categories of a dominant language were universal, natural, and more adaptive. But as the materials in this book show, communicative realities are not all the same.

In the literature about storytelling cultures, for example, the emphasis on orality and its previousness to writing, implicitly (often through coded language that appears analytic) signify a lack of civilization, a backwardness associated with so-called primitivism. The hegemony of Western communicative practices is tied up in assumptions about orality and the need to put other communicative systems within the conceptual space of what Michel-Rolph Trouillet (1995) has termed "the savage slot," a linear way of thinking in which the Western world uses language and narratives to define others as implicitly backward in time and inferior in status. The story the West continues to tell itself is that of its so-called civilizing capacity, the white man's burden, that of being more "developed" or advanced than the world's other cultures.

Western communicative hegemony is based on the orality-literacy distinction and the notion that orality is both previous to and inferior to writing. Walter Ong (1982), one of the most celebrated literary scholars of "orality," struggled to understand what it might be like to live in a world defined by orality, a world without alphabetic writing and without the technologies of literacy. In a taped lecture, "Writing Is a Technology That Restructures Consciousness," Walter Ong poses the question of how life might be if one did not have access to printed documents, where one "never looked anything up"—a world supposedly without texts.[5] Ong speculated how strange such a way of living would be and developed a hypothetical model termed "primary oral cultures," cultures that lack the technology of literacy, texts, and writing.[6]

In this model, primary oral cultures, although interesting to think about, are technologically, socially, and intellectually inferior to cultures of "literacy." Literacy is a more advanced and superior philosophy of communication, one that permits development in the Western sense of material and scientific advancement.[7]

Such a theoretical position, one that implicitly ranks "orality" as inferior to "literacy" (Ong 1967, 1982), is a good example of how Western communicative hegemony is considered to be natural and self-evident, for Ong's ideas resonate with the Western narrative of self-superiority via technology, machines (Hornborg 2001), and language. Ong's neo-evolutionary way of thinking is shared by some anthropologists. Jack Goody (1968, 1977, 2000), for example, has followed an Ongian line of thought informed by extensive fieldwork in Africa. What these theories share is that they prioritize the Western theory of communication, a theory that weights the linguistic theory of language and its relationship to technology as the pinnacle of human achievement.

Research has showed how the orality-literacy distinction has been linked to the rise of capitalism, Western metaphysics, colonialism, nationalism, and modern forms of power (Foucault 1975; Derrida 1967; Anderson 1983). In this sense, David Guss's discussion of Yekuana views of "literacy" are relevant, for they provide us with a powerful critique of the Western theory of communication from the perspective of a so-called primary oral culture, a culture that supposedly lives without "texts" or complex analytical thought.

The Yekuana, who subscribe to a mythological view of the world, see real "power" (which for them is spiritual) as deriving from the invisible realm of soul doubles, which all things possess. These assumptions about the world are embodied in their culture hero Wanandi, who represents power and the good life in the Yekuana view of things. Wanandi, however, has a brother named Odosha, and unlike Wanandi, Odosha has been deceived by the forces of darkness and illusion. In the Yekuana mythological complex, darkness and illusion—embodied by Odosha—are associated with the European conquest, Venezuelan colonialism, and Western materialism, while good is associated with Wanandi and Yekuana culture. In this dynamic reality, which we can read as a critique of Western civilization, the Yekuana view literacy as just another manifestation of Western materialism and Odosha's ability to deceive people (Guss 1986). Real power, as Guss is able to show, lies in Wanandi's teachings, which are centered around the Yekuana's own forms of textuality: weaving, gardening, house-making, and other social practices of inscription that involve orality (Guss 1989).

Yekuana mythology, thus, is a complex that provides a rich comparative critique of Western communicative hegemony.[8] While literacy defines the colonial Western communicative philosophy, the Yekuana live out a different communicative philosophy defined by their own notions of textuality. These relations are embodied by Wanandi, who, in his own way, "deconstructs" the Western communicative regime. The anthropologist David Guss (1986:426), for example, writes, "The Yekuana, in acknowledging the primacy of literacy in the creation of a more advanced technology, are not concluding, as have Goody and others, that this technology has resulted in greater power. Their elaboration of this chain of events has been done to demonstrate the reverse: to show how literacy, and particularly sacred literacy, has led to a direct diminishment of power." In other words, for the Yekuana, "literacy" (in the Western sense) represents an extension of colonial psychology and hegemony, a political project of Western materialism. Yekuana notions of textuality, embodied by Wanandi, are counter to Western assumptions of communication because they involve different value forms that structure what counts as the good life. These Yekuana notions of textuality, and the discourses that accompany them, work back upon Western hegemonic forms as "counterpower" (Graeber 2004.35–37; see also D. Whitten and N. Whitten 2008:256), a way of reorienting perception so that the assumptions of the colonial order are reversed (see chapter 8).

Ruth Finnegan (2007) has concluded that the West has used its assumptions about communication (and specifically language) to construct a hegemonic complex that explains away much of the richness of other expressive systems as inferior. She writes: "The linguistically driven narrative . . . presents a profoundly evocative and compelling account. Europe fulfils the foreordained human destiny through its attainment of writing, and above all print, buttressed by the successes of modernising science and rationality to which this led. Human history is to read through the glass of language and its technologies" (Finnegan 2007:205). Just as many grand theories of early anthropology reflected Western assumptions about "civilization" and how people ought to live, so too does the notion of orality's inferiority to writing reflect Western hegemony in communication. The fiction of orality without textuality tells us more about the stuff of Western thinking about others than how people in other cultures view and express themselves.

The philosopher Jacques Derrida, perhaps more radically and powerfully than any other scholar in the Western world, has challenged the implicit ethnocentrisms of Western philosophy that are concentrated within the very notion of "literacy." Derrida, in his book, *Of Grammatology* (1967), traces the origins of writing to the origins of language itself, but this is a difficult point for many modern people to accept; they are invested in their literacy and their superiority of being alphabetically literate. When one considers the possibility that writing is culturally and historically constituted, then language and communication become political propositions. Writing and literacy are social assumptions that dominate most Western people's lives and that should be extended and imposed on others. Other ways of living are unimaginable.

In our reading of Derrida (1967), it is socially liberating and revolutionary to see language itself as concurrent with writing. Indeed, a whole host of socially meaningful distinctions become irrelevant: the social distinction between literate and illiterate people, the categorical difference between writing and art, the opposition of "text" to "real life," and lastly the opposition of the voice with inscription. In following Derrida's line of thought, people who use the voice also make patterned encryptions of meaning, if not on "paper" then on cave walls, ceramics, the ground, the body, and in cultural practices that include ritual and storytelling.

As we show, it is not possible for human beings to live in purely "oral" worlds, worlds without inscription or textuality. Furthermore, it is methodologically unsound to continue to theorize generally about "orality" as if were the same in all times and places. "Orality," one aspect of the semiotic expressiveness of a culture, is not the same everywhere, for oral expressiveness involves specific cultural assumptions about the voice, sound, the body, and textuality. The power of culture is that it can organize and create systems of communication, systems that are philosophically and aesthetically different from those that define the Western world.

Understanding the semiotic complexities of Quichua communication and storytelling, we argue, reveals that Derrida (1967) helps a great deal in exposing the ethnocentric theory of language behind Western philosophy. We follow Derrida in seeing the critique of language as necessarily based on the critique of the orality-literacy distinction, on redefining writing as synonymous with language itself. We point out, however, that Derrida's insights do not develop a critique of communication from the practices of other cultures and their capacity to engender alternate visions and social practices.

It is here that our detailed ethnography enters the scene, in direct articulation with the radical Derridan idea that there is no human system of language and communication that does not also inscribe. We show the reader how a contemporary, living, community of real people creates inscriptions and "lines" of meaning in ways philosophically and semiotically distinct from how things are practiced in the West. As we show, Amazonian Quichua storytelling practices can only be understood in the context of a complex and multidimensional whole, one that is inseparable from the vocal and textual presence of rainforests, rivers, and other beings that delineate an inscribed landscape of community, memory, and power.

But unlike Derrida (1967), we do not refer to these practices as "writing" but rather as "textuality" and "somatic poetry" so as to leave some conceptual space for the elaboration of cultural differences and aesthetic sensibilities. For the categories of the aesthetic communicative world of Quichua speakers are not easily replicated in other languages, and English must be creatively employed in the process of trying to describe Quichua communicative realities. No term, no gloss can really capture the essence of what Amazonian Quichua speakers do with their communicative practices and through their poetic traditions. So we work various angles and provide different perspectives on what is a complex and rich experiential world, a world where words are only part of the story.

Amazonian Communication and Perspectivism

Stories in the Amazonian world are often referred to as "myths," and although we call them "stories," the practices we describe here have complex mythological as well as aesthetic qualities. As Lawrence Sullivan (1988:22) has argued, myth conveys a "religious reality," a quality of "imaginal existence" that defines human landscapes. For the people who use it and live by it, these works are texts whose social and cultural meanings are inscribed upon the landscape, the body, and upon material objects. Following Arnold and Yapita (2006:8), we conceptualize mythological storytelling as creating a textual regime, an alternative system of textuality that overlaps with alphabetic literacy and newer forms of technological literacy such as computers, audio, and video (see chapter 4).

Like other indigenous peoples of Amazonia, Amazonian Quichua-speaking people see the world as a place where all living things, including stones and other features of the landscape, can metamorphose into different kinds of corporeal forms. All of these forms share a common soul substance that circulates throughout the world (Descola 1992; 1996a). These principles can be contrasted with the Western ontology of naturalism, where society and nature are divided by a clear social boundary (Descola 1996a). In Amazonia there are social and communicative relations between natural beings and human beings. "Nature" is a social domain full of subjectivities, sexuality, and human qualities, so much so that to call it "nature" is to distort how Native Amazonian peoples inhabit landscapes and relate to the things in their world.[9]

The Brazilian anthropologist Eduardo Viveiros de Castro (1998) is the main proponent of a theory called "perspectivism," which describes these relations of humanity and "nature" in Amazonian societies in a very synthetic but also abstract way (see also Arhem 1993). Perspectivism is the idea that all living things, and some inanimate things too, possess "souls," subjectivity, and communicative intentionality, a complex field of social relations in which messages, energy, and stories circulate among human and nonhuman beings alike (Fausto 2007). Perspectivism is an Amazonian theory of the body in which perception and communication are grounded in the necessity of all things to speak from a specific bodily perspective. Part of the richness of Amazonian communicative culture is that different corporeal states require different modes of communication, but the body is never static; it is always changing, transforming, metamorphosing (Vilaça 2005, 2009). People and other beings can transform their bodies, and in transforming they can acquire new communicative, social, and even magical abilities.

The action and experience of bodily refashioning is a common philosophy of life, a religious way of looking at the world that is shared by most Amazonian peoples. Vilaça (2002:351) emphasizes this religious quality when she writes: "What enables the permutability of the body is precisely the equivalence of spirits: all are equally human, equally subjects. By modifying the body alimentation, change in habits, and the establishment of social relations with other subjects, another point of view is acquired: the world is now seen in the same way as the new companions, that is, the member of the other species." The key point here is that by modifying the body, one takes on a new experiential point of view of that of another species or living being in the world. In such practices, communication extends beyond the just human and involves sharing messages with other living and nonliving subjectivities.[10]

Acquiring a new bodily perspective, a new species point of view, however, is almost impossible to explain because such transformations are grounded in experience and are not part of a doctrine or theology. How, for example, can a book translate for the English-speaking reader what it is like to experience the world as a plant, bird, or a jaguar? We can try to describe how Quichua speakers feel their metamorphoses, but the only way to truly know it is to experience them.

One strategy is to study the aesthetic practices of Amazonian peoples, for perspectivism, as we show, is congealed within the poetic and musical traditions of the Amazonian world. Storytellers, artists, and musicians produce artistic texts that demonstrate and manifest the lived reality of perspectivism, as many stories and songs feature multiple voices and bodily perspectives, such as grandmother Jactina, for example, turning into a dove and singing to the world from a musically elicited bird perspective (see chapter 4) or Verna invoking the subjectivity of Chiuta Mountain through a combination of gestures and ideophones (see chapter 2). Communicating perspectivist relations require multiple expressive competencies, competencies that draw on the body's power to invoke textuality. As we detail, unlike Western notions of textuality, the texts in the Amazonian world must be continually co-created by performer and audience, and the text itself is never finished, nor is it a strictly human endeavor. The text extends back to the beginning of time and forward into the future, and creating and recreating the text is part of the productive process of making social relations. Storytelling is about the continual communicative relatedness shared by all living and existing things.

Translation and Place

A major challenge to translators of stories and music is that the cultural categories of the more dominant language (English in this case) impinge upon the translation and recontextualize the original as something "foreign." A translation can be recognized as very good but still frame the source "text" in a way whereby the original context and genre are severely distorted. Whereas the very idea of translation itself implies communicative equivalence between two different languages, the underlying reality is that translation usually involves incommensurate cultural categories (Sakai 2006:71–72).

We bring up these problems, and the incommensurability among communicative systems, because they make our task of trying to translate Quichua stories very difficult. Mediating English and Quichua realities is not easy, for these language systems are connected to different philosophies of being in the world. For example, we feel these differences when we return from Ecuador to the United States and experience a sudden change from living in our home in the Amazonian-Quichua world to the North American English-speaking world. Not only does our place change, our "selves" feel as if they change too, as new possibilities and dependencies arise in our relatedness to all things around us. Because the bulk of our relatedness to place is somatic and experiential, language is but a mere part of the way people become defined by living in a locale. We can translate words, but it is impossible to convey the whole of the "crudity of experience," to borrow a phrase from the philosopher William James (1967:135), of living in any one place (see chapter 7).

While speaking Amazonian Quichua, for example, the world looks, feels, and sounds more perspectivist and fluid—full of vital energies that influence and play on human consciousness and actions—rather than mechanical, technological, and commercialized (Hornborg 2001). In the Quichua world, the mind-body dualism of Cartesian thought dissipates, the body becomes more powerful and sentient, our ecological surroundings come alive socially and pragmatically, and nonlinear mystical realities, mainly dreams, become part of everyday life.

Place, the philosophy of being connected deeply and intimately to a locale or region (Cruikshank 2005; Casey 1993, 1997, 2001), is one way of conceptualizing these differences, as communication, language, and culture are aspects of the human condition that are intimately tied to place. Edward Casey, the well-known philosopher of this subject, has explored place in numerous publications and books as one of the defining problems of Western philosophy. Casey has consistently showed how modernity's regulation and control of geographical relations have created alienation from place. He calls this alienation the rise of "space," a process of social abstraction in which experience and relatedness are rendered unimportant to other priorities, such as state power, economics, administration, and politics, which take over and define local geographies.

Consider, for example, the social and political processes that are unleashed when a state transforms a living social landscape of place relations into the economic flows of space (Ingold 2007). The shift toward space now threatens many Napo Runa communities, which are located within the national geography and project of intensifying petroleum extraction. This spatial geography emphasizes the social relations and flows of the capitalist market, flows that can be traced by following the growth of underground pipelines, petroleum wells, and roads. These transformations are fueled by the power of capital but are organized by a politics of "development." The threat upon the environment is not just natural. It is social, cultural, and linguistic. To use a Napo Runa metaphor, petroleum threatens to damage "the body," which, in Quichua thinking, flows into and through the land, trees, rivers, and local ecology.

Casey (2001) argues that place, the meaningful world in which we live, is a means of entextualization, an entextualization that defines the self and that works through the body. He writes, "Because we have a body and are ensconced in a landscape, place and self alike are enriched and sustained, enabling us to become enduring denizens of the place-world to which we so fatefully belong" (689). The relation here is not one of cause and effect but of internal relatedness, one in which each aspect of being—the body, the landscape, place, and self—are part of a complex whole that shapes and defines how people experience and perceive the world they inhabit. Most striking is Casey's insistence that, in the broad perspective of the human condition, humans are meant to be grounded and entextualized, not just to each other, but also to the locale and region in which they are rooted.

The problem of the place and its relationship to the self is a crucial but often unexamined aspect of storytelling, for in many cultures groundedness and growth are root metaphors in the way the world is organized. This is certainly the case among Quichua speakers, whose notions of time and space, or should we say time and place, are linked to cycles of plant growth, maturation, death, and new growth. Like plants, humans follow these same cycles and are rooted in *allpa*, the earth, which defines temporal and spatial deixis. In Quichua as well, time and place are not separated, as a temporal moment is always also a material reality, an experience of what Quichua speakers term *pacha*, which means "time" and "world," as well as "earth." As William Hurtado de Mendoza (2002:72) has argued, Quechua (Quichua) speakers see the past (*ñawpa*) as a "seed," the present (*kunan*) as "the fruit," and the future (*washa*) as a new "seed." Implicit in this temporal unfolding, however, is the notion that time occurs within place, within *allpa*, the landscape of one's historical and future relatedness. There is no reality that is not part of place, and like plants, humans grow, mature, die, and reproduce within locales of species rich cohabitation.

These implicit forms make translating Quichua stories into English problematic and almost impossible. How can one translate stories if basic notions of self, world, and communicative categories are not the same in the source and target languages? Indeed, given these differences and challenges, a perfect translation of Amazonian stories is not possible.

Our translation strategy, however, is not to provide the reader with the sense of a perfect translation but rather a good translation. A good translation, in our view, must go beyond just words to address the textuality of place and the way the self is defined in the other culture, Amazonian Quichua in this case, through their own communicative notions and practices. The cultural and social constitutedness of storytelling, and its place-context, are just as much a part of the story as the stories themselves. By providing information about the way stories relate and are related to place, self, communication, and sociality, we hope that readers will gain a deeper appreciation for the way stories shape perception, create relations, and invoke feelings for the people who inhabit the storytelling world.

In conveying Napo Quichua storytelling realities, we draw on anthropological and ethnopoetics theory to help describe cultural differences and to bring to attention the problems of intercultural translation. Without the use of theory, readers might fall back into their own assumptions about orality and textuality and, in the end, learn little about Amazonian philosophies and practices of communication. Our use of theory, however, has a specific purpose in that we are attempting to use theory to provide a perspective that will do justice to the complexity of relations and experience that defines the Napo Quichua storytelling world. Theory, in other words, is a part of the process of attempting to translate stories—stories, as we show, must be given context in the larger anthropological perspective of differences, cultural embeddedness, power relations, and fields of social action. Without theory, stories and other cultural information would slide into the West's "savage slot," thus undermining the point of translation itself—to better understand another culture's achievements and contributions. Theory and poetics are complementary practices.

Verse-Analysis, the Spoken Word, and Digital Translation

Most of the stories here are transcribed according to the Hymesian style of "verse-analysis," in which stories are transcribed according to lines, verses, stanzas, scenes, and acts (D. Hymes 2003). These conventions are tools to help readers better appreciate the complex and artful relations that move through different levels of a story, relations that involve everything from plot to structure to the aesthetics of grammar and sound. We also, however, are equally indebted to Dennis Tedlock (1983) and his pathbreaking insights about the aesthetics of sound and how sound, together with language, also defines performances of stories and songs. Tedlock's notion of the "spoken word" emphasizes the power of the human voice to create relations that interpenetrate the grammatical and symbolic structures of a story. The musicality of the spoken word, as we try to show, is crucial to the art and sociality of the storytelling world.

In our scheme of presenting the translations, lines are usually defined by predication, but they can also be defined by subordinate phrases, subjects, repetitions, ongoing actions, and pauses. Pauses, strategic silences of meaning, often define lines, especially when they are purposely and crisply deployed by narrators. Sometimes, however, pauses do not define lines, as storytellers sometimes search for the right words or become momentarily distracted during a telling. Although sometimes it is impossible to tell the intentionality of a pause, most of the time, when a line ends, there will be some sort of a pause. Pauses, however, can be incredibly short as narrators often speed up their speech. The pause, in other words, is not something that works as a "formula" but rather is one aspect of a much more complex storytelling patterning. As we show throughout this book, pauses, vocal prosody, gestures, awareness of surroundings, dialogue/overlapping, and structural concerns of grammar all work together in the patterning of lines and other forms that define stories.

Verses, which are indicated by indentation of all but the first line, are groupings of lines that share aesthetic "equivalence" (Jackobson 1960; D. Hymes 2003) in the sense of being an artful whole of similar but varied relations.

Often things like grammatical parallelism, quotations, or repetition define verses. Stanzas, which are indicated by capital letters (A, B, C, etc.) are larger aesthetic configurations that subsume verses. Stanzas can be detected by the use of time words or other "turns" of talk. After stanzas come scenes, which are indicated by lower-case Roman numerals (i, ii, iii, iv, etc.). Scenes involve action in the story and changes of location, action, or subjectivity. Lastly, long stories are divided into acts (represented by capital Roman numerals I, II, III, etc.), broad themes that divide stories into two or three major parts. Readers who wish more information about verse-analysis should consult chapter 5, which contains a more detailed discussion of the method in relation to Amazonian Quichua narratives and Quichua grammar.

Following Dell Hymes (2003) and Dennis Tedlock (1983), we have made the effort to create aesthetic translations that are accurate but not overburdened by technical information—our goal is to create English poems imbued with the spirit of Quichua aesthetics. In this sense our translations are Quichua-English hybrids. Our translations are based on complex mixed methods of translating that involve taking into account the grammar of Quichua and structural relations, ideophones, and the musicality and rhythms of the storyteller's voice. For some stories, which were videotaped, we have included notes about gestures and small images of them, a technique introduced by Janis Nuckolls (2000) in relation to Pastaza (Amazonian) Quichua narratives. These techniques should help readers get some sense of not just the words but also the prosody, structures, and bodily movements within the Quichua storytelling world. While no translation method is perfect, having an explicit framework does help in organizing and bringing to attention certain (not all) aspects of performances. Verse-analysis is a good method for conveying the structures of grammar as well as other features such as time words, quotations, and parallelisms that define the aesthetics of stories told in many of the world's indigenous languages (D. Hymes 2003).

The use of digital technology will improve our translations. First, digital technology will allow readers to hear the sounds of actual Quichua speech that are integral to Napo Runa mythology. The reader, by accessing media files on our companion website (http://spokenwordecology.com), can listen to the original sounds of Quichua speech and music while reading the translations via subtitles. Here, the prosody of the storyteller's voice interpenetrates the translation. Second, our use of digital technology allows people to read nonlinearly, to follow information in ways that will help them to connect a greater amount of relations more gracefully. By following their interests, readers can follow lines of thought and relations of thought, poetics, place, and meanings that loop among and intersect within the various stories. Quichua storytelling, as we show, is circular rather than linear, so it is appropriate to move around in the materials rather than explore them in linear order. Readers, we hope, will gain a fuller appreciation for the whole of relations that define the stories..

Third, the use of technology has also allowed us to include maps and images that will enrich many of the stories presented here that would otherwise not be included in a printed text, mainly for reasons of economy. With photographs, drawings, and images online rather than in the printed text, readers will have access to related images that help to communicate the visual lifeworld of Quichua storytelling. These images are not, in our view, tangential to the argument of the book; they show how words and experience work together in ways in which the inscribed meanings upon the landscape, and geography, come to life in storytelling performances. Storytelling competence, as we show, involves a great deal of visual information as well as visual forms, patterns of "seeing" and "experiencing" the world.[11]

Lastly, the use of the Internet will also allow readers to access some of the stories and songs in video format. While not all of the performances in the book were videotaped, those that were reveal the rich use of gestures and the body in the aesthetics and semiotic complexities in storytelling. For example, Verna's tellings of the great flood and the Iluku stories involve imagery brought into being by gestures. Interestingly, Verna's use of gestures is often linked with ideophones, which, like gestures, are used to create images. These gestures and ideophones bring movement into presence, through the use of the body, such as the emergence of the axis mundi, shape-shifting, and moments of transformation. As well, in videotaped stories, facial expressions and postures are visible, allowing readers to sense some of the emotional qualities and interactions that define a storytelling scene.

For the rest of the materials, which were recorded using audio technology, video-making software has made it possible to create movie files that enhance our ability to communicate more complex information and relations gracefully. These "audio-movies" include the original audio file, subtitles with the English translation, and a photograph of the storyteller. These "works" are an innovation upon the conventional method of only including an associated audio file with a printed translation. While the old way made it difficult for readers to relate the poetics of the original language to the translated text, the new way allows for a more dynamic experience of a translated story.

The use of subtitle technology allows for a closer association of the actual sounds of Quichua speech with the translated text; especially ideophones and nonlinguistic poetic features come through with more impact as their location within the translation is more precise. Also, including a photograph of the storyteller helps the reader associate a face with the stories and songs and provides an aura of his or her presence, an aura that is often lost in the book format or in the straight audio file.

In two cases (see chapters 3 and 7), we have provided audio files of actual performances of our translations, performances inspired by Dennis Tedlock's (1983) notion that translations too can be performable works of art based upon the aesthetics of the original performance in the Native language (see chapter 3). Performances of translations are important anthropological works, especially if performed in front of an audience or within a group. Not only does the story come through more cleanly and elegantly (if the performance is a good one), but a performed translation captures more of the sociality of storytelling as a human exchange of voices, gestures, and relations. Storytelling is not really about reading books. It is about practicing a living, aesthetic tradition, a tradition that can also be practiced by anthropologists and others.

While this use of new technology will hopefully improve our translations and the academic quality of the book, we realize that even the best technology is no substitute for the experience of actual practices in their original context. Indeed, we are aware of the way that videos, when watched from distant places, create "context collapse," a social process where "an infinite number of contexts collapsing upon one another [go] into that single moment of recording" (Wesch 2009:23). While the pioneering media scholar Edmund Carpenter (1972) was wary of the damage to "traditional" notions of the self and sociality caused by new media, Wesch's recent work has demonstrated that people from indigenous cultures (Papua New Guinea in his research) do not simply lose their culture because they are exposed to Western media technologies (Wesch 2009:32). Furthermore, the research by Terence Turner (1991b, 1992) has shown how video and new media technology, when appropriated and used by indigenous peoples, can help raise political and cultural awareness, as well as become an additional tool in the fight for cultural and linguistic revitalization.[12]

The issue of context collapse does create problems for appreciating the implicit poetic and social meanings involved in stories. Using our website and this book, readers will be able to access multimodal presentations of Quichua storytelling materials, but people not familiar with the context will still lack experiential knowledge of the places and people involved in the tellings. They will also be deprived of other senses that are important to knowing stories—specifically touch, smell, and even taste. But most importantly, the intimacy of stories with experience and a grounded sociality in situ will be lost. Indeed, one of the central tenets of Amazonian storytelling is that the story and life itself, which are connected to the earth and the people that are rooted in it, all converge. To really know a story one has to live it, breathe it, feel it, grow from it, and be it. Storytelling and experience are convergent realities, for experience is the lifeblood and essence of the storytelling world.

Hearing and seeing a digital copy of someone's story is not the same as being there. But it is better than not hearing a voice at all or just reading a story in a book. Books too have some advantages, however, in that readers can take their time in reading a translation, contemplate complex arguments and their citations, and enjoy the visual aesthetics and relations that verse-analysis congeals onto the page. There is also a lot of joy to be gotten out of the sensory experience of a book, the feel and smell of the pages, the "voice" that emerges in the mind's eye as one follows words on a page. Our strategy, as the reader will see, is to enhance the printed word with digital technology's ability to facilitate nonlinear, multiple perspectives of thought and relatedness quickly and gracefully. We hope that this hybrid strategy will help readers see communication, language, orality, and textuality in new ways as well as provide more information about the relations that constitute the Amazonian communicative world.

Authorship and Description of the Chapters

The chapters in this book were written at different times and in different places, with many of them written in our home in Napo, Ecuador. Although the chapters develop different angles and considerations of theory, they all confront our engagement of Napo Quichua storytelling practices as a holistic complex of communicative practices. These practices, as will become evident, are not just of anthropological interest to us. They are also defining of who we are and how we, a Quichua-, English-, and Spanish-speaking family, relate and imagine the world.

While the bulk of the specific language in the book, which is English, was written by Michael, Edith's participation in the project has been equally significant as she is a Native speaker of Napo Quichua who has a personal history linked to the stories and storytellers we present. The arguments and nuances of Quichua communicative philosophy and sociality would have been totally lost to Michael without Edith's efforts in helping him to understand this world socially. As well, the translations, which were painstakingly and carefully wrought over weeks, months, or years in some cases, have been enriched through Edith's participation. While Michael is the specialist in anthropological and ethnopoetic theory, Edith is the expert in the textuality, semantics, aesthetics, and intertextuality of the materials presented here. Without her, the stories behind the stories would have been lost or oversimplified, a common deficiency in many storytelling or folkloric approaches. Although the use of the first person plural "we" obscures these details, it does justice to the teamwork involved in carrying out this book project.

Unfortunately, it is often assumed that Native speakers are "informants" in the background of anthropological works, but studies of this kind are significantly shaped by Native speakers, individuals with names and personal histories, who are the real experts of living their communicative worlds and cultural realities. Teamwork among anthropologists, those trained in the theory and broad scope of cultural and communicative differences, and Native experts allows for a richness of detail and texture that is also theoretically powerful. Anthropologists help, for example, in getting peoples' messages out and can publish in international journals, presses, and other prestigious venues. This kind of collaboration, which is practiced by many anthropologists who have been influential in our work, allows for greater appreciation of the implications and complexities of other ways of life.

Anthropology is a small discipline, but it remains a powerful and influential area of academic practice that continues to shape how people view the human condition as a complex and varied kaleidoscope of cultures, languages, and peoples. Like many anthropologists who work in close association with indigenous groups, we position our work and life's mission as anthropological and political. As members of a larger world of intercultural relations, we insist that diversity, respect, cooperation, and mutual understanding among the varied cultures and peoples of this world are essential social principles that should be fostered and fomented by governments, states, and local institutions. While these goals seem obvious and good to many people, they are indeed political, for such principles are under attack in many sectors of the contemporary world, and even in many institutions of education and higher learning. Today, money, domination, and control—political projects fostered by anti-anthropological "one dimensional thought" (see Marcuse 1991)—are the implicit priorities behind many governing bodies, local, national, and international.

Anthropological practice, however, requires a different way of thinking and acting in the world, one in which people are respected and differences appreciated in social practice and daily life, not just in rhetoric or in printed statements. For anthropologists, no singular way of life is more "evolved" or innately superior to another. Each culture is a different manifestation of the human condition, and all cultures deserve respect and social support. As a practice, anthropology is a vocation where listening and building deep friendships with others, distinct from ourselves, are guiding moral principles. As a listener, the individual becomes humbly linked with the wisdom and knowledge of a specific culture and its individuals, an apprentice to a different way of life. Anthropology in this sense is one kind of voice overlapping with the voices of many others, academic and non-academic alike (Friedrich 1988), a necessary condition for a more peaceful world (Latour 2007).

For those familiar with Native South American cultures, the specificities of the stories here to link individual lives into networks of texts should be evident as a patterning of *ayllu*, or extended-family relations, the defining form of social organization in the Quichua-speaking world (see Uzendoski 2005). Indeed, all of the storytellers here are relatives by some tie of blood, marriage, or residence. The storytellers are our elders, who, in sharing their knowledge with us, have tried to teach us Quichua truths about how to live life's aesthetics and experiences to their fullest. Hopefully, readers of this book will gain a deeper appreciation and insight into what the stories have taught us. It is with their shared enthusiasm and desire to share their knowledge with others, that we have written this book.

In chapter 1 we describe a healing experience that Michael experienced in Campo Cocha with Fermin Shiguango, a *yachak*, or healer, with whom Michael lived during his first fieldwork period in 1994. We also present the poetics of Edith's brother Eugenio Calapucha's manioc poem and the shamanic song of power of her uncle Lucas Tapuy, or Chuyaki. All of these materials reveal the multimodal and multisensory complexity of Quichua storytelling, music, and ritual performances. These expressive modalities and events connect people to each other, to unseen forces, and to the landscape. The organizing principle of this chapter is somatic poetry, the practice of experiencing stories holistically through and with the body's interconnectedness to multiple textualities, textualities of vital energy.

In chapter 2, we discuss two stories and a song about *izhu punzha*, or judgment day. *Izhu punzha*, as we show, is a primordial story of destruction and remaking of the world. These stories teach that the world is constantly in flux and that no order, no state, no state of dominance will last forever. *Izhu punzha* is both a past and future reality, the beginning and the end of the world.

We next present two stories about celestial transformations, the Iluku story and Origin of the Sun, in chapter 3. As we discuss, Iluku, the mother of the twins or culture heroes, is the analogical mother of the Amazonian Quichua community. The sun, by contrast, is a one-eyed anaconda, a being whose presence is analogic of masculine potency and human procreation. Both of these stories involve complex aesthetics of experience and rainforest ecology. As well, axis mundi imagery and the interconnectedness of the celestial and terrestrial worlds define both stories.

Chapter 4 is a detailed study of six woman's songs, the "breast song," "dove woman," "rubber tapping woman," "birds and flowers," "Huallaga," and "Fish."

These songs are defined by feminine shape-shifting relations between birds and women, fish and women, and similar mimetic transformations in history, such as the rubber boom. Music is a mode of expression in which the spoken word is condensed and empowered. The cultural theory of communication, as we show, is one where sound attracts power to the body for use as social action.

In chapters 5, 6, and 7 we provide a detailed analysis of stories about the culture heroes of the Napo Quichua world, the Cuillurguna or Twins. The sons of the union of the moon man and Iluku, the Twins, make the world habitable for human communities. Chapter 5's main theme, "becoming a jaguar," shows that the Twins are shape-shifting beings, mythical humans infused with jaguar substance and power.

Chapter 6 describes how the Cuillurguna overthrow the oppressive regimes of the jaguar father-mother and the birds of prey. Chapter 7 features a story about the Twins' relatedness to petroglyphs and a story-poem, coauthored by Edith and Michael, of the Twins ascending to the sky to become stars. In this same chapter, we describe our own discovery that storytelling in the Quichua world creates a stirring of the soul, a hidden power to evoke one's own relatedness to the world as aesthetic and imaginary as well as social.

In chapter 8 we describe the modern musical genre Runa Paju, a genre that features clever Quichua lyrics, electronic amplification, and eclectic use of instruments and musical styles. Our focus is not on musicology but on the social dynamics of the music and its relationship to Quichua cosmology and mythological thought. We argue that, although Runa Paju is a new, modern genre, it follows the same communicative and social assumptions of storytelling as traditional genres. Runa Paju brings into artistic contour the experiences of life's problems and experiences with a larger narrative of cosmological destiny. By targeting the human soul, Runa Paju musicians must "reverse" many of the superficial or apparent relations of modern life and revert destiny to shared cosmology. The threads of Quichua life become newly interwoven into musical pathways of cosmological communitas, a moment of community-wide experience of the circularity and relatedness of all things.

We end our journey into Napo Quichua storytelling with a few concluding thoughts. We tie things together by arguing that somatic poetry—the thread that ties together all the materials in this book—is a shared philosophy of life and art that connects the individual life to the history of a community and its landscape. We also call for a more nuanced and sympathetic treatment of the communicative practices of other cultures, different forms of textuality, and the poetic power of the multimodal bodily expressions.

CHAPTER 1
SOMATIC POETRY
Toward an Embodied Ethnopoetics

In Amazonia, communicative action is not limited to humans but also includes spirits and beings from the nonhuman phenomenological world. Throughout Amazonia spirits, plants, and other nonhuman beings possess communicative agency, but these beings communicate with humans through dreams, ritual states, feelings, visions, telepathy, or other means besides language.[1] This Amazonian religious philosophy, which has been written about extensively, is commonly glossed as "perspectivism" (Viveiros de Castro 1998), a philosophy of life that attributes agency, souls, and subjectivity to all living things, including some inanimate things. Most of the literature on perspectivism is densely packaged theory. However, others, inspired by the beauty of "perspectivist" realities, have emphasized the poetic and experiential qualities of these interspecies relational systems (Uzendoski, Hertica, and Calapucha 2005; Kohn 2007).

We explore here the poetic qualities and nuances of the art of ritual healing, a genre we term "somatic poetry." Flowing out from the emphasis of the body as a site of social and cosmological action in the Amazonian world (T. Turner 1995; Fausto 2000), somatic poetry is multimodal art created by listening, feeling, smelling, seeing, and tasting of natural subjectivities, not just those emanating from human speech or from the human mind (see Uzendoski 2008). Somatic poetry involves the creative use of words and music and also plants, animals, and the landscape—entities recognized as having subjectivity and creative powers, powers that are internal rather than external to the art.

Somatic poetry is the poetry of place and experience, an art that recognizes and builds upon the expressiveness of ecology and ecological interrelations. In our usage of "poetry," we draw an analogy with the ancient Greek notion of *poiesis*, which conveys "making" or "creating" something of beauty (Heidegger 1971:212; Ziarek 1998). In this sense, we are attempting to disentangle "poetry" from its Western specificities and defining characteristics so that other, more holistic traditions can be appreciated in their own cultural terms and context. "Somatic poetry," however, is not a thing. It is a term to describe what Amazonian Quichua people do in creating multimodal works of art that draw upon the body's interconnectedness with the larger world, a genre that has been honed over thousands of years and that is the lifeblood of Native aesthetic practices. We emphasize the poetics of the body, because, in indigenous practice, there are no poetics or use of artful words that do not also involve bodily subjectivities. Verbal art in the indigenous world is somatic. Its embodied nature flows through and is expressed through words, but words are but one aspect of a more complex multimodal aesthetics that also involves images, smells, tastes, feelings, sounds, and unseen vital energies and powers.

As we attempt to show, Amazonian somatic poetry is not just "oral." On the contrary, somatic poetry can be viewed as a process of textual creation (Arnold and Yapita 2006; Derrida 1967; Finnegan 2007; Hanks 1989), one in which individual poems become interconnected and woven into others to create infinite, looping lines of artistic creations, creations that as a whole define experiences and human histories of specific places (Ingold 2007). As a process of oral textuality, somatic poetry organizes the voice and the body as privileged agents of creation. Rather than allow the printed word to dominate the body in the disciplinary sense of Foucauldian biopower (Ziarek 1998), somatic poetry allows the body not just to create but also to become the text (Guss 1986). As we show, the voice has an incredible force in somatic poetry. Not only can it heal and invoke unseen powers, but it can also inscribe meanings on various mediums: the body, the land, stone, the air, and even the imagination.[2]

It is worthwhile to consider the larger implications of such work. Following Dell Hymes (1981, 1985, 1992, 1994, 2003), Dennis Tedlock (1983), Jerome Rothenberg (1994), Seminole poet and artist Elgin Jumper (2006), Juan Carlos Galeano (2000, 2007), and many other poets we have met throughout our lives in Amazonia, one can appreciate that poetry is not limited to alphabetic writing or to bookish people. If anything, this point has not been made forcefully enough. Amazonia provides a striking example of somatic poetry, poetry that transcends the boundaries of human agency and includes multi-authoring through the visceral social subjectivities. Amazonian people create spectacular poetry, but we still fail to understand its social power, healing efficacy, politics, and beauty—in short, its genius. We lack sustained experiential knowledge of their art, despite very good research by anthropologists and ethnomusicologists (Basso 1995; Conklin 2001; Graham 1996; Guss 1989; Hendricks 1993; Hill 1993; Oakdale 2005; Olsen 1996; Seeger 1986; Urban 1991).

Let us provide one example of Amazonian somatic poetry, a healing practice called *kushnirina*, a medicinal vapor bath designed to cleanse and provide energy for the body. We then comment on Federico Calapucha's manioc story and a shamanic song performed by Lucas Tapuy in 2007. All of these examples show that somatic poetry—the lifeblood of shamanic potentialities and an animated universe of flowing energies—is about creating loops of intersecting relationships with different species and unseen subjectivities of the landscape and the spirit world.

Part 1: Vapor Poetry

Years ago, we returned to Ecuador for a summer of fieldwork among the Napo Runa, Amazonian Quichua speakers of Ecuador. Although Edith had returned a few times to visit her family, we had not been to Ecuador together since Michael's dissertation fieldwork in 1997. Having just defended the dissertation, Michael had a general feeling of bodily malaise. His Quichua was rusty, and he was terribly out of shape. He felt generally tired, nervous, and ill at ease. So we went to visit Fermin Shiguango, a *yachak* (one who knows or healer) with whom he had lived during an extended period of fieldwork. When we arrived at his house, Fermin noticed that Michael had a bad cold. He said that Michael appeared weak, *sambayashka*. He told us what was needed was a treatment he referred to as *kushnirina*, a medicinal vapor sweat bath designed to cure illness, cleanse the body, and give strength. Fermin had told us that he was practicing this kind of healing in addition to his long expertise in *wanduk* (*Brugmansia suaveolens*), a vision-inducing plant. He claimed that these two areas were his best specialties of knowledge, or *yachay*. Fermin told us he had recently cured (*alichina*, to make better) an ill foreigner, one addicted to drugs, through a treatment of various *kushnirina*. He did this treatment for those in his community who requested it, or for anyone else who visited him.

Michael had never seen this kind of treatment during almost three years of fieldwork between 1994 and 1997, including a whole year of living in Fermin's house. He was at first skeptical and could not understand why Fermin was so excited about the vapor baths. Michael could not see the connection between these vapor baths and being a *yachak*. At best, he considered the vapor baths to be a kind of medicinal healing, but they did not seem to be related to the spirit world or to other anthropological markers of shamanic practice like soul travel or altered states of consciousness.[3] Edith, however, knew better because she had seen these practices from childhood.

Fermin invited us into the forest to see what plants were used to make the vapor bath. Michael had his audiotape-recorder and camera in hand, and we set out on a hike that took a few hours; many of these plants grow only in the primary forest. Fermin knew where each plant was located, and as we walked gathering them, he explained the names and various uses of each plant and invited us to sample their aromas, tastes, and textures. Fermin stressed that for the treatment to be effective, the right kinds of plants must be used. He did not show those of us present all of the plants, as there were some that he wished to keep secret.

The first plant Fermin showed us was *chiriwayusa* (*Brunfelsia grandiflora*), a smallish-looking shrub with very aromatic leaves. This plant, he explained, was good for alleviating the body of any malaise and especially a hunting curse. Fermin noted that one of the great benefits of *kushnirina* is that it entails the use of *chiriwayusa*, which helps hunters stay sharp by cleansing their body. The traditional way to "ingest" *chiriwayusa* is through a vapor bath.

Chiriwayusa, like other medicinal plants in Quichua, is identified by its pungent taste and distinct aroma. When showing us the leaves, Fermin made a point of breaking off the leaves and smelling them. Their aroma was evidence of their power. After harvesting some of the leaves, we moved on to look at other plants. We next came to a plant called *kiru panga* (possibly of the family *Melastomataceae*), which had stalks with a distinct lemony flavor that people often "drink" to quench thirst while in the forest. The flowers that protrude from the stalks are distinctive and look like large white teeth, the mimetic quality from which the plant gets its name (*kiru* means tooth, *panga* means leaf). The plant often attaches itself to the trunk of a large tree, but it can also grow on the ground. Because of the poetic and mimetic qualities of Fermin's description, we present his words in verse form (Hymes 2003). Fermin stated:

> from each stalk from the tree it comes
> > the flowers are its life force (*kawsay*)
> > > its power (*urza*)
> > those flowers are on each leaf
> look at this vine
> > this vine has a flower
> > > look, this one is about to flower
> ones like this I collect
> > collecting
> > > to get their powers (*urzauna*)

Why did Fermin describe in such detail, and so poetically, the form of these flowers? He might have simply mentioned that the flowers contain more of the forest's *kawsay* (life force) than other living things, picked them, and been done with his demonstration. However, Fermin chose to organize his description in a poetic way, using parallelism, imagery, and the aesthetics of the plants species themselves. The flowers, for example, were described in a way that conveyed the idea that they were like "shamans," in that they contained and personified power (they were "strong" and "powerful").

The notion that life force circulates among all living things was aptly conveyed in the way Fermin described and showed us the flowers, especially the vine flower *kiru panga*. Fermin made a point of indicating that the flowers of the plant *kiru panga* came from their vines. The vines in turn "were fed" by the tree, and the trees "fed" off the earth. Fermin then showed us some other flowering plants, which he described also as having *ushay* or power, a term often used interchangeably with *kawsay*. He showed us the plants *awa uchan panga*, *awa kruz panga*, *arete panga*, *sacha lamar panga*, *malagri panga*, and *sacha ajo* (*Mansoa alliacea*). He then indicated a vine called *kutu chupa* (howler monkey's tail) and said that the power of this vine is that it gives you *urza* (power) "like that of a monkey." We broke off and tasted the leaves and stalks of some of the plants. We just smelled others. They all had bitter or aromatic qualities, the kind of taste that would stay in one's mouth for a long time and give one a subtle "buzz." Fermin described all the plants as *asnak* (aromatic) and *ambi* (medicine or poison).

Later that afternoon, Fermin prepared the herbal concoction. He boiled the herbs and flowers in a large pot of water, covering the top with a lid made of leaves. Once the concoction was ready, he had Michael sit on a small stool in the middle of the floor. He placed the pot between Michael's legs and gave him a large wooden spoon. Fermin then carefully covered Michael with blankets in a way that would not allow vapor to escape. It was totally dark inside. When he was ready, Fermin said, "Now break the seal." Michael took the wooden spoon and punctured the leaf top and was soon overwhelmed by heat and the strong aroma of the herbs and flowers. The first ten minutes were the most difficult, as the heat is intense and causes profuse sweating. Michael could hardly breathe and asked Fermin if that was enough, but Fermin shouted, after laughing, "No, you must stay there for at least fifteen minutes more." After ten more minutes, Michael noisily coughed up a large ball of mucus that had been dislodged through the vapors. Hearing this, Fermin stated, "There it is." After the time was up, Fermin removed the blankets. Michael emerged completely drenched, dizzy, and disoriented. He was given a towel to wipe off the sweat and vapor that covered his body.

Fermin instructed Michael not to bathe for 24 hours, for the cold water could make him ill. We asked Fermin to explain the healing theory of the vapor bath. He said that the bath allows the healer to transfer the power of the plants into the body of the patient. The healer replenishes and augments the *kawsay*, or life force, of the patient by using the plant energies that contain much of the forest's power. He also said, however, that the plants alone do not work unless the healer also "puts his power [*ushay*] in there too," a power thought to emanate from his flesh, his *aycha*. The defining aspect of this liminal state of healing is created through a poetic synesthesia of words, visual effects, heat, aromas, taste, and sweat. In this process, the body is "opened up" to receive the power of the rainforest. This process is described as *paskarina*, or "to open up," and this is the same term used to describe how tobacco smoke works on the body of patients in an *ayahuasca* (a plant-derived mixture in which the main ingredient is *banisteriopsis caapi*) ceremony. The term *kushnirina* has multiple meanings. In one sense, it means to vapor oneself in a reflexive sense. *Kushni* means vapor or smoke. *Ri* is the reflexive particle, and *na* is the infinitive ending. *Rina* also means to go or to travel, however, so *kushnirina* can also mean to travel into the vapor.

This additional meaning resonates with the mimetic processes of moving inside of a sensory experience. For example, reflecting on his work with healers in Putumayo, Taussig (1987) considers how nonvisual senses work mimetically and cross over with vision to create powerful bodily reactions such as nausea, which he experienced while working with medicines in Putumayo: "the senses cross over and translate into each other. You feel redness. You see music . . . seeing is felt in a nonvisual way. You move into the interior of images, just as images move into you" (Taussig 1993:57–58). What occurs is an experience where vision is but part of a larger mimetic whole in which the senses cross over. "Seeing," Taussig (58) writes, "is felt in a nonvisual way."

Sensory crossing over is explained by reference to cosmological processes in the ritual space of Napo Runa culture; it is not simply a psychological phenomena but is also an aesthetics that is essential to healing. Fermin explained that during the process of being inside the vapor bath, the patient becomes "opened up" to the powers of the forest spirits, spirits who come into direct contact with the soul substance of the patient. The healer guides these actions. As Fermin explained, the healer's body does the work, and there is not any real effort involved. The healer intends to heal, so his *aycha*, or flesh, sends out power of its own accord. This power also "goes into the vapor bath" and augments its healing power. This is the body's subjectivity, its shamanic self.

Because the ritual is both beautiful and theatrical, we find it useful to see it as a dramatic social process structured by the storytelling, narrative shape of onset, ongoing, and outcome (Hymes 2003). The ritual space of healing in the *kushnirina* is a transformation (*tukuna*) that responds to the social connectedness of people to hostile others, both human and nonhuman. In any healing ritual, the healer assumes that the cause of illness is dark shamanism or a spirit, both of which often send invisible darts or bad energy into the flesh of victims (onset). In the ritual space of healing, the healer removes these foreign objects from the patient's body and reinforces the patient's weakened soul substance (ongoing). The patient gets better, but healing might also involve the ritual assassination or "sealing off" of the offending shaman, for to heal a sick patient often requires that the healer "kill" or quarantine the enemy (outcome).

While Michael was under the blankets, and after each of his complaints, groans, and labored breathing, those around commented with such phrases as "ah-hah" (yes)—comments identifying the invisible struggle going on in the afflicted body. When Michael spat up the ball of mucus, Fermin became animated and excited and urged him to get rid of even more of the mucus. This moment of drama reflected the implicit knowledge that the spirit pathogens were being forced out of the body. When using visionary plants, for example, at that time spiders, thorns, darts, and lizards (all of which are the perceived sources of shamanically caused illnesses) appear in the body as wrapped in purple mucus.[4] The shaman sucks out these entities, swallows them, regurgitates them, and sends them away, often aiming them back at the originating source.

Kushnirina, like visionary healing, removes such spirit pathogens, but through the power of the vapor rather than "sucking." Language expresses many of the aesthetic qualities of *samay* (breath, soul substance) in the healing ritual, and language works together with imagery, sound, smell, and taste to produce a holistic communicative experience. We saw how Fermin described flowers as having the animistic qualities of *kawsay* and *urza*—terms of strength and power that reflect the assumptions of a perspectivist world. He also framed the *kushnirina* ritual in terms of the recognized shamanic terms of *ushay* and *alichina* (to make better) and using healing plants. The healing process elicits cleansing and spiritual strengthening, but as patterned against the background of cosmological violence and ever-present spiritual attacks.

The qualities of *kutu chupa*, for example, are said to transfer the power of the howler monkey to the patient. The furry-looking vine is not a mere "copy" of the monkey's tail; it is a mimetic relation with the monkey's invisible soul power. The vapors that are released when the patient punctures the top of the pot are also defining of the ritual's imagery and its name; because the vapors are medicine, they cannot be wasted and must be released in concentrated form and in intimacy with only the patient. The vapors (*kushni*) circulate through the patient's body and are felt as well as seen. They flow into and move through the nose, eyes, and pores of one's skin—mimetically imbuing the patient with refortification.[5]

As a patient, one goes from feeling ill to feeling overwhelmed by extreme heat to feeling cleansed and refreshed. The aesthetics create a sense that one's illnesses are being assaulted and purged by a more powerful healing force.[6] The plants, in this sense, are an ideal means to this end. Their beauty and aromas intimately connect with the aesthetics and ontology of the Napo Runa "soul," for they, like shamans, have powerful internal essences, essences that "work" on others and the world in specific ways. Merleau-Ponty said that "whether it is a question of another's body or my own, I have no means of knowing the human body other than that of living it, which means taking up on my own account the drama which is being played out in it, and losing myself in it" (1962:198). Although we do not think that all bodily experiences must be dramatic, Merleau-Ponty's point that somatic experiences are central to many of life's dramatic events resonates with what Quichua speakers have taught us about vapor poetry.[7]

Part 2: The Lines of Federico's Manioc Poem

We now wish to explore some further semiotic dynamics of somatic poetries, dynamics that we were able to discern by recounting other genres of somatic poetry. We have thus far argued that somatic poetry is dramatic as well as artful, and that it involves creating and performing relationships with natural beings and spirits. These are not just entities in the abstract but, rather, subjectivities that are linked to geography and the experiential contours of the landscape.

As Julie Cruikshank (2005) has eloquently discussed, when studying "oral traditions" or mythological realities it is useful to follow the philosopher Edward Casey's distinction between space and place (see the introduction). Space is modern Western theory of the land as mapped, measured, and easy to fix using Cartesian coordinates (Cruikshank 2005:67). Place making is a different process of becoming connected to a landscape, of having a history and specific social meanings tied up with specific locations.

Place takes on unique and complex characteristics in relation to somatic poetry. For example, many Native cultures do not separate space from time. In Quichua, for example, *pacha* conveys both time and space, a "world" of experience where "time" cannot be divorced from the place it happens.

There are countless examples of somatic poetry and its relationship to place and the experiences of daily life in all the communities in Upper Napo. After one person recounts his or her own somatic poem or story, others join in and share theirs. Sharing one's somatic poem, even a simple one, invites others to share theirs and create new relationships. These stories, taken as a whole, reveal the meaning of *samay,* or soul substance, as a kind of energy that is crucial not only to life but also to storytelling. Within this gigantic looping of mysteries and interrelations exists an infinite potential for somatic poetry and multiple genres (see chapter 8).

Federico Calapucha, Edith's brother, for example, often recounts the history of Edith's *ayllu* (kindred group) by way of a metaphor about a manioc plant. In telling his story, he draws on the imagery of the segmented stalks of the plant to analogize human relatedness. This imagery is combined with arm gestures that convey processes of human-plant reproduction. Federico says, "The plant grows, bears fruit, and is harvested, but it is replanted and continues to grow and reproduce in the same spot. This is how we are." Federico gesticulates in a precise way the growth lines on the stem of the manioc plant, each of which represent a segment of human and manioc growth.

For this somatic poet, the plant's shape and line structure express perfectly the rootedness, vitality, and continuity of human-vegetable *samay* in both place and time. Indeed, manioc is one of the most meaningful plants throughout all of Amazonia, the source of all life, and associated with the production of children (Descola 1996a; Uzendoski 2005). Manioc can reproduce itself from its own body without any need for seeds, and its gardens are mimetic extensions of the feminine body. In expressing the *ayllu* by reference to a manioc plant, Federico expresses the mysteries of human bodies as defined through the complex lines of vegetable matter and its tangled rootedness in the earth, or *allpa*. His somatic poem is intertextual. It is built up on all the other manioc poems and myths he has heard in his life. Indeed, somatic poetry is full of such lines, lines in the sense described by Tim Ingold, who aptly writes:

> I have suggested that drawing a line . . . is much like telling a story. Indeed, the two commonly proceed in tandem as complementary strands of one and the same performance. Thus the storyline goes along, as does the line on a map. . . . Far from connecting points in a network, every relation is one line in a meshwork of interwoven trails. To tell a story, then, is to relate, in narrative, the occurrences of the past, retracing a path through the world that others, recursively picking up the threads of past lives, can follow in the process of spinning their own. But rather as in looping or knitting, the thread being spun now and the thread picked up from the past are both of the same yarn. There is no point at which the story ends and life begins. [2007:90]

Ingold's notion that the story and life are "of the same yarn" provides insight into the relational and social dynamics of somatic poetry in Amazonia. As we have recounted, Quichua speakers create experiences and poetic relationships for themselves and for others that bring the community itself into the imaginary spaces of mythology and its rootedness in specific landscapes.

That Michael's journey began in Omaha, Nebraska, the place of his birth, does not make these processes inauthentic. On the contrary, Quichua speakers in Ecuador find these threads enriching, and they are masters at integrating the experiences of others, including historical and all sorts of "modern" and globalized phenomena, into their own traditions of somatic poetry. In this sense, the "power" of their world is affirmed. The *samay* and forces, powers, and eternity of the forest, rivers, and mountains of the Amazonian world "inverts" the inequalities of the modern, technologized "machine world" (Hornborg 2001; N. Whitten and D. Whitten 2008).

Somatic poetry, as we have shown, is constituted by lines that loop through past lives, history, myth, the body, and the myriad and various subjectivities of the Amazonian landscape. This is place making, which can be contrasted with some modern notions of abstract space. Place lines are written into the landscape in countless other ways, by way of petroglyphs, other large stones, trees, paths, animals and plants, gardens, and even familiar sounds (see chapters 4 and 5). Indeed, place, lines, and somatic poetry are all part of the same reality, one whereby people, their environment, and the past share in a common destiny, one in which life and the story are one and the same pathway.

The Cubeo Henhénewa of the Vaupés region describe their world through the somatic "lines" of anaconda spiritual and soul substance. They say that the anaconda's "heart and soul enter into the river itself: into its fish, birds, and fowl, into trees, into human houses, and through hallucinogens, into ritually engaged human beings" (Goldman 2004:33). The semiotics of anaconda reality involve complex transmutations of form, social relations, meaning, and geography. These relations are not external to the body but occur within it and work through it. They are the dramatic contours of the cosmic body (Uzendoski 2010a), of the body's shared substantiality and coagency within a myriad of natural and spiritual beings.

To conceptualize these interrelations demands that one become a poet, in that thinking poetically is the key to knowing the system in its own terms, terms we might describe as evoking mystery, power, and beauty. It is to participate in an "extraordinary anthropology," one in which "transformative events lived with others in their world cannot be wished away" (Goulet and Miller 2007:7). Let us now look at another somatic work of art, Lucas Tapuy's *takina*, or his shamanic song.

Lucas Tapuy's Shamanic Song: A Poetics of Shamanic Circularity

Napo Quichua people use shamanic music and gestures to inscribe "lines" of power and spiritual connectedness with the landscape. Although it is well documented that shamanic music is for calling spirits, organizing visions, and achieving states of ecstasy, there is a lack of work that analyzes the aesthetic relationships of shamanic music to specific landscapes, family and individual histories, and place. There is also surprisingly little work that looks at the poetic features of such songs and the relational histories that they create among people and places that root them.

We contend that shamanic music is more than formulaic or just a mechanical neurophenomenological means to enter into non-ordinary reality (Katz and Dobkin de Rios 1971; Belzner and Whitten 1979). On the contrary, we appreciate that shamanic music is a kind of somatic poetry that allows people, both singers and hearers, to experience a *samay* interconnectedness to the primordial forces, subjectivities, and myriad detailed and subtle qualities of place—of a landscape inscribed with and defined by unseen power. Shamanic music is complex and difficult to decipher, but like poetry, understanding its semiotic dimensions and situated context are the keys to unlocking some of extraordinary qualities, qualities that give shape and life to the music.

Lucas Tapuy, otherwise known as Chuyaki while he was alive, was known as a healer and a person with a special connection to the spirit world of Sapo Rumi. Chuyaki, Edith's maternal uncle, suffered a terrible accident while he was working for fruit plantations on the coast of Ecuador, and as a result he lost one of his eyes. In his old age, he lost the ability to walk, and his good eye deteriorated to the point of blindness. Despite these physical limitations, people often came from far away to seek out Chuyaki's healing abilities, sometimes in the middle of the night due to a health emergency.

Chuyaki's main talents were cleansing rituals performed with leaves, smoke (mainly tobacco but other plant substances as well), and massages done with sugar cane alcohol or *cachiwa*. Although Chuyaki had participated in the visionary world of *ayahuasca* (mainly when he visited his other shaman friends), he did not regularly organize ceremonies. Chuyaki, however, could sing *takina* songs, one of the defining powers of a healer, or *yachak*, and Chuyaki was especially adept at engaging the realities of the spirit world through his dreams. Chuyaki was also a talented storyteller. In the next chapter we present his telling of the great flood narrative.

In one of the last conversations we had with Chuyaki before he died, he talked about his spiritual power. Chuyaki mentioned that he was extremely powerful, that he possessed an incredible amount of *yachashka samay* (power /

knowledge breath), and that his "blood" was some of the strongest in the world, stronger than many *yachak* who currently practiced *ayahuasca* rituals but who were "weak" in power.

It was the summer of 2007 and the first year we had brought students to Sapo Rumi to participate in an ethnographic field school we organized through Florida State University. Seven undergraduates gathered in the *cabaña*, or meeting place, and we called Chuyaki to come over and to share with us some of his shamanistic knowledge and practices. Chuyaki and his wife, Carmela, came over and sat down in the *cabaña*. Federico, Edith's brother, offered Chuyaki a natural cigarette of homegrown tobacco and a drink of *cachiwa*, or sugar cane alcohol. The event started out as an interview, with Michael translating between Quichua and English.

To begin the event, which took place in the evening, Michael introduced Chuyaki to his students. Chuyaki claimed to be over 100 years old but said he still felt really young and didn't get sick very often. Michael then asked Chuyaki where his *yachay* (knowledge) and *ushay* (power) for healing people comes from. Chuyaki responded, *"chi rumimanda"* (from that rock over there), pointing to a large boulder near the river. In Sapo Rumi, this large boulder, larger than a bus, is named Supay Rumi, or stone of the spirits. Chuyaki explained that Supay Rumi was the home of two spirit women, called *yaku warmiguna* (water women), who look like *gringas* and visited him in his house during the evenings. During the night, Chuyaki says that he doesn't sleep sometimes: "I am seeing at night . . . and these beautiful women come and kiss me and keep me from sleeping." He also stated that there was a landing pad next to the rock and that during the night they would take him in a "green helicopter" to their world, a spirit-world city, underneath the rock. Chuyaki was the *dueño*, or owner of these women and, by extension, the rock that they inhabited, which was the portal to the underworld and a great source of shamanic power.

Chuyaki and his wife told stories of all of the people that Chuyaki had cured. He explained that he could cure not just regular illnesses but also supernatural ones like "bad wind" or various *pajus* like *malagri supay*—illnesses caused by spirits or evil shamans. He told a story of a woman named Dolora near Pano who was ill and couldn't be cured by any of the other local shamans. One shaman took *ayahuasca* two nights in a row and "blew" and "sucked," but he couldn't cure her. So her family brought the sick woman to Chuyaki. He drank two bowls of manioc beer and a glass of sugar cane alcohol, and then he performed his special massage involving pressure points. The next day the woman was better. During the story Chuyaki's wife stated, "the others couldn't cure her, but he [Chuyaki] made her better right away."

Chuyaki spoke of the mountain overlooking Sapo Rumi, a large mountain called Wasila. He noted that there was a lot of *malagri supay* (a type of predatory spirit that appears as a priest and omits a deadly sweet odor) up on the Wasila Mountain, and one could smell them when one hiked up there, as they smelled like perfume.[8] However, Chuyaki said that he took care that these spirits didn't hurt us or others. He used his "breath" to send them away so that things were safe. Esteban, another of Edith's brothers, then blurted out, "we need a song . . . a song here is lacking." Lydia, Esteban's wife, stated that Chuyaki needed to cleanse one of the students, and Vanessa came up front and sat down in front of Chuyaki, who had a natural tobacco cigar in his hand and a cup of sugar cane alcohol at his feet. Carmela, Chuyaki's wife, said, "hey bring him some of the cleansing leaves." Chuyaki continued to use his speaking voice but began speaking *takina*-like words that resembled a chant or poem of power. Chuyaki spoke only three lines:

I am from all those mountains, all of the beautiful mountains
    chaaaa malagri supay
    a person of substance

Then Chuyaki started humming and broke into song:

CHUYAKI'S SHAMANIC SONG

ri ri ri ri ri ri ri ri. . . . .
from all of the mountainsssssss
Wasila [Mountain] from
    that mountainnnnn
I am a singing legendary
    person—lla
from Huallaga a substantial person
    a legendary person
an attractive
    just so beautiful, beautiful
      beautiful, beautiful
        legendary person
ir ri ri ri ri ri ri ri ri. . . . .
    mmmmmmmm. . . . . .
attractive attractive person
    legendary person
Huallaga [from] a substantial person
    legendary . . .
      ri ri ri ri ri. . . .

ri ri ri ri ri ri ri ri. . . . .
tukuy urkumandachu
Wasila ña urkumanda runachu

ñukalla tokashachu uyaringa
    runami—lllla
Huallaga ashka runachu
    uyaringa runami
gustu
    munaylla, munay
      munay, munay
        uyaringa runachu
ir ri ri ri ri ri ri ri ri. . . . .
    mmmmmmmm. . . . . .
gustu gustu runachu
    uyaringa runami
Huallaga ashka runachu
    uyaringa . . .
      ri ri ri ri ri. . . .

Here, Carmela interjects that Chuyaki should use the *abiu* leaf (to cleanse Vanessa, the patient). Chuyaki then gently chides her for interrupting him and states, "how can I sing with someone saying that?" Chuyaki then continues his song.

. . .

a person of many energies	caran tunu runami
a person from many different energies	caranmanda runami
from ICHU Mountain [he has] a bunch of women	Ichu urkumanda warmi muntunlla
the mother woman sang and there stood	madre warmi kantashka uku . . . shayaunga
an attractive little person	gustu runa shituchu
Wasila now on that mountain	Wasila ña urkupi
hmmmmmmmmm. . . .	hmmmmmmmmmm. . . .
a beautiful green helicopterrrr	gustu virdi heli-cop-i-t-sha
that group of women stand him up	warmi muntun shayachisha
an attractive little person	gustu runa shituchu
a singer of shamanic songs person	takinagalla runamari
ri ri ri ri ri ri ri . . .	ri ri ri ri ri ri . . .
a person who did the wedding	bura rashka runami
everything legendary person—lla	tukuyra uyaringa runami—lla
beautiful person from this rock right here—lla	gustu kay rumimandachu—lla
it is not a rock from this [world]	mana kaylla rumichu
it is a rock full of substance	undashka rumimi
ri ri ri ri ri ri ri.	ri ri ri ri ri ri ri. . . . . .
ri ri ri ri ri ri ri ri ri. . . .	ri ri ri ri ri ri ri ri ri. . . .

While Chuyaki is finishing the last lines of his song, Carmela comes in and comments to the students:

—when someone has a headache
when he does this
when he is warm
we nicely massage it
it works [really well]

After the song, Carmela comments that Lucas is good at giving people head massages and that these massages cured not only cured headaches but other ailments as well. Chuyaki then cleanses and gives head massages to several of the students who felt that they had some sort of malaise or pain, and lastly to Michael.

There are many poetic as well as shamanic features to the song, aspects of it that cannot be separated, and the song traces lines that connect Chuyaki's dream world, his life experiences, and his embodied connectedness to the landscape that defines him and his power. The salient metaphysics of the "lines" invoked in the song are various circular relations. Lucas, for example, mentions several sites of power—the mountain Wasila (which overlooks Sapo Rumi), Ichu Mountain, and the Huallaga River. The Huallaga River is located in Amazonian Peru, and the Napo Runa was used to travel there to obtain salt in past times (see chapter 4). These are all places to which Chuyaki has traveled, if not in real life, in memory and in spirit, and they define him as a being full of forces and powers of an extended geographic spirit world. The path of his musical journey, however, leads back "home" within the house in which we are now all sitting.

The defining feature of the landscape that Chuyaki mentions is "this rock," which he refers to as not belonging to "this world." The rock he refers to is Supay Rumi—the site where his spirit women take him into the underworld in a green helicopter, referred to near the end of the song. Taken as a whole the song reflects a kind of spirit or "soul" journey that Chuyaki has traveled before and continues to travel. It is as if each place he visited during his waking life can also be visited during a dream state or through the shamanic consciousness. In a sense, all of these places are part of Chuyaki, part of his person, his house, and his community.

That Chuyaki's life is a circle of relations is what he means when he says he is a person of many different energies. Although the term "substance" is a poor translation of *tunu*, which in Quichua means "kind," the phrases Chuyaki uses imply that he is a person of many different energies, powers, and qualities. We choose "substance" in the sense that it resonates with our translation of *samay* as a kind of soul substance. When Chuyaki refers to himself as being made of many different things, he is specifically talking about his *samay*.[9]

The poetic features of the song also convey a marked competency in using sound, sounds that go beyond linguistic meaning, to invoke power and to touch the human soul. The phrase "ri ri ri ri ri ri ri" is a common sound-form among shamans of Upper Napo, and these sounds are used to call spirits to the body and presence of the shaman. In one place Chuyaki follows up the "ri ri ri ri ri ri" phrase with humming, "hmmmmmm," making a nice couplet with parallel but contrasting sounds. Throughout the song, Chuyaki returns to "ri ri ri ri ri ri ri" to mark sections in the song, and "ri ri ri ri ri ri ri" is almost always bracketed by meaningful, purposeful pauses (D. Tedlock 1983). This same phrase is also used in the beginning and ending of the song. These sounds create the shamanic circle in which words are encompassed by spirit sounds, sounds that, in the Native view, orchestrate energies and powers in and through the body.

The words themselves are not complete thoughts, nor are they a kind of discourse. Chuyaki uses words to create images and to make circular relations among and between lines. Sound is a big part of making these connections. Throughout the song, Chuyaki refers to himself—not his "social self," but rather his invisible spiritual self— as "attractive," "beautiful," powerful, and well traveled in life. He creates images of mountains, rivers, and other sites on the landscape, sites that are inhabited by the spirit women that "teach" and "help" Chuyaki. Lucas uses the ending phrase *-lla* (just or little) to add emphasis at the end of lines, creating a kind of "circle" of sound within a song that is defined by circular relations. Other circular features are the inversions of endings of *chu* with those of *mi*. *Chu* refers to a question or uncertainty, while *mi* indicates a speaker perspective and speaker certainty, what linguists refers to as "epistemic modality" (Nuckolls 2010). The alternation between *chu* and *mi* creates a dual relationship, but one in which the speaker's presence, his embodiment of power and knowledge, encompasses its contrary of doubt, a dualistic structure that is also a circle.

The gestures used by Chuyaki also work in tandem with sound and language to convey circularity and elicit the presence of the powers and subjectivities invoked in the song. Michael is suffering from headaches, and after singing his song, Chuyaki massages his head by applying pressure to specific points. After doing this massage, Chuyaki then begins cleansing Michael by blowing with sugar cane alcohol.

The rhythmic sounds and blowing action whisk away bad energies and transfer *samay* from the healer into the body of the patient. These blows (*sssssuuuuuu*), which are repeated seven to ten times, are punctuated by a final blow (*sssssuuuuuu*) that is louder, quicker, and followed by a short hum (*hmmmmmm*). The short hum, followed by a pause, works something like a stanza, an arc of sound patterned by lines and verses. The two stanzas, A and B, are each made up of two verses (indicated by indentation).

CHUYAKI BLOWING

A   *sssssssssuuuuuuuuuu*
     sssssssssuuuuuuuuu
      sssssssssuuuuuuuuu
       ssssssssssssuuuuuuuu
        sssssssssuuuuu
        ssssuuuuuuuuuuuu

sssssssssuuuuuuu
sssssssssuuuuuuu

tssssssssssssssssssssssssssssssssuuuuuuuu
hhhhhhmmmmmmmmmm

B   *sssssssssuuuuuuuuuu*
sssssssssuuuuuuuuu
sssssssssuuuuuuuuu
sssssssssssuuuuuuuu
sssssssssuuuuu
ssssuuuuuuuuuuuu
sssssssssuuuuuuu
ssssuuuuuuuuuuu
sssssssssuuuuuuu

tsssssssssssssssssssssssssssuuuuuuuu
hhhhhhmmmmmmmmmmm

masha

The final word that Chuyaki utters, *masha* (son-in-law) signals the end of the healing process. In this brief example of somatic poetry, gestures and gesture sounds do the "work" of transferring Lucas's *samay* from his body into the body of the patient.[10] There are no words, no discourse involved—only gestures, sounds, and pauses.

Now that Chuyaki has crossed over to the other side of life (he passed in 2008), he is now considered to be with Yaya Dios or Father God[11] as well as to frequent those places that defined his shamanic consciousness and about which he sang on this evening in 2007. He always used to say, "those women are going to take me any day now. They really want me to become part of their world." Now part of their universe and traveling around in a green helicopter, Chuyaki has become a presence on the landscape. He, like many others, has become what he used to dream.

Conclusion

In this chapter, we have discussed somatic poetry, a multimodal, relational form of poetic expression involving the body and its interconnectedness to the world. Specifically, we showed the example of vapor bath healing, where one experiences the beauty and power of plants through all of the senses. This beauty and power moves from the forest, into the vapor, and finally becomes part of the body. As we have tried to demonstrate, the poetics of the Quichua language, imagery, the artful use of aromas and heat allowed the healer to create a multisensory work of art. We have also discussed other somatic poems, specifically Federico's way of describing his *ayllu* (family group) by analogy with manioc plants. As well, we looked at Chuyaki's shamanic song as a striking example of the multimodal use of sound, words, images, gestures, and the landscape to create circular forms, forms that connect various subjectivities and relations into a pathway of interconnectedness between this world and the spirit world, between life and death, between space and time, and between illness and healing.

We describe these experiences as somatic poetry to emphasize the body's central role in the creation of artistic meaning, meaning that takes on qualities of being substantial, visceral, and dramatic. Somatic poems, which are defined by experiences and relations as well as language, are untranslatable in their full beauty and complexity.

Somatic poems are socially as well as aesthetically different from Western poetry, a particular kind of art linked to the social and cultural transformations of alphabetic writing, the printed word, and the social history of the Western world (Ingold 2007). Somatic poems connect the individual life to the history of a community and its landscape in a way in which experience becomes tangled up with the stories and history of the place. Indeed, if nothing else, we hope we have provided some sense of the social dynamics of somatic poetry to connect individual lives to the larger narrative of a community's connectedness to place, the subjectivities of that place's ecology, its history, stories, and traditions, plants, animals, and people, both living and dead.

CHAPTER 2

PRIMORDIAL FLOODS AND THE EXPRESSIVE BODY

This chapter deals with voices that speak about the great flood, glossed as *izhu punzha* in the Napo Quichua vernacular. *Izhu* is an Quichua adaptation of the Spanish *juicio*, which indexes biblical notions of judgment, but the concept of the world ending and remaking itself through floods predates the arrival of Christianity to the region.[1] The term *izhu* likely derives from the proselytizing voices of colonial Jesuit priests from times past, religious specialists who occupied and were expelled from Napo two times. Between the 16th and 18th centuries, the Jesuits established over 74 reductions (concentrations of indigenous peoples for missionization and colonization) and brought together several tens of thousands of Natives throughout Amazonia (Taylor 1999:223). Napo, a key corridor between the Andes and Amazonia, was an intense site of Jesuit activity.

As the religious studies specialist Lawrence Sullivan (1988) has demonstrated, many South American cultures feature myths of primordial destruction. As he explains, these myths speak to an ongoing "ontological questioning" of the world and its order, as stories of catastrophe provide a complex symbolic language by which transformation, rather than fixity, is posited as the essence of things (Sullivan 1988:51). Indeed, the implicit message in South American myths of destruction is that society and order are subordinate to greater forces, namely the mysterious and powerful subjectivities of various others that are nonhuman, subjectivities that are integral rather than external to human reproduction (Fausto 2000; Uzendoski 2005; see also chapter 3). These meanings are all inscribed upon the landscape and "read" aloud by storytellers, people versed in the nuances of sound, movement, and transformation of phenomenological others.

Floods are processes of social destruction, but in destruction floods also generate new relations. Traces of these transformations, and the voices that define them, are embedded in the features of rock formations and the peaked lines of mountain ranges, entities that can make people dream or "feel" their hidden realities. Flood sociality engenders a view of the human condition in which human life and death are deeply intertwined with chthonic forces, forces of the underworld that emanate from *kallari timpu*, or beginning time-space. Being present during a telling or singing of *izhu* allows people not only to feel the presence of chthonic subjectivities but also to come into contact with them.[2]

In our presentation of the materials, we have attempted, in translated form, to highlight the principles of form, images, personality, voice, gestures, and style that define the *izhu* myths. The textuality of the mythological world of *izhu* is brought into presence using a variety of poetic techniques, especially gestures of vertical space and vertical movement, that take advantage of the whole expressive body. Our argument is that these narratives show transformations of subjectivity in which phenomenological others and humans possess different but interrelated communicative perspectives within the cosmological order. Mountains, for example, define the landscape and are eternal, while people, who are mortal, live within it. Mountains are considered to be places where animals and spirits reside, and are social actors with voices and unseen powers. Mountains are conduits between the earth and sky and, as we show, are associated with divinity and the upper world. Possessing what anthropologists often gloss as "shamanistic power," mountains are healers and life-givers; their power, as we discuss, manifests in their ability to communicate, shape-shift, and save people from harm. We present translations of two flood stories and one song. Each myth is introduced separately, and the end of the chapter provides a synthesis.

On our companion website, we include not only videos of the storytelling performances but also a map and drawings of the *izhu* story by school children of the Escuela Intercultural Bilingue Venancio Calapucha of Pano. The drawings, which show mythology as outlined by the hands of children, give the basic image-relations of the *izhu* complex, mountains, water, people, and the *cucha mama,* or anaconda.

The Great Flood as Told by Verna

The *izhu* myth presented here was told in 2003 by Verna Grefa, a man who is now over 80 years old. When Michael asked Verna to tell the *izhu* story, he initially recounted an oral version of Genesis 6–9 in Quichua. Fermin Shiguango was with Uzendoski this day, and Fermin then politely asked Verna to tell "our [Runa] version of the story." Here we present our own textual version of that telling.

Verna's story has three main acts: "Prophecy," "Mountains and Water," and "Receding and Reproduction." There are three main mountains that define the mythological landscape, and all three have voices. The first is Chiuta, a small mountain located at the outskirts of Tena, which is the cultural hearth of Upper Napo Quichua speakers. Next is Sumaco, the famous Amazonian volcano. Lastly, Verna mentions Cula, a mountain in the southern region near the city of Puyo. As is common in most tellings of this myth we have heard in the Tena region, Chiuta is always the central mountain, the metaphorical tree of life that "defeats" competing mountains from other areas. In the moment of struggle against the waters, the mountains cry out "MAAAAAAAAAAAAAAAAAAN!" to each other. The term "man" or *kari* in Quichua refers to power and strength; it is a common phrase in Napo Quichua vernacular for sonically projecting one's power (Uzendoski 2005).

The first act begins with a household of godly people who are informed by an angel that they should either save themselves on a balsa or climb a mountain. These people spread the word of imminent disaster. Wise people choose to climb up Chiuta, but others build balsa rafts and climb other, seemingly taller mountains. The next act is about the flooding and the rising waters. As the waters rise, the mountains grow, fueled by human agency as people "pray to God." The mountains call out to each other, and Chiuta establishes his superiority. In the end, Chiuta both grows the highest and sinks the lowest because of his power. The last act speaks of human salvation and reaffirms the vertical and cosmological superiority of Chiuta and, interestingly enough, Cula Mountain over Sumaco.

Janis Nuckolls (1996, 2000, 2010) has brought to light the centrality of gestures and imagery in Quichua narratives. Here, we follow her methodology in providing small images of gestures in the appropriate moments of the text. In this way, the gestures are linked to words—rather than divorced from them—allowing the reader a better appreciation of the body's power in storytelling experience. Furthermore, readers who wish to access this story online can observe the full movements of Verna's gestures and facial expressions.

Verna's gestures are central to the imagery, especially vertical imagery, of the story. Gesture 1, which takes place at 1:17 of the telling (see the gesture illustration next to line 48 on page 46), is a raising of the hand that conveys the rising water and complements the ideophone (a more technically precise term for what is sometimes referred to as onomatopoeia) ***aparrrrrilllla*** (pulling), which conveys the water rising in a steady fashion. Gesture 2, which takes place at 1:47 of the telling (see the gesture illustration next to line 64 on page 46), is a miming gesture of the people praying to God to save them. Gesture 3, which takes place at 2:03 of the telling (see the gesture illustration next to line 74 on page 46), accompanies the ideophone **Tsssssssssssuuuuuuuuuuuuukkk** and conveys the movement of one body arising out of another. Here the gesture is one of motion. Verna uses both hands to show that the mountain suddenly rises up out of the water and grows taller.

Gesture 4 occurs at 2:28 of the story and is a two-part gesture (see the gesture illustration next to line 93 on page 47). First, Verna moves his hands toward the ground to convey that there is a sound arising from inside the earth. Then Verna raises both arms suddenly upward to convey the mountain growing again for the second time. This gesture is complemented by the ideophone **drrrrrrrrrrrrrrrrrrrrrrrrrrrrr**, the sound and feeling of shaking "like a lightning bolt."

From this point, up through 2:54 of the telling, we have no information on gestures, as the camera operator, Fermin Shiguango, pans the camera to show the firepit and other details of Verna's house, but it is likely that Verna uses a series of gestures to convey the "growing, growing, growing" of the mountain toward the end of this scene. This hypothetical gesture, which we have observed in other tellings of this story, would be the inverse of gesture 7, which involves hand gestures downward instead of upward (see below). Gesture 5, thus, is left with a question mark (see the gesture illustration next to line 98 on page 47). Gesture 6, at 3:36 of the telling, is a quick downward hand motion that conveys the descent of Chiuta Mountain in returning to its original size (see the gesture illustration next to line 127 on page 48), and Gesture 7, at 3:43 of the telling, is the last one (see the gesture illustration next to line 132 on page 48). This gesture involves the aforementioned series of gestures downward that show Chiuta Mountain shrinking down, "even, even, even, even," with the water as it is drying up.

Although gestures are usually left out of transcriptions and translations of stories, here the reader will observe that the use of gestures in Napo Quichua storytelling enhances the storyteller's ability to convey images and movement in stories. The salient imagery and concomitant gestures in this story are vertical; they convey the connection of the earth and sky realms via mountains. These relations, sometimes referred to by specialists as an "axis mundi," or conduit that connects different realms of being (see chapters 3 and 4), are gestured into being, and it is no coincidence that the vertical imagery of this story is associated with divinity and God. Words simply cannot express these imagined relations of the story as succinctly and elegantly as the hands.

As we discussed in the introduction, the story is presented following the conventions of "verse analysis" in which the narrative is broken down into lines, verses (groupings of lines signaled by indentation), stanzas (A, B, C, etc.), scenes (i, ii, iii, iv, etc.) and acts (I, II, III). (See chapter 5 for a more detailed discussion.) Gestures, which are an integral aspect of the narrative's poetics, are indicated by corresponding images to the right of the text.

IZHU PUNZHA BY VERNA GREFA

```
I/i/A      now
             in our living
                Ecuador
                here in the rainforest
             there was just the same [implicit that he refers to Genesis 6–9]      5
B          when the judgment water was going to arrive
             one
                sin-
                   avoiding
                      peace-loving                                                 10
                         inti [full of] children
                            inti [full of] sons
                               household
ii/A       an angel came down they say
             "some of you                                                          15
                make a balsa raft and save yourselves
             some of you
                climb a mountain and save yourselves"
             [the angel] said, they say
B          and so being                                                            20
             they
                decided to climb the mountain they say
                   half the people
iii/A      here at the headwaters of the Tena River
                the mountain named Chiuta                                          25
                   stands
                      a tall mountain
             they climbed that mountain they say
B          and so being
             there was another mountain they say                                   30
                at the headwaters of the Ansu River
                   the mountain named Cula
C          with that one
             just the same
```

	people climbed it they say	35
	to the top	
D	and so being	
	there was another mountain they say	
	this	
	from where we are	40
	you can see it	
	named Sumaco	

people climbed it they say 35
   to the top

D and so being
there was another mountain they say
this
   from where we are 40
      you can see it
named Sumaco
   an even bigger mountain!

II/i/A three mountains
when the judgment waters covered them 45
   covered them
they grew they say
like pulling the water up [apaaarlIllIlla]   * Gesture 1 [upwards, one hand]
   it grew they say
those climbers on top of the mountain 50
   were there they say

B and so being
those floating on the rafts too
   were floating they say
lots of people 55

C however
when they tried to land on Chiuta Mountain
   [he] would not let them get close they say the mountain
      only those that climbed before were there they say

ii/A and so being 60
now the water

   when it was going to cover the top of the
      mountain kneeling   * Gesture 2 [praying]
   putting hands above
      they prayed to God they say 65

B "like this we are going to die" saying
  "ay ay ay God" saying
    "please bless our mountain of salvation"
      they cried they say
        kneeling 70

C and so doing
the mountain again
tssssssssssuuuuuuuuuuuuukkk   * Gesture 3 [sudden raising]
made noise
   it grew they say 75
      the water stayed below it they say

iii/A   while that was going on
       now they were there for a long time they say
    and while they were there
       the water rose to the top again   80
         water

B   again they shouted they say
       to Father God
         kneeling

C   and so doing   85
    just the same
    water
    made even more noise
       from inside the water
    the mountain made sound they say   90
    drrrrrrrrrrrrrrrrrrrrrrrrrrrrrr   * Gesture 4 [inside then raising]
       it sounded like a lightning bolt
         it climbed higher they say

D   and so doing

    growing [iñasha]   * Gesture 5? [possible raising]   95
      growing [iñasha]
        growing [iñasha] it went they say

III/i/A   since it grew
       the people were able to save themselves
    water now stopped there they say   100
       right there
         it didn't cover them anymore they say

B   looking there
    Cula Mountain shouted they say
    Chiuta Mountain shouted they say   110
    Sumaco Mountain shouted they say

C   just those three
       all the other big mountains
    were lost they say

D   only water was visible they say   115
       everywhere like the sky
        looked like glass [chhiiiiiiiiiiiuuuuuuuuuikllaaaaaaaaaaa]

ii/A   only those three mountains
    not being lost they shouted they say
    and you "**MAAAAAAAAAAAAAAAAAAN**"   120
       they shouted they say
    and I too "**MAAAAAAAAAAAAAAAAAAN**"
       they shouted they say

B   and while they were shouting
        Sumaco grew only so high they say   125
            not any more
                because there weren't people there
                    he didn't have any more power they say
      in trying to descend too   * Gesture 6 [downward]
            he couldn't do it they say   130

iii/A   on the other hand
      Chiuta Mountain
            having lots of people

      when the water was drying   * Gesture 7 [leveling then 4 downward motions]
      starting   135
      even [pariju]
            even [pariju]
                even [pariju]
                    even [parjiu]
                        descended they say   140

B   and so doing
            the people could be saved they say

C   Cula Mountain
            just the same grew they say
                with people   145
      a growing mountain then
            sat back down
      if you see it now only in your mind
            does it look like a tall mountain
                it seems like a small mountain   150

D   Chiuta even more
            even though it's a very high mountain
      when you look at it from far away
            a small mountain appears

iv/A   and so   155
      that's how things seem here
      from this here
      our people reproduced
      this is how our old people told the story

B   like this   160
            and so being
      about the judgment waters this much of the story exists
            here
                about the world
                    we live in   165

The Great Flood as Told by Lucas Tapuy (Chuyaki)

This myth was recorded using cassette-tape audio equipment in 1996 in Sapo Rumi, Ecuador. The storyteller, Lucas Tapuy (nicknamed Chuyaki) is Edith's late uncle, and he was known for his irreverence and his brash sense of humor. Like Verna, Chuyaki told this story when he was very old. Chuyaki, as well, liked to tell stories about his connection to a very large stone near his house and how *yaku warmiguna* (water women) visit him at night in his dreams, stories that are related to his shamanic song (see chapter 1) of this experiential reality. Taken as a whole, both his songs and stories invoke the power and reality of the chthonic world.

The reader will notice that Chuyaki's style is nonlinear and more metaphorical and visual. In telling his story Chuyaki relies on the listener's ability to connect implicit social and geographical knowledge with the images he creates of kinship relations, mountains, and movements. Although we present an accurate translation, the story is almost impossible to understand out of context, and its plot is very weakly developed. However, Chuyaki's intent in this telling is social and metaphorical.

The narrative contains two main acts, "Mountains" and "Flood." The first act focuses on the interaction and competition between the two mountain peaks, Sumaco and Chiuta. Act I ends when Chiuta, the smaller of the two mountains, grows up high and the water passes over Sumaco. In this rendition, however, Sumaco cries out loudly, but Chiuta's power is reflected in his quietness, a figure-ground reversal of Verna's telling. It is not that Chiuta can't cry out; it is that he chooses to communicate by being silent. Chiuta stays above water, and Sumaco is defeated. The second act focuses on the destruction caused by the flood and the human perspective. It features the death of the *auka* (a term that refers to a non-Runa Native who is not Christian and who also kills Runa people) and places the narrator's ancestors on top of Chiuta. The concluding scenes speak to the kinship flow from the ancestors to the present generation.

In the beginning of the story Chuyaki refers to "father." In Napo Quichua kinship, substance flows of descent often move through time and space, collapsing many generations into one. This technique is like "time-travel" applied to the domain of kinship and connects current inhabitants to the very beginnings of time and space. Indeed, after telling us this story, Chuyaki comments that his father personally "knew" the twins, the mythical culture heroes of the Napo Runa featured in later chapters.

Here is the story.

IZHU PUNZHA BY LUCAS TAPUY

I / A	in that beginning times
	in that epoch
	talking about *izhu* times
	the water . . . to water . . . father (says with certainty)
	father at first 5
	at first he had been tested by water
B	from there later there were the Cuillurguna [The Twins], those guys
C	at first now
	tested
	everything 10
	in doing whatever the water
	when the water explodes
	when that happens
i / A	now
	izhu times 15
	the red headed woodpecker
	just this plume headed woodpecker
	escaped they say
B	he didn't get tired they say
C	now everything **tun** [something closing and becoming dark] 20
	nothing to see they say
ii / A	being so now this water
	in this
	Sumaco
	it passed over that valley 25
	that water filled and passed over
	Sumaco
B	that water he
	he'll win saying he had shouted that mountain father
	he'll win he had said that mountain 30
C	he'll win
	when he said
	he
	Chiuta
	did not speak he 35
	umbas [being really quiet, not moving]
	he did not speak he
	the mountain
iii / A	being so
	this looking from Chiuta 40
	they escaped

	my father's fathers	
	there	
	white cacao stand there now they say	
	on top of that mountain	45
	where they escaped	
B	my father's father's *grandfathers* [Spanishized word, "abueloguna"]	
	they escaped	
C	there . . . there in escaping	
	from there we have reproduced	50
	they used to say	
iv/A	and so being in that	
	that Chiuta	
	when they were looking	
	those elder living ones looking	55
	with the mountain	
	it now was passing over they say	
	that water	
	Chiuta	
	the valley was full	60
B	in that a big lake was formed they say	
	that beginning times water that water was there they say	
C	it was deep they say	
	he didn't let anyone climb up they say	
	he was a spirit [*supay*] mountain they say	65
	that mountain	
v/A	doing like this	
	this Chiuta	
B	again with the water coming	
	up	70
C	again with more water coming	
	up	
	again more water	
	up	
	he grew even more they say more	75
vi/A	doing like this	
	they did not die these people	
	Sumaco	
	covered	
B	covered	80
	passed over	
	that valley	
	that valley right in the middle	

C	became defeated they had said	
II/i/A	doing like this . . . that . . .	85
	Runa people now	
	all	
	savages were there they had said	
	savages that killed Runa people	
B	the water carried them off	90
	from there	
	shoutiiiiiiiiiiiiiiing standing they were looking they say (from Chiuta)	
C	[turning over] (**tian**)	
	from there being	
	[turning over] (**tian**)	95
	one from there being	
	[turning over] (**tian**)	
ii/A	from that mountain we enjoy it they say they	
	they were enjoying they say they from there	
B	who who who would catch hold they say like that	100
C	all **tun** covered [completely filled up]	
	when there were just two mountains who grew	
iii/A	in so doing	
	they had gotten away they had said	
B	from there we reproduced they said	105
	my fathers told	
	all that like so	
iv/A	how we had escaped	
B	if it wouldn't have been so	
	this Chiuta now . . .	110
	if the water would have passed over	
	nobody would have lived	
	reproducing	
	or not reproducing	
C	it would have been over	115
v/A	in doing so	
	now reproducing they [people] live	

Camilo's Flood Song

The last *izhu* story we present is the genre of violin music, a common practice among the elders, who not only told stories but also created music out
of mythological experience and realities. This *izhu* song is sung by Camilo
Tapuy, Edith's elder cousin, who is nearly 70 years old. Camilo learned this
song from their grandfather, Ñachuyaya, and grandmother (see Uzendoski,

Hertica, and Calapucha 2005). Ñachuyaya taught Camilo how to play the Amazonian violin and gave Camilo his *paju*, or "magic," of music.

The violin, which can be seen in the video of this performance, remains an important part of Napo Quichua musical culture because of its central role in wedding rituals and its association with "tradition." The violin is also used in *ayahuasca* rituals to call spirits. In contrast to modern Runa Paju, violin music is considered old-time music, that is, music associated with past generations. We have more to say about Napo Quichua musical culture in chapter 8, but as in many cultural traditions, Napo Quichua people use music and song to tell stories and evoke mythological realities.

Unlike the European violin, the Amazonian violin is played by sitting with the body of the instrument in one's lap like a cello. It is usually bigger than the Western violin and has three rather than four strings. The musician traditionally made his own violin out of *cedro* wood (Spanish cedar), and often the face of the violin was covered with an old piece of tin. The bow, also made by the musician, is a piece of wood that is strung with palm fibers rather than hair. Today, many violin players buy Western violins in town and play them in the Amazonian style, but the majority of people use the violin to make Runa Paju, a modern eclectic style of Amazonian Quichua music rather than the music of beginning times made by Camilo (see chapter 8).

Traditionally, the violin was a masculine instrument that was almost always accompanied by a feminine singer, except in *ayahuasca* rituals, where men would sing *takina* songs that were enhanced by the violin playing (see Belzner and Whitten 1979 for a recording and analysis of Napo Quichua shamanistic violin music). The Amazonian violin, as well as all music, is a means of relating to the spirit world, and as Camilo has told us, the violin is metaphorical of a spirit woman. One of its defining sound qualities is that it is played so that it "wails" evoking the voice of the spirit-woman, and in the old days violin players would carve heads of women into the handles of their instruments. Fermin Shiguango, a *yachak* from Campo Cocha, once commented that the violin, like all old-time music, is a way of expressing one's *ushay*, or spiritual power. This basic idea fits with Norman and Dorothea Whitten's (2008) notion that, for Amazonian Runa, beauty and power are closely associated, and that the production of beauty is a shamanistic action of *samay* (breath/vital energy) expression.

The first time we heard this song was during a father's day celebration in 2003 that took place in the church. We have seen Camilo perform this song many times, usually spontaneously, and community members often help out with the singing. The performance is never exactly the same twice. While

Camilo can dictate from memory the lyrics of most of his songs, there are possibilities for improvisation during the performance.

Unlike the previous two stories about *izhu*, here the anaconda, referred to as the *cucha mama*, or mother of the deep, is the implicit generator of the flood because she is angry. The *izhu* song emphasizes the death of all things more than the stories. There are only two acts, "The Flood" and "Salvation." There is a stanza, repeated various times throughout the song that deals exclusively with the death of birds, people, jaguars, and all things.

The performance presented here took place in the communal house of Sapo Rumi in the summer of 2004. It was videotaped using a stand, and there were a number of people in our family present, including Chuyaki, whose flood story we just finished recounting. Before singing, Camilo introduces the song in a speaking voice. Like Chuyaki, who is sitting next to Camilo in the performance, Camilo elicits kinship flow from the past by mentioning that his "fathers" invented this song in the beginning times. When the video starts, one can see Carmela, Chuyaki's wife, Chuyaki, and Camilo in the scene. On the far left is Ernesto, a nephew of both Camilo and Chuyaki. Camilo describes the song as "the flood" and refers to the "beginning times." Here, he points to Chuyaki. This brief gesture (0:02) is an acknowledgment of Chuyaki as a man who is connected to beginning time-space and someone who "knows," a *yachak*, of that realm (see chapter 1). He then says that this story is "about the coming of the *izhu* waters" and begins to play.

Camilo's use of the violin creates an altered sonic space, which begins the song. Then the human voices join in and put words into the song, but unlike the words of the storyteller, the words of the singer are much more condensed and at times nonlinear; hearing them creates powerful images in the imagination, but only if one implicitly knows the story. At the 58-second point, one can observe that Chuyaki interjects a statement during the song. He makes a comment that if their ancestors had not climbed up that mountain we "would have not been here today." Here we can see the interaction among storytellers, whose somatic poems overlap and complement each other.

The video shows about 40 seconds of postperformance interactions, interactions that are socially significant. Camilo, now speaking, reiterates that he just performed the song of the "flood" and "Chiuta Mountain." He puts down his violin and smiles. Michael says "that was beautiful," and Chuyaki repeats, "if they wouldn't have been saved we wouldn't be here today." Then Federico, Felicia's brother, suddenly enters the scene and offers Camilo a drink of trago. Camilo empties the glass and then adds tree resin (*copal*) to his bow fibers. These postperformance interactions are moments of communitas, moments when all participants feel the reality of the storytelling world as defining of the place and people with whom they share life.

The reader should be aware of some important differences between mythical storytelling through discourse versus mythological storytelling through music. Musical storytelling is much more condensed and emphasizes specific images and transformations of mythology (see chapters 4 and 8). The power of mythological song is that words are given new capabilities and qualities when they are musicalized. The use of couplets, for example, a defining feature of all Quichua storytelling, is enhanced by paralleling melodic contours. The music, a complex set of relations that are felt rather than seen, enhances the implicit mythological truths of all things being defined by flow and transformation. Music helps one to feel myth in the bones.

In our translation below, the song is organized into stanzas. As the reader will note, each stanza contains two couplets, but sometimes Camilo adds a third line to his couplets, which does not alter the basic structure. Each verse, made up of two lines, is a couplet, and each stanza contains two verses. The refrain is a bit more complex, as there are three verses that make up the stanza, with each verse being a couplet but the whole being a triad. These dynamic relations of twos and threes are repeated so that the song, like Chuyaki's shamanic song in the last chapter, is a circle of relations. Here is the song.

IZHU PUNZHA SONG BY CAMILO TAPUY

speaking introduction

Camilo: the *izhu* [flood] of the beginning   *GESTURE Points to Chuyaki   1
Michael: *izhu* day?   2
Camilo: *izhu*, *izhu* waters   3
about the coming of the *izhu* waters   4

I/ The Flood
violin introduction

A   when the *izhu* water comes
       when the *izhu* water comes
       the whole forest got covered
       the whole forest got covered
B   the birds died   5
       the birds died
       the animals died
       the people died
       everything died
       everything died   10

violin solo

Chuyaki: if. . . . we wouldn't be here today

C   For forty days
       For forty days
       it really rained like hell
       it really rained like hell
       it really rained like hell   15

D   when the mother of the deep [implicit=anaconda] got mad
       when the mother of the deep [implicit=anaconda] got mad
       the whole forest got covered
       the whole forest got covered

violin solo

E   the birds died   20
       the birds died
       the people died
       everything died
       everything died

violin solo

II: Salvation

A   there was only one mountain left   25
       there was only one mountain left
       that the *izhu* waters didn't tear down
       that the *izhu* waters didn't tear down

B   they climbed the Chiuta Mountain   30
       they climbed the Chiuta Mountain
       many people were saved
       many people were saved
       many people were saved

violin solo

C   at the headwaters of the Tena River   35
       at the headwaters of the Tena River
       Chiuta Mountain stood
       Chiuta Mountain stood

D   climbing Chiuta Mountain
       climbing Chiuta Mountain   40
       many people were saved
       many people were saved

violin solo

E   there the saved Runa people!
       there the saved Runa people!
       we are still happy up until now   45
       we are still happy up until now

F	there the saved Runa people!	
	there the saved Runa people!	
	we are still happy up until now	
	we are still happy up until now	50

violin solo
violin conclusion

Postperformance Conversation

Camilo [speaking voice] that is the ancient flood	1
Chiuta Mountain	2
Michael: that is very beautiful	3
izhu day	4
Chuyaki: if they wouldn't have been saved, we wouldn't be here today	5

Conclusion

In this chapter, we have presented translations of three flood stories. The first was a story by Verna Grefa, the second a story by Lucas Calapucha, and the last one a song by Camilo Tapuy. We have argued that the social theory implicit in flood myths is that mountains and humans possess different but interrelated communicative perspectives within the cosmological order. Humans are beings who live within the landscape, but mountains are timeless, or *wiñay*, in Quichua. They define the landscape, vertical space, and root the cosmological order. Traces of these relations, and the voices that define them, come out in the socially active communicative space of storytelling. Storytellers, as we have seen, draw out the textuality of mountain subjectivities by using a host of techniques: discourse, ideophones, metaphors, imagery, quotations of phenomenological others, perspective-changing, gestures, and music. All of these techniques employ the power of the whole expressive body, which, in the Quichua world, has multiple and synergistic communicative potentialities.

Flood sociality engenders a humble view of the human condition that is distinct from the arrogant Western idea that "nature" is meant for resource extraction and human domination. Floods of destruction teach us that human life and the landscape in which it exists are linked socially, communicatively, and spiritually. While it is difficult to talk directly to mountains, Quichua speakers acknowledge that mountains are beings with subjectivity and communicative potentiality, living conduits of vertical space that link the upper world and the chthonic domain. The communicative relatedness that Quichua speakers create with mountains, rivers, and other features of the landscape, roots them socially and spiritually within a textual reality that is philosophically as well as aesthetically complex.

CHAPTER 3

THE ILUKU MYTH, THE SUN, AND THE ANACONDA

The Axis Mundi: Ladders, Bridges, and Tunnels

In this chapter, we share the Iluku story and the origin of the sun story, two beginning-times transformations of celestial relations in Upper Amazonian Quichua mythology. In the first story, Iluku brings into existence an axis mundi of the cosmos through a sound channel of love and desire with the moon man (N. Whitten and D. Whitten 2008). In later episodes of the mythology, Iluku becomes the birth mother to Napo Runa civilization. Through her pregnancy with moon man, she brings into being the Cuillurguna, the culture heroes of the Amazonian Quichua world.

The origin of the sun involves a family that has an anaconda for a child. The anaconda takes a human wife and transforms into a handsome man, but in a passionate moment the woman puts out the anaconda's eye with a dripping candle. Angered, he leaves this world and ascends to the sky. His remaining eye becomes the sun. Like Iluku, this story also invokes axis mundi relationality of the cosmos through an axis mundi of love, desire, and sorrow. Both celestial bodies, the moon and the sun, like many plants and animals of mythology, were at one time part of the human domain and integral to cycles of human reproduction.

Poetically, these stories demonstrate how Quichua speakers create oral textuality using sound, imagery, and experience. Ecological others, perceived as humans in transformed states, come alive through the musicality of the spoken word and the human voice. Oral textuality is also created through the invocation of a specific imagery that scholars have referred to as the "axis mundi," which, as Lawrence Sullivan (1988:131) has written, is a center that allows access to other cosmic realms. Both stories, for example, create complex axis mundi relations that interconnect this world with the upper world and interrelate people with celestial bodies, birds, and snakes.

The axis mundi can take the form of a tree, mountain, pillar, vine, or conduit. The imagery of the axis mundi establishes "communications between spiritual planes," and it is common in the Native South American world for the axis mundi to also exist within the house or as the house itself (Sullivan 1988:133). The center post, for example, can often represent the "center" of the world in many South American traditions (see Guss 1989). Amazonian Quichua people associate the axis mundi with a number of phenomenon, phenomenon that include the Iluku bird song, the moon, the sun, and the rainbow, which is said to be the manifestation of an anaconda's energy body traversing the sky. In terms of the house, or *wasi*, the fire pit (*nina*) is a social space with associations with vertical travel among different realms of the cosmos; people gather around the fire pit, usually in the early morning hours, to tell stories, make music, drink *wayusa tea*, and analyze dreams. As one Quichua person commented, "the fire is our *kawsay,* or life," a place of energy and transformations.

In Quichua the term *chakana* signifies "ladder," and the image of a ladder is also often a central image of mythology in the Andean as well as Amazonian world. As Michelle Wibbelsman has written, "the *chakana* stands for the interrelatedness of everything and the interpenetrability of different time-spaces" (Wibbelsman 2008:2). In Amazonian Quichua mythology, the *chaka*, or "bridge," as well as caverns, can also signify such relations, as ladders, bridges, and caverns are present in crucial scenes of the mythology. The Iluku story, for example, contains the ladder as a central image (see later in this chapter). The Cuillurguna story we present in chapter 5 features a bridge. The mundopuma story of chapter 6 features a cavern. In the Amazonian Quichua world, there is no single image or phenomenon that is the axis mundi. It is a plural concept that is all about the interrelationality and interpenetrability among all things living and existing within and among the different levels of the cosmos.

We argue that the significance behind these stories is axis mundi relationality and a human condition defined by poetic relations with celestial, ecological, and spirit others.[1] The relatedness among birds, people, rocks, rivers, the wind, the landscape, and various other presences provides people with a deep emotional and social attachment to the ecological world around them. The poetics of these narratives and songs derive from experience of this rich landscape. The stories, as we show through text as well as sound, emphasize the dependence of people on spirit and cosmological others in the larger complexity of life and its varied transformations.

Iluku and the Moon

Iluku is the name Amazonian Quichua speakers used to describe the common potoo (*Nyctibius grisens*, Nyctibiidae), a nocturnal bird that is known throughout Amazonia to sing in the presence of the full moon.[2] As the story goes, Iluku was impregnated by her brother, the moon, who was visiting her at night as a stranger and making love to her. In Quichua this act of lovemaking is glossed as *killayachina*, or "to make the woman lazy" (see Orr and Hudelson 1971). To find out who her lover really is, Iluku smears *wituk* (*Genipa americana*) on his face one night. When her brother is discovered the next day, he ascends into the sky but retains the "spots" from the *wituk* pigment. This separation of Iluku from the moon is the initial transformation, and the "painting" of the moon's face is the initial image, one that can still be observed today with the "spots" on the moon's surface.

Iluku wants to follow her "husband" into the sky but due to the moral fault of *killa* (laziness, carelessness, sexual "looseness" [Swanson 2009]), Iluku fails and remains on earth saddened. There are two major images that emerge in this part of the tale. The first is the creation of a ladder by which Iluku is supposed to climb to follow her husband, but that falls apart. The second is Iluku's skirt coming undone and "falling out" behind her. The first image is reminiscent of vines in the forest (N. Whitten and D. Whitten 2008), while the second is mimetic of the tail of the common potoo, which fans out in a distinct way.

The last and most important aspect of the story is the sonorous call of Iluku. Every time the moon comes out, it is said, one can hear Iluku calling out to her lover, "luuu, luuu, luuu, luuu," a mimetic outpouring of her desire, sadness, and longing to be with her "husband." The story of Iluku's loss can be heard from a storyteller in the human voice or from Iluku herself in her bird voice. Both are performances, however, and they speak to a mythological reality shared by humans and birds. Whether it is Iluku or the storyteller, the mimetic sounds of Iluku's song elicit the meanings, images, emotions, and outcomes of her story.

English Translation of the Iluku Story as Told by Verna Grefa, Summer 2006

This version of the Iluku tale was told by Verna Grefa to both of us in his house in 2006. The performance was videotaped. Although it is not a long telling (3:43), the musicality of the storyteller's voice in creating mimesis with the actual song of the common potoo bird made this a special recounting. Also, in this telling, Verna's use of gestures is remarkable, as he uses

17 gestures to express the complex relations of movement, transformation, and relationality present in the narrative. The gestures depict imagery and movement that bring the story to life. In scenes iv and v, the mimesis of the phrases "oh my beloved husssband [ñu-ka ku-sa-lla]" and "Iluuukuuuku cries [il-lu-ku-mi nin]" with the common potoo bird's song is pure poetry; the pitch as well as pauses match, as both human and bird voices fall out into lines of sorrow and longing. While vocalizing Iluku's song, Verna uses a head gesture that imitates a bird's form while singing out to the moon (see gestures 11, 12, and 17 below).

The video also reveals how Verna uses gestures to invoke crucial images that are central to the story, specifically the use of the hands to invoke movements, shape-shifting, and the vertical relations of the axis mundi. Here we describe the gestures, which can be observed in a more dynamic way through the video online. The gestures are depicted though a small image and labeled in the transcription below on the right.

Gesture 1, which occurs at 1:11 (see the gesture illustration next to line 36 on page 63), is one in which Verna uses his hands in outlining the skirt that Iluku was wearing. He moves his hands up his torso and then around his waist as if he were tying a skirt. Gesture 2, at 1:21 (see the gesture illustration next to line 40 on page 63), is a pointing gesture to show the trail that moon man took when he left Iluku. Gesture 3, at 1:25 (see the gesture illustration next to line 42 on page 63) is a torso-neck gesture that mimics moon man turning around to see if Iluku is following. Gesture 4, just a few seconds later (see the gesture illustration next to line 45 on page 63), is another skirt gesture. Here Verna mimics the skirt of Iluku coming loose and her retying it again. At 1:38 gesture 5 (see the gesture illustration next to line 48 on page 64) is a pointing gesture to indicate the trail taken by moon man as he leaves Iluku. Gesture 6, at 2:11 (see the gesture illustration next to line 61 on page 64), is another skirt gesture, and gesture 7, at 2:22 (see the gesture illustration next to line 65 on page 64) is another trail gesture, but this time the trail is the one taken by Iluku as she turns into a bird.

Gesture 8 (see the gesture illustration next to line 66 on page 64) is a two-part gesture that marks the central transformation of the story. First, a brief trail gesture is used to indicate Iluku's path, but then Verna opens his arms wide and up above his head to show Iluku's transformation into a bird. These gestures are complemented by the ideophones *waaaannn* (spreading out) and *paklllaaan* (opening up) that express Iluku's skirt becoming the tail of the common potoo bird. Gesture 9, at 2:30 (see the gesture illustration next to line 71 on page 65) is a brief leveling hand gesture that shows Iluku landing on a tree branch. Gesture 10 (see the gesture illustration next to line 72 on page 65) is another trail gesture, and gestures 11, at 2:41 (see the gesture illustration next to line 75 on page 65), and 12, at 2:45 (see the gesture illustration next to line 76 on page 65), are head gestures in which the same gesture is repeated twice. Here, Verna mimics the bodily form of a bird singing out its song.

Gesture 13, at 2:52 (see the gesture illustration next to line 81 on page 65), is a two-part trail gesture, in which Verna changes the path of moon man's trail from horizontal to vertical ascent. Gesture 14, at 2:57 (see the gesture illustration next to line 85 on page 65), is then another vertical trail gesture to indicate moon man's arrival in the upper world. Gesture 15, at 3:10 (see the gesture illustration next to line 89 on page 66), is a pointing gesture to express the precise link between Iluku and her song, and in gesture 16, at 3:12 (see the gesture illustration next to line 92 on page 66), Verna then opens his hand to show the roundness of the full moon. Gesture 17, at 3:15 (see the gesture illustration next to line 95 on page 66), is the head gesture of a bird song as Verna again repeats Iluku's crying.

Readers who watch the video will also see the moment of communitas toward the end of the story. Verna laughs heartily as Michael says "aaaaahhh," an expression of understanding what has just been told, recognition of the story's textuality. These moments of coming together, of storyteller and his or her audience, reveal the shared world of experience and relations that define the communicative community.

Here is an English translation of Verna's telling in 2006 presented in the form of verse analysis. Gestures are labeled to the right.

THE ILUKU STORY BY VERNA GREFA

I/i/A   in the beginning times
        there was Iluku
            who was here they say as a person
        and so being
        at that very same time   5
            there was also they say
                the Moon person he was named
        in this, this very world they lived they say
            Moon
        he was a nice looking man they say   10
            white, a good man
B   and so being
        that
            he got this woman named Iluku
        and so being   15
            after a **looooong** time

          loooong time
            a **loooong** time they lived together

ii/A   and so being
        Moon one day said   20
            "now my day has come
                my Lord is calling me
                I am going to the heaven above" he said

B   to his wife he said this
            "you, don't make any mistakes   25
                with me together
                    getting all your things
                        follow me up there"
      saying this he spoke

C   when he said this   30
      "it will be fine" she said
            it seemed like she was getting ready they say
      and while she was getting ready
      in that time they wore a skirt called the *pacha* which

            wraps around the body [**yes**]
      and like that Moon said   *** Gesture 1 (showing clothing)** 35
      "now I am going"
          saying

          "let's go together" when he said
             he, the man, was going they say
             like this he was going they say   *** Gesture 2 (trail)**
                                          40

iii/A   "are you coming" he turned around to look   *** Gesture 3 (turning around)**
      "no" saying
         "my skirt

          wrapping is coming open" saying   *** Gesture 4 (skirt undone)**
             she grabbed the belt and wrapped it again they say   45
                again she wrapped it they say, that *pacha* skirt

just going two or three steps   * **Gesture 5 (trail)**
    again the skirt opened up they say
        becoming like that she couldn't keep up they say

B   and so without being able to keep up   50
    Moon wanted to take her with him
        "but like this you can't keep up"
            "what happened to you?" saying
                "are you an Iluku mama?" saying
                   "falling down like that   55
                      and turning back" he got angry they say

iv/A   and so being
        right there
    "yes I am Iluku for God's sake!" saying she said they say

that long skirt fell out and out   * **Gesture 6 (skirt)** 60
    as it was very very long it would have fallen out all over they say
B   like so that long long thin

"I am Iluku" saying she said   * **Gesture 7 (trail)**

running she flew away they say   * **Gesture 8 (trail, shape-shifting)**
    waaaaan taking off   65
        into the **opppppppppennn [pakklllaaan]** sky
            with that flowing skirt behind she was flying
                she sat on the end of a tree branch they say

* Gesture 9 (leveling)

C and so being

* Gesture 10 (trail) 70

her man now was **angry, angry**
  Iluku looked at him while he went away
saying to her man

* Gesture 11 (head)

   "**oh my beloved husssband** [ñu-ka ku-sa-lla]

* Gesture 12 (head)

   my beloved husssband"
    saying [ñu-ka ku-sa-lla]
    she cried they say

75

D and while she was crying
   her husband

* Gesture 13 (trail)

   left her for good they say
    she saw him as he disappeared at the top they say
     as if he were climbing a mountain   80
      going into the clouds he went up they say

* Gesture 14 (trail, upward)

E he went up they say
  and so going he abandoned her

v/A that's how it was!
  and every time the moon comes out she must cry
  seeing her husband's face makes her cry they say

* Gesture 15 (pointing)

85

   whenever it is a full moon
  and so being
  "my beloved hussssband" [ñu-ka ku-sa-lla]
   she has that distinct cry

* Gesture 16 (hand=moon)

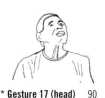

 her man responds
  "Iluuukuuuku cries" [il-lu-ku-mi nin] saying
   they named her Iluku
   yes (laughs)

* Gesture 17 (head) 90

B that is how Iluku became
  yes her name

95

C and so being
 there are stories like that
 if one knows them
  they are there
   yes about our way of life
   yes

100

Incest and Ladders in the Iluku Story: Poetic Play and Variation

Let us now discuss a few more relations that can be elicited by considering
other versions of the Iluku story. Verna's telling, unlike the more complete
"traditional" story, uses the notion of Christian death as the prime mover.
The moon man leaves earth because God calls him, and moon man asks
Iluku to follow. In Orr and Hudelson's (1971) book, *Cuillurguna*, however, the
authors present a longer version of the Iluku story in Quichua and in Spanish

translation. In this version, the authors provide a narrative that includes a scene where incest between the moon man and Iluku, rather than Christian death, sets the story into motion. As well, this longer version contains a scene where moon man builds a ladder, and ladder imagery is explicit. This is how the story begins (our translation here is from the Quichua):

in the beginning times the Cuillurguna did not exist.
a man made his own sister loose [**killayachishka**=to make loose]
at night when he made her loose [**killayachikpi**]
his sister waited to wipe **ituk** [a pigment] on him
while she lay waiting for him to come and sleep with her she had the **ituk** ready
    she **huii** [rubbed] it on his face
when she rubbed it, he got scared and ran away
in the morning he did not wake up
    he was just lying in his mosquito net

This version of the story begins with a mysterious man sleeping with his own sister. As discussed earlier, the poetics of this union are described as *killayachishka*, or "to make loose," a term that implies sexual relations, but the root of the word, *killa*, also means "moon," "lazy," "careless," as well as "sexually loose"—the negative value embodied by Iluku herself.

In order to discover who has made her "sexually loose," the woman, who has not yet become Iluku, decides to wipe *ituk*, a black tree pigment, on the face of her lover. So she waits for him and wipes it on his face. When his sister wipes the *ituk* on his face, the moon man, certain he has been discovered, runs away and refuses to get up in the morning.

Ituk is the Quichua word for a black tree pigment (*Genipa americana*) that does not wash off. If a person is painted with *ituk*, the pigment will stay on their skin for a month or longer. Traditionally, *ituk* is used for face painting and protection from evil spirits and dangerous animals. However, in this story, the *ituk* serves a crucial purpose of marking a social transgression and transformation. *Ituk* becomes a marker of incest and sets the story in motion; it is because of the anger of their parents, in realizing that their daughter is pregnant through incest, that the moon man decides to ascend to the upper world. Quichua speakers say that the spots that appear on the moon are the stains from Iluku wiping *ituk* on his face.

Also, in this version of the story, the moon man builds a ladder out of bamboo arrows and tells Iluku to follow. When her skirt keeps falling off, she is unable to keep up and falls to the ground because the ladder does not hold. He then calls the birds to carry her upward, but she again falls down. Here is the scene.

her man had now climbed to the above
the bamboo arrows
from the top
    tía tía tía [things coming apart]
      they had by then come apart
her man had said if you don't tie your skirt right you will have to stay
when she couldn't climb
    her man got a lot of birds together to make her fly
but she still couldn't climb even though she was getting them together and flying
    she fell right back down to the earth

This scene features the idephone, *tía*, which connotes two things coming apart. Here, *tía* marks Iluku's demise through a sound-image of arrows, stuck together, that begin to come apart. As the arrows fall to the earth, the ladder is destroyed and the path to the upper world gone. Like in Verna's telling, a few lines later, the moon man directly asks his wife if she is Iluku. He then names her:

are you Iluku or what?
I am like Iluku
I am just a little bit like Iluku yes she said
stay here in this place
you couldn't [keep up]
you are the Iluku woman he said

This version portrays Iluku's crying as "luuuu luuuuu luuu," a mimesis of the common potoo's song, but this way of telling is more generic than Verna's more precise, "my be-lo-ved hus-band" and moon man's response "Ilu-ku cries." Also, in contrast to Verna's telling, this version does not contain the scene where Iluku transforms into a bird and her skirt becomes her tail, but the Orr and Hudelson (1971) version contains two short scenes where moon man tries to raise Iluku up by sending flocks of birds. Both attempts fail, and Iluku remains trapped in this world.

This quick comparison of these two versions of the same story show that there are considerable differences in storytelling and in telling the Iluku story, even at the level of scenes. Verna prefers to emphasize God, the transformative effects of carelessness, the image of Iluku's skirt-tail, and the song of Iluku. The Orr and Hudelson (1971) story emphasizes incest, the ladder, and the birds who try to make Iluku ascend. Unfortunately, because this story was found in a book, we do not have audio information about the character of the sounds beyond the words nor do we have information about gestures or the storytelling scene.

Despite these variations, there are relations—mostly images but also sounds—to the Iluku story that are unchanging because the story would not be the same without them. The skirt and Iluku's failure to tie it up correctly, as well as the mimesis of her crying with the sound of the common potoo bird's song, are vital to all tellings of this tale. The axis mundi imagery and the ascent of moon man and the failed ascent of Iluku are also essential, but as we have tried to show, storytellers have considerable poetic play in how these relations are brought to life. But why is this so? What really defines the similarities among different versions of a story?

Here a few words about "oral formulaic theory" (Lord 1960) are in order, for the notion that Amazonian Quichua speakers use "formulas" in performing consistent stories and myths is a tempting and, in many ways, convincing idea (see also Finnegan 2007:100).[3] But to reduce what Quichua speakers do in storytelling to the notion of "formulas" would be to distort the communicative and social complexity that defines storytelling practices. As we have seen, for example, the sonic contour of the common potoo bird is part of experience. It exists in the world. To call it a "formula," to pay attention only to the words, would distort the complexity and beauty of what is a much more complicated and multidimensional textual reality, one where creativity and innovation meet tradition and experience.

Storytellers elicit textualities and shape them poetically via individual styles. Sometimes, as we have seen, they use similar phrases and turns of talk. Storytellers—Quichua storytellers, at least—are not automats, as the notion of "formulas" implies (Lord 1960). All the storytellers that we know are creative, socially linked people who share in a textual and communicative world of experience. They are defined by competence (see D. Hymes 2003) rather than formulas.

The Origin of the Sun

Norman and Dorothea Whitten (2008:194) argue that by focusing on the "imagery" that Amazonian mythology evokes, one can appreciate the aesthetic power of stories to create a "transformational tunnel through which lore and history are projected into contemporary life." Among the Pastaza Runa, a different group of Amazonian Quichua speakers, Iluku (called "Jilucu" in their dialect of Quichua) is also the ancestral mother and the originator of the clay that defines the ceramics tradition practiced by women potters, but the Iluku story also explains the "seed beads" prevalent in Native Amazonian regional exchange as well as the Jesuit-era salt mines in the Marañón River system. Out of the great transformations of the primordial incest between

Iluku and the moon is a great flood and the rise of the sun (*Inti*) out of a cave. As the sun rose into the sky, many "tiny colored bubbles flew outward, as did thousands of white ones. The colored beads became seed beads. . . . The white bubbles became salt" (N. Whitten and D. Whitten 2008:190).

In the Napo Quichua tradition, Iluku and moon mythology are linked with the origins of the sun, but the link is figurative rather than linear. The Iluku cycle is usually followed by tales of the Cuillurguna in the Napo Quichua world. The origin of the sun, a much more rare narrative, is another story located in *kallari timpu* (the beginning times) before the Cuillurguna come to this world. It is temporally consistent with the theme of the creation of the celestial world, the diversification of the world itself.

In the Napo version of the origin of the sun, the world begins in a state of darkness and with people who have no manners, and it is implied that they are unable to copulate properly. God, who is referred to as "our eternal father" by the storyteller, sends his bird-of-prey soldiers to teach people manners, a scene in which a baby is conceived as a result. The "divine child" image here is a common theme in many mythological as well as religious traditions, but the divine child in the Amazonian world is an anaconda.

As the story goes, the couple is surprised when they give birth to a log. Upset and confused, they throw the log into the swamp. After many years pass, there is a knock at the door. A very large anaconda has come to visit and claims he is the lost son of the couple. He reprimands them for throwing him into the swamp, and the couple finds a place for him to live in their house.

After some time the anaconda decides he wants to marry the daughter of a "king" (*rey*) who lives nearby. His father goes several times to ask for her hand in marriage and finally gets the king to agree. The anaconda's father brings the king's daughter home and performs a simple ritual to marry them.

The woman is afraid, however. So the anaconda tells her to lock herself in her room and have candles ready so that they can be lit in an instant. There is a noise that night, and the anaconda enters her room. She lights the candles but is surprised to see a beautiful man. The man explains he is the anaconda and has transformed into a handsome young man. They begin to hug and kiss, with the woman taking the top position. However, she accidently drips resin from the candle into the eye of her husband, and his eye explodes. When it explodes he immediately turns back into an anaconda and, in a fit of rage, decides to ascend into the sky.

He gets tired, though, and stops to rest halfway. There he becomes the sun. That is why we only have one sun and that sun provides us with just enough heat. If the anaconda's eye had not exploded, we would have had two suns and would have burned up.

The origin of the sun, like the Iluku tale, is all about an axis mundi of failed love, desire, and sorrow. The sun, like the moon, is masculine and leaves his beloved in this world as he ascends into the upper world. The relations parallel those of the Iluku complex, but they elicit other meanings, emphases, and mysteries of the ecospiritual world. Specifically, the myth shows the interpenetrability of relations in cycles of reproduction and procreation.[4]

This story might also contain a trace of the various forays of the Inkas into Upper Napo that occurred in pre-Hispanic times. An account by Warvin (1927 [1993]:684) documents a Napo Runa person telling a story of how the "Pope of Rome sent the *Rey Inca* [King Inca] to instruct and teach us [The Napo Runa] Quichua and Civilization." As the story goes, the Inkas tried to establish a city on a mountain in Napo Runa territory, but the attempt failed, so the Inkas were forced to locate their capital in Quito.

In the narrative, the anaconda-man marries the daughter of a *rey*, and the storyteller (Bolivar) uses the Spanish word *rey* (rather than a Quichua term such as *apu* or *kuraga*), which was often used to describe the supreme Inka in many colonial accounts. The use of the term *rey* here is significant, as it indicates a greater degree of otherness and status. For example, the peoples and cultures of the Upper Napo region never had a form of social organization that involved "kings," and the preferred Quichua term for leader is *kuraga*, a term that is more in line with chiefdom than with empire sociality. Historically, the pre-Hispanic peoples of Napo Runa were chiefdoms that intermarried across social and cultural boundaries to form complex networks of trade, warfare, and the exchange of people without forming states or empires (Uzendoski 2004a; Cuellar 2006). It is well documented that the Inkas "conquered" people not just by force but also through intermarriage with different groups and their complex calendar and ritual cult of the sun. We can only speculate that the story might reveal a trace of a struggle or failed alliance among the Napo Runa groups and the Inkas for control of territory, social organization, and sun ideology. In Upper Napo, the anaconda, and by extension the Napo Runa, are the descendants of the sun and the sun's power that flows through all things.

The origin story of the sun was told by Gerardo Bolivar Andi (who holds an MA degree in ethnology and history from a university in Bulgaria) during the annual fiesta de Pano in 2002, at which Edith, Michael, and other community members were present. Michael videotaped the performance, but others were using recording devices as well. In the video, a boy can be seen holding a tape recorder next to the speaker's microphone.

The story was originally known and told by Wagra Uma (tapir head), a now deceased elder from Pano, who told this story to Andi when he was in the sixth grade. We have only seen one other reference to this story in a book written by our compadre, Carlos Alvarado Narvaez (1994). Andi, one of the most knowledgeable people of Napo Quichua mythology, has told us that he has never known anyone else in Napo to have known this story except for Wagra Uma, deceased for many years, who was the original source.

The social context of a "fiesta" and telling a story to an entire community public creates some different performative demands and relational dynamics. First, the presence of a stage and amplification are two elements that change social dynamics. The microphone allows the speaker to project her or his voice, but it limits gestures because one hand is tied up holding the microphone. In a fiesta, storytellers (and other participants) become part of a larger "scene" of other performers, government authorities, and indigenous beauty queens, girls who are referred to as *ñustaguna* and who are named after plants (as in *sara ñusta,* or the corn queen). In a fiesta context, storytelling takes on a different dynamic of community-wide interaction and the celebration of Quichua traditions. The storyteller is no longer within the intimate domain of the fireside but rather in the center of the community. Here is the narrative in translated form:

THE ORIGINS OF THE SUN BY GERARDO BOLIVAR ANDI

I/i/A   in the beginning times
      when the world was still young
      there were people living

B   and although they were living
      on this world there was no sun
      without the sun
         night and the day
         night and day
            there wasn't [any light]
               there was only darkness in that time

ii/A   and at that time there was a family living they say
      an old man
         and a woman

B   those people
      were living without having children they say

C   and so being
      in order to try to conceive a baby
      they used to speak like this
      "your vagina is mine"
      and the woman would say back
         "your penis is mine"

                    "my vagina yours"
           speaking like this they lived
D   and so speaking like this
           our eternal life-giving father
           sent they say
           his bird-of-prey people
                    to tell them
                        "that is no good"
                            "you aren't supposed to speak like that" saying
           and so they left them teaching them how to speak properly
E   and in that the woman conceived a baby they say
                    and she was pregnant
iii/A   and so being pregnant
           the baby now came out
                    it was time
           that baby came out they say
                    but it wasn't a baby
B   although it [the baby] came out they say
           [it was] a tree stump
                    it [the baby] was a log they say
C   and so the man and the woman looking at it [the baby-log]
                    spoke
                    and were afraid
                        "how can this be our child?" saying
                            "it is a tree stump" saying
D   and so being
           that stump that log they grabbed it
           and threw it in the swamp they say
                    right next to the house there was a great big deep swamp
E   and after they threw it into the swamp
           they made a big corn field right next to that very same swamp they say
           and so planting the corn they sent all the felled trees right into the swamp
                    every single tree right into the swamp
           and after doing that the swamp became gigantic they say
F   and in that!
           many years passed
           fifteen
                    sixteen
                        seventeen
           about that many years passed
II/i/A   and in the middle of the night
           there was a knock at the door they say
                    in the middle of the night

B   and so knocking at the door
       the house door opened [**tsaraslla**]
       and when they looked to see who it was
       it was a big, big anaconda that came they say
          a big anaconda
C   and so doing those anacondas in the beginning times
       could talk just like people
          they could have conversations
             they could talk
ii/A   and so coming he spoke to the man and the woman they say
       "no father" saying
          "no mother" saying
             "I am your son" saying
       when he was born
          "like this when I was a stump"
             "a stump"
                "a stump"
                   "you threw me in the swamp" saying
B   and so "and now"
       "turning into an anaconda I come"
          he spoke
             "I am your son" he told them
C   his father and his mother
       a house, one . . .
          they made him a nice little room to stay in
       and the anaconda would go out to get food for his father
          hunting
             he would bring his parents all kinds of game and fish
                and they lived eating well
iii/A   and so that anaconda one day spoke they say
       nearby [hmmmm]
       there was a king [*rey*] living they say
B   "go ask for that king's daughter" he [the anaconda] spoke they say
       and so being
       his father didn't want to
       "no way son" saying
          "how the hell will he give her?" saying "his daughter"
             "he won't give her"
                "you are an anaconda so he won't give her"
C   and so after his son begged him so much he went they say
       he went right there and spoke
          "king" [*rey*] saying

                    "I have come for my son to ask for your daughter"
                    saying
                        "my son like so
                            is a great big young anaconda"
                            he spoke
D   and so being
        he didn't want to [give her away]
            "how the hell will I give my daughter to an anaconda?" saying
E   and so he came [father] home
        and he spoke again
        his father said "son" saying "he won't give her away" but
        [anaconda answered] "no" again he begged him "go father" saying
F   and when father went the king [rey] had the same answer they say
        and so he came home again
III/i/A and after sending him three times the anaconda spoke
        "no father" saying "he will now give [her]" he said
        "and when the king [rey] gives her"
            "tell him to send her to me immediately"
                "and tell her to bring seven candles"
                    "and seven locks" he said
B   and so doing the king [rey] gave her and sent his daughter
        and when she arrived at the house
        the father spoke
            "son" saying
                "here is your wife" saying he spoke
        and to his daughter-in-law he spoke
            "daughter-in-law" saying
                "here is your husband now"
                    he spoke
ii/A   and so being
        that new bride spoke
            "how the hell will I sleep with an anaconda husband?" saying
B   and so being
        the anaconda spoke to his wife
            "don't be afraid wife" saying
                "go inside the house and sleep" saying
                    "and from the inside have those seven locks ready" saying
C   "with those close yourself in and sleep" saying
                "and have those candles ready to light" saying
                    "those seven candles"
                        that he had asked her to bring

iii/A   and so!
              in the middle of the night
                  there was a noise [**tzaras**]
                      those seven locks were opened they say
B   and so opening he entered
              and just as he had told his wife
              she had been sleeping and lit the candles [**dzas**]
                  in the beginning times they had tree resin candles
C   and so being
              lighting the candles
                  when she looked
                  that anaconda
                      was a young man
                          looking very fine
                              he was a young man they say
D   and so looking the anaconda
              the anaconda had turned into a person right there
              and so turning [into a person] he spoke to his wife
                  "I am an anaconda"
                      "but I turned into a person and came to you" saying he said
E   when his wife saw a beautiful loveable looking man
              she hugged and kissed [him]
              doing that they started kiiiisssing
iv/A   and so doing
              the man was lying underneath they say
                  his wife on top
                      she had a candle in one hand they say
B   she had it in her hand
              and when she bent down like this to kiss her husband
              that tree resin dripped down they say
                  that candle
                      it dripped into his eye they say
              and so doing
              his eye exploded they say that very instant
C   and when that happened
              he turned back into an anaconda
                  an anaconda again
                      that man
                          again turned into an anaconda when his eye exploded
D   and so doing he got mad at his wife
                  he got real mad
              he got mad saying "I am leaving you"

v/A   and so being his wife cried
       "It wasn't because I was mad that this happened this has happened
          to you" saying
       "I wasn't angry" saying
B   his parents woke up
       and they cried too
          "don't go son " saying
              "stay here" saying
C   and when they tried to stop him
          he wouldn't obey
              "I am going" he really meant it
D   and so doing
       again our eternal life-giving father sent his bird-of-prey people they say
       they tried to stop him [the anaconda]
       and when they tried to stop him
       not obeying
       to the upper world that anaconda climbed they say
vi/A and climbing
       up to the upper world halfway there
       he was tired and stopped to rest they say
B   and in that
       the anaconda turned into the sun they say
          with one eye exploded he had climbed
C   and it is for this very reason
       the sun. . . now there is just one sun that we have they say
       if that anaconda's [eye] hadn't exploded
       we would have had two suns
D   and if there would have been two
       we would be burning
          we would have been burned to death and passed
              unimaginable horrors
E   but with just one eye
          it is just right
              perfect for living
                  like this the sun gives us heat and gives us life they say
F   and so saying!
       when I was in sixth grade I heard this story

Conclusion

In this chapter, we have presented two eloquent and poetic stories about the
celestial world. Both the Iluku and Origin of the Sun stories are about axis
mundi relationality and the existence of channels of love, desire, and sorrow

among different levels of transformation. The celestial bodies, the moon and the sun, like many plants and animals of mythology, were at one time part of the human domain and integral to cycles of human reproduction.

The polysemous and condensed meanings of these stories define and inform some core principles of the Amazonian Quichua philosophy of life. First, Iluku's complex and failed motherhood is transformative, but her actions embody a negative value of Quichua life—*killa*, or laziness/carelessness/sexual looseness—which, as in other Quichua origin stories, creates differentiation among people, plants, and animals (Swanson 2009). The narrative creates a mythological flow that analogically links femininity and "love"/"sadness," or *llakina*, with local ecology and the axis mundi. In the Amazonian Quichua world women are said to share the destiny and feelings of Iluku. Not only is feminine ritual wailing mimetic of the Iluku bird song, but women are often described as being *Ilukus* if they have lost their husbands to death or abandonment, especially if this loss is due to a fault attributable to the woman's behavior.

The sun story also features a woman who makes a mistake, but the story does not emphasize the notion of *killa*. The wife, the daughter of a king, is terrified of having to sleep with an anaconda, and the storyteller implies a lack of understanding between the anaconda and his human relatives. The emphasis here is the danger and difficulty of maintaining healthy, sustained relations with powerful others, especially the anaconda, who is a predator and master of the Amazonian world. The paradox, however, is that the story also teaches that these powerful others, especially the anaconda, remain central to human procreation and the reproduction of all life itself.

Through the stories in this chapter, we have tried to show the oral textuality of axis mundi relationality and a human condition defined by poetic relations with celestial, ecological, and spirit others. This Quichua poetic relatedness among birds, people, the moon, the sun, rocks, rivers, the wind, the landscape, and various other presences provides people with an aesthetic and emotional connectedness with the world around them, a "zest" that "adds itself like a gift to life" (James 1967:759). This is not just an "imagined" world. It is also an experiential world where people and various human and nonhuman others engage in communicative exchanges that involve the whole expressive body.

The way Quichua speakers achieve the relations, however, are not limited to restricted formulas or canned phrases; storytellers, as we have shown, have considerable freedom in eliciting axis mundi relations and the defining transformations of myth. As we show in later chapters, the poetics of perception, relatedness, and transformation are communicated in diverse and multiple ways through various genres: stories, songs, and even modern Quichua music called Runa Paju.

CHAPTER 4

BIRDS AND HUMANITY
Women's Songs
With the Assistance of Mark Hertica

A Few Words on Feminine Power

In this chapter we present translations and interpretations of six women's songs that speak to the power of the feminine voice and the feminine soul. These songs feature feminine shape-shifting relations between birds and women, fish and women, and similar mimetic transformations in history, such as the rubber boom. In this context, the spoken word becomes musicalized, and the body realizes different cosmological capacities.

The materials here show how the poetic structures of the voice, grammar, and music evoke the Native theory of the body's potency and its ability to attract desirable things, powers, qualities, and people. In confronting the aesthetic and cultural complexity of these songs we draw on a variety of theoretical approaches, among them French and Brazilian structuralism (Descola 1992, 1996a, 1996b; Taylor 1993, 1996; Viveiros de Castro 1998, 2001; Vilaça 2002; Fausto 2000), embodiment (Csordas 1990; Merleau-Ponty 1962), mimesis (Taussig 1993), ethnopoetics (Hymes 2003), and ethnomusicology (Feld 1982; Olsen 1996; Seeger 1987). However, our main goal, in addition to translating these songs and identifying their main aesthetic features, is to convey their meanings as phenomenological acts. Throughout this book, for example, we have implicitly followed philosopher William James's (1967) method of "radical empiricism," a method in which experience is the basis of knowledge and more highly valued than synthetic theories that are ex post facto linguistic abstractions from experience (Jackson 1995).

We show that the aesthetic features of these songs resonate with the mythological and metaphysical qualities of the Iluku bird, discussed in the previous chapter. As we have argued, the Iluku complex and its resultant imagery of the axis mundi (a channel of "love" and "attraction" between gender complements) are at the core of how Quichua speakers of Amazonian Ecuador view and experience lived reality. "Mythology" in this world is not simply "discursive" but rather is multimodal, polyphonic, metaphorical, and experiential in multistranded, complex ways.

We argue that these women's songs are a form of shamanic practice in which the singer experiences her body as a special locus of subjectivity as defined by relations with birds and other alters. When women sing, they report feeling the power (*ushay*) "in their flesh" (*paygunác aychay*) of the birds or animals about which they sing. The Runa view *takina* and *kantana* as *ushay* and believe that shamanic songs allow people to embody power by mimetic association with powerful alters. Singing elicits and reflects the power (*ushay*) of the singer, a *sinzhi warmi* (strong woman) (Nuckolls 2010).

In publications and discourses about Amazonian Quichua cultures, the masculine *yachak* ("one who knows"; often translated as "shaman") has attracted considerable attention and is often assumed to be a public role occupied only by men (Cipoletti 2007). This notion is incorrect. Women too can occupy the role of *yachak*, but it is more common for people to refer to a woman with shamanistic power as a *sinzhi warmi,* or strong woman (Nuckolls 2010), a category that overlaps with the notion of *yachak* but that refers specifically to feminine power.

As the sociologist and Napo Quichua native Sharimiat Shiguango explains in his detailed study of Napo Runa shamanism (2006), the notion of *yachak* involves hundreds of interrelated concepts and associated practices. *Yachak* is an umbrella term for four basic classes or specializations that include the *pajuyuk* (those possessing magical power), the *muskuyuk* (those with powers of dreaming and prediction), the *samayuk* (those possessing much *samay* or embodied energy as well as an understanding of the cosmos), and the *yachak* proper (those who possess all of the above qualities plus regularly cure sick people as a vocation) (Shiguango 2006:71).

The practicing *yachak* is a social role that affords status, but many people who fall under the umbrella term of a *yachak* avoid the public profile for all sorts of reasons. One such reason is personal safety, because shamans are often persecuted due to the close association of the *yachak* with sorcery (Uzendoski 2005, 2010b; Whitehead 2004). Many people, including women, "shamanize" and posses shamanistic power without necessarily taking on a public profile of a *yachak* (Uzendoski 2005, 2008, 2010b; N. Whitten and D. Whitten 2008).

Shamanism ramifies throughout Napo Runa culture so deeply that it is hard to find any daily activity or ritual action that does not involve *samay* (breath or soul substance), *muskuy* (dreams), or *paju* (magic). It is a mode of perception defined by the perspectivist idea that all living things possess hidden subjectivities and energies, and human survival depends on being able to interact and communicate with these unseen forces and subjectivities.

The notion of a "strongwoman" has been carefully studied by Janis Nuckolls (2010), who argues that feminine notions of power have not been sufficiently analyzed among Amazonian Quichua peoples, mainly because feminine power is "marked" in relation to masculine power, which is assumed to be dominant (as well as complementary to feminine power). However, as Nuckolls (2010) discusses, feminine strongwomen do not see their powers as inferior or subordinate to those of men. Grandmother Jacinta, a strongwoman from Pano, compares her power to that of a *yachak* and does not see herself as lesser in any way. Strongwomen successfully oppose masculine dominance at various important junctures. They possess, as argues Nuckolls (2010), a great degree of freedom and control over their lives. This social power derives from their internal spiritual energy.

The women's songs we analyze here pick up and provide details about such themes; they speak to the theme of feminine soul potency and the feminine body's refashioning not just in relationship to birds but also in relationship to gender, kinship, and history. They demonstrate the transformative role of music in the fabrication and experience of the body as a locus of power and attraction, a feminine practice of shamanistic imagination and power.

Takina or Music: A Way toward Attraction

Music among the Napo Runa is generally termed *takina*, and people say that all *takina* originate from *samay* (soul substance or breath). In the past people used to make a distinction between *kantana* to refer to women's songs and *takina* to refer to *ayahuasca* songs and music, but today *takina* is used to refer to all Napo Runa music. Generally speaking, people consider that *takina* songs are action, social acts that *attract* energy, qualities, people, and power, and, if used for the purposes of sorcery (*sagrana*, *brujuna*), can make others ill.

Singing these songs requires great courage and confidence in one's own internal strength. To make one's songs public, for example, is to enter into a social context in which one's imagination, *samay,* and shamanic power become visible to others. In the world of Amazonian cosmological relations of predator and prey, shamanic actions often elicit counter-responses from rival shamans or spirits (Whitehead and Wright 2004); traditionally, women's songs are part of this field of relations, thought to influence life, death, sickness, and health.

Many women's songs are performed in secret, at night in the river or when the woman is alone in her *chagra* (garden), but women also perform their songs in public, during fiestas or other social gatherings. Because the intent is to "make people happy," these songs are not dangerous, but they continue to be regarded as expressions of *samay* and power. Their intimate connection with emotional states (Harrison 1988:147) resonates with the notion that they embody powers of attraction and have influence over the *samay* of others. They evoke memories of the ancestors who sang these songs earlier and the emotions linked to them, and singers of songs are the most respected women in Napo Runa society.

Some young people are beginning to relearn the songs of their grandparents and great-grandparents, and men are beginning to perform women's songs, arguing that men among the Shuar and Achuar sing, and there is no reason they should not (see Descola 1996b; Karsten 1998). Women continue to compose new songs that relate to their intimate experiences and visions of the contemporary world. These songs may never be studied by scholars, as they are expressions of shamanistic action aimed at controversial problems (for example, a woman may be seeking to attract a man who is someone else's husband or may be trying to win her husband back from another woman). Some of the most meaningful and powerful women's songs in Napo Runa culture will forever remain secret. Because of their complexity and their private, emotional, and esoteric nature, they are difficult to study (Harrison 1988).

The songs we examine emphasize the power of the spoken word and music to act upon the body, which, in the Quichua world, is defined by its *samay* relatedness to others, including ecological and human others. In these songs, women experience the world from various corporeal perspectives defined by rhetorical forms of mimetic relations and transformation.

The Metaphysics of Power and Sexuality

Regina Harrison's (1988) pathbreaking work on the intimate connections among the body, power, spirit, and music in women's songs from Napo has revealed that gender and sexuality are central to their shamanistic qualities. Singers acquire power and seduce men. Attraction, more than just a feminine preoccupation, is one of the defining characteristics of shamanistic action and is the cornerstone of animal-human relations, central to hunting and to masculine agency as well (Uzendoski 2004b). Michael Brown (1985:88–90) has discussed the importance of attraction in Aguaruna magic and in hunting and singing and points out that attraction is a property of powerful plant substances as well.

In Napo it is often said that the anaconda attracts its victims "like a magnet." Anacondas also appear as beautiful men and women (attracting humans of the opposite sex). Male anacondas are said to impregnate women in their dreams by appearing as handsome men (Harrison 1988:162). Just as animals seduce humans, humans can use the *ushay* of animals or plants to seduce other humans. Two plants, *simayuka* and *puma yuyu*, confer powers of attraction, although the former is renowned as love magic.

Among the Napo Runa, the complementarity of gender and gendered sexual energy mediates most animal-human relations. Some women have male spirit / animal lovers from whom they acquire special energy and power. Men also acquire female spirit or animal lovers who help them to attract and control Runa and the animals and fish they seek. Women's songs connect the singers with the spirit power of birds, turning them into predators who "hunt" men. In Napo Runa culture, men do not simply "dominate" women. Men and women see themselves as equally powerful and indispensable. Napo Runa women's songs help us to understand something of how their singers experience power and demonstrate the centrality of aesthetic performance to perspectivist cosmologies. In Robert Plant Armstrong's (1981) terms, they have an affecting presence.

Song Forms and Equivalence

The texts of the three songs presented here consist of ordered sets of lines that can be considered as representing scenes, stanzas, and verses (see Hymes 2003:303). As in myth narratives, the predominant poetic features of Napo Runa music are couplets, repetition, grammatical parallelism, syllabic patterning, and rhetorical initial words and ending words (Mannheim 1998; Uzendoski 1999). High-pitched singing marks couplets and indicates beginning of a line or verse. These vocal moves convey motion and perhaps elicit flight, both the flight of the imagination as a bird and the flight of a song to its social target. Drawn-out vowels form a complementary opposite to the high-pitched tones. Found at the ends of verses, they have a descending quality and signal closure or outcome, a transition to silence or pause. These features create what Hymes (2003:304–5) has termed "succession," the equivalence of form that gives shape to action (see also Nuckolls 2000; Jakobson 1960).

The succession here is something like an aesthetic form for the elicitation of *ushay*. Opposites often come together to form a third entity that transcends them (Uzendoski 1999). Taussig (1993:106), speaking of the Kuna chanter, says that he "chants himself into the scene. He exists not just as a subject but also a mimeticised Other. . . . He creates the bridge between original and copy that brings a new force, the third force of magical power, to intervene in the human world" (Taussig 1993:106). Similarly, the singer in these songs sings herself into a person of power and embodies this power in her performance. In so doing, she intervenes in the world both as a shamanic actor and as a *sinzhi warmi* (see D. Whitten and N. Whitten 1988; N. Whitten and D.Whitten 2008; Nuckolls 2010).

The Breast Song by Gervacio Cerda

The Breast Song was recorded by Santiago Calapucha, Edith's father, in the early 2000s on a trip to Limoncocha, a large community in Lower Napo. The singer is originally from the Tena area and narrates and sings in the Tena dialect of Quichua. The recording includes four parts, an opening narrative, a violin introduction, the song, and finally the story. The most salient feature of this performance is the details Gervacio gives about the social meanings and the shamanistic power of the song to attract a faraway man. Structurally speaking, the singer and Iluku (discussed in chapter 3) occupy the same position of subjectivity—they are women who sing or cry to their lost men in hopes of restoring the relational wholeness of masculine-feminine complementarity. In both the narrative and the song, Gervacio uses the terms *wakana* (to cry) and *kantana* (to sing) interchangeably, as both meanings are inherent in the power of the feminine voice to elicit and evoke strong emotions of sadness. Unlike men, who do not have this power, women utilize the energy flows of "love," "desire," and "sadness" to influence and transform relations.

THE BREAST SONG BY GERVACIO CERDA

Part 1. The introduction to the Breast Song is spoken by Cerda in a narrative voice.

now
your man
if he abandons you
nowadays men are leaving [their women] so much
you all should know this well   5
    this singing
    this crying
if you know it you can call your man
    if you don't know it you can't call your man
he will just leave you   10
    yes that is how it is
and so being how women call a man

Part 2. Here Gervacio plays the violin and introduces the song.

Part 3. Here Gervacio sings the song, which is organized into couplets.
The song is directed at the woman's man, who has left her.

A   my breast hurt-t-t-s
    oh ho ho ho
    ho ho hooooo
  my breast hurt-t-t-s
    oh ho ho ho   5
    ho ho hooooo
B   to wherever [he] may go
  just back to me you will come
  to wherever [he] may go
  just back to me you will come   10
C   three days lat-t-er
  just back to me you will go
  three days lat-t-er
  just back to me you will be
D   my breast hurt-t-t-s   15
    oh ho ho ho
    ho ho hooooo

Part 4. Here Gervacio tells a story about how a woman used this song to call her man back.
He then concludes by speaking to the value of the song and its power to call men back.
He implores listeners to learn the song and use it when necessary.

a long time ago way before us
a man went and left his woman
when he left his woman
the woman cried holding her breast
  the woman's breast, the woman's breast is big!   5
holding her breast
she pointed it at the path down which her man left her
pointing it
  crying
crying or singing   10
  my breast hurts saying
three days later
just back to me you will be saying
  she cried
  she sang   15
there the people who heard about it didn't believe
  they didn't believe as he had left her
  you have been left saying

and so being
in three days   20
the man came back
there a lot of people were frightened
this song is very valuable
in this area I teach it to everybody
    I even teach it to whites   25
the whites know how to call back their men
    to here
learn it you all
    if your man leaves and abandons you
        sing like this to your man   30
so he will come back in three days or maybe a week

Gervacio not only performs the song but also interprets the song and explains how women use songs to call their men back to them and, in the process, reinvigorate their relationship. Although Gervacio emphasizes that this song should be used for wives to "re-seduce" their abandoning husbands, one can see how this and similar songs might be used to attract the men or husbands of other women. The song is indeed a kind of feminine shamanism, which, like other forms of magic, can be used for purposes of healing or sorcery, a tension that exists in all shamanic practices and powers.

The song works through the power of the woman's breast, emphasized by Gervacio when he makes an emphatic point about women's breasts being large. This is a special kind of feminine shamanism where women use their unique bodies to work magic on men's souls and sexuality.

Women's Songs and the Younger Generation

THE BREAST SONG BY CAMILO TAPUY AND HIS GRANDCHILDREN

The Breast Song, like many other women's songs, is currently being performed by the granddaughters of Camilo, the violin musician featured in chapter 2. This music group of youth organized by Camilo and Michael listened to the song on Michael's computer and decided to integrate it into their repertoire (for the movie file of Camilo and the young musical group performing the Breast Song see the companion website). In addition to the Breast Song, this group knows various other women's songs, and they meet every Sunday to practice. During 2009–2010 the group performed the Breast Song and other Quichua songs at several public events in their home community of Pano.

Unlike their ancestors, however, these youth, who are alphabetically and computer literate, take advantage of the written word and digital technology to learn their songs. As can be seen in the video, which is a practice session, these songs have passed through various textual mediums of which written words and computer technology are used as intermediate steps to facilitate the learning process. The ultimate goal, however, is the somatic internalization of the music, a transformation in which the principles and aesthetic sensibilities of oral textuality are reasserted. The group leader, Camilo, a retired school teacher, always emphasizes that to know a song well means embodying it, knowing how it relates to experience and history, and being able to perform it like the ancestors did. Although this is a topic for more in-depth future research, written, oral, and digital textualites are combined and converted in ways that reflect the cultural priorities of Quichua people and their embeddedness within a globalized world (see chapter 8).

Grandmother Jacinta's Songs

The next two songs were recorded during a taping session in 2002 with Grandmother Jacinta Andi, who lives in the community of Pano and who is known for her strength, wisdom, hard-working nature, and artistic abilities. Jacinta is related to us by way of the wives of Edith's brothers Federico and Esteban, who married sisters. These women are the granddaughters of Jacinta, but because of the fluidity of Napo Runa kinship, we also consider Jacinta to be our grandmother, as do many people in the community (see Uzendoski 2005).

Like Gervacio, Grandmother Jacinta begins her performance with a story. While she is telling her story, we and other relatives are surrounding her, and nobody is actually sure that Jacinta will sing a song. After imploring by the participants, Jacinta finally breaks into song. Her performance consists of five parts: a general introduction, the introduction to the first song, the song Dove Woman, an introduction to the next song, and the song Rubber Tapping Woman.

Part 1. In the general introduction Jacinta Andi talks about how women would take over for men in hard work when men would get tired. She then talks about her power as a "strong woman" to make manioc beer (the substance of life in Napo Runa culture) and know when to serve it. She discusses her genealogy of power, which derives from her mother, who, even though she was "illiterate," knew more and had more wisdom than the younger generation that learns only in school. The audience then asks Jacinta to sing, and she responds that "it will be sad."

DOVE WOMAN BY JACINTA ANDI

we in beginning times used to get around in canoes using only our
    hands and poles
when our men got tired
we would grab the poles and that way we got upriver
having strong manioc beer made, giving to drink, making them happy
    hiiia hiaaa   5
        shouting they came home
if not, we would grab the poles and get us upriver
    all night long
wherever we went
that is how I am   10
I always had manioc beer ready
in whatever
and so being now
I have served my husband more than was needed
    since I was a young girl I have served him   15
whenever manioc beer was ready
    everything
    everything
    my husband didn't have to say anything
he didn't have to tell me   20
"make manioc beer"
to tell me to give to drink to visitors
no saying
my own heart already knew what to do
    because in my young days I had been taught   25
now if I teach my children in the same way
    they don't understand
and so being
in what language do you want me to speak in?
    they don't want to understand   30
even though my mom couldn't read writing [alphabetic]
I have her wisdom and the wisdom of all my aunts and uncles in my heart.
    I have it all in my heart
[they taught me] "doing like this working one will eat"
    "doing like this one will drink"   35
        "doing like this one will give her man to drink"
they taught me everything
I don't leave that behind even though I have gotten old
everything
EDITH——now do you want to sing?   40
    do you remember?

PEDRO—sing
    you should sing while you are still living
FERLIMONA—we are taping it
JACINTA—it will be sad   45
PEDRO—for the children
FERLIMONA—mom for us to listen to when you die

Part 2. In the introduction to Dove Woman Jacinta explains the meaning of the song. The song is about her man abandoning her while they are on a canoe trip. The singer turns into a dove and restores the unity of the husband-wife complement.

I am going to sing about my travels downriver (Lower Napo)
    travels downriver
from downriver
    coming back up
when my husband abandoned me   5
I would make it back all by myself
this is the kind of woman I am
coming to the beach
while he is there drinking
turning into a dove   10
I am a returning woman
That is what we sing about

Part 3. In Dove Woman the singer turns into a dove to return to her husband, but he tries to shoot her. Jacinta, however, is too quick and powerful and eludes her husband's shot. She succeeds in restoring their complementary wholeness.

i / A   I am a little woman
      when my man gets mad and leaves me
      I
      right behind him would come up!
      Andi woman little Rosita saying   5
      I am a woman no one can compare to
B   my father
      is Mariano
      my father
      I am an Andi daughter!   10
ii / A   arriving there my little husband
      upon the beach's edge
      carrying standing
      me, there

B	turning into a dove	15
	in the shadow of the sun, a little woman coming	
	him, a dove saying	
iii/A	getting his gun	
	to shoot saying	
	when he runs over	20
B	I	
	turning into a dove	
	going to the base of the mountain	
	in the shadow of the sun, a little woman coming	
iv/A	my man together	25
	now	
	getting old I am suffering	
	like an abandoned orphan left behind	

RUBBER TAPPING WOMAN BY JACINTA ANDI

Part I. Jacinta introduces her next song about when she used to collect rubber during the "times of rubber," or the rubber boom. Jacinta probably has memories of this epoch as a child and is also expressing, through her song, the embodied the experiences of her mother. Then she says:

> now here I, my travels as a rubber tapper [I will sing]

Part 2. Here Jacinta performs Rubber Tapping Woman. In this song, she speaks to her traveling and to her movement across the landscape and vertically through the axis mundi. Toward the end the song becomes a lamentation for her sadness in being separated from her son. Jacinta wonders if her son still thinks of her. The song ends as Jacinta cries and everyone falls silent.

i/A	I a little woman rubber tapper	
	turning into a little orphan	
	carrying	
	up the side of a huge mountain	
	traveling back and forth	5
B	to the Ichu Mountain base	
	a litttle walking woman gone everywhere	
ii/A	Andi women are never found lacking	
	arriving anywhere	
	arriving to the top of Verde Yaku [mountain river]	10
	clouds laid out pouring all over	
B	I am a little walking woman	
	from when I was young	
	my working hand	
	was never lacking	15

```
             in my little death approaching
             my working hand will then be lacking
   iii / A   let's drink vinulla [manioc wine] husband
             helping together let's drink
             let's drink banana-manioc beer [warapu]                    20
             little man while we are still living
             let's drink this together
             little husband
   B         as little death approaches
             will we stop this                                          25
             my little man
   C         now without a son
             only having one little son
             leaving he has left
             thinking of my son I am getting sad                        30
             does he remember us?
             together
             having given him to drink
   iv / A    when my son desired vinulla [manioc wine]
             when he desired manioc beer [asua]                         35
             whatever he wanted
             I had given him it all to drink
   B         I am crying about his abandoning us
             and leaving us
```

Serafina and Vicente's Songs

The last three songs we examine here come from a copy of a tape recorded
in the 1980s by Timoteo Tapuy, Edith's cousin and Camilo Tapuy's son (now
deceased). The tape features the music of Edith's grandfather (Vicente Calapucha) and grandmother (Serafina Shiguango), the founders of the Native
community of Sapo Rumi. Vicente plays the violin and Serafina sings. Vicente
and Serafina were well known for their musical powers when they were alive.
They used to make their music daily during their morning *wayusa* tea-drinking
ritual, and their affinity for music was a sign of their status as strong people.

A note on the transcriptions is in order, for here we follow a hybrid translation strategy that combines Dennis Tedlock's (1983) concern with voice and
Dell Hymes's (2003) use of verse, a method we have not used thus far in the
book. High-pitched singing is represented in all capitals (upon MY FLOW-
ERRRRR) and drawn-out vocals are represented through repetition of letters
so as to give a visual image of a longer line (is flyinnnnng).

Part I. This first song, Birds and Flowers, features a woman turning into various kinds of birds, visiting flowers, flying through the sky, and calling on her husband to wait for her. The birds it mentions are the *siccha,* the *kindi* (a hummingbird), the *suyuguna* (a bird that flies in flocks high in the sky), and the duck. The song has four scenes that correspond to a transformation from one bird form to the next. Each scene is made up of two or three stanzas. Its main poetic features are repetition, couplets, parallelism, imagery, and rhythm, and its main theme is transformation into birds. While singing, the woman takes on the subject position of four different birds and visits flowers that provide her with nectar. She ascends and descends, moving between the heavens and the earth, and as a duck, she visits water and the snow-covered mountains. She refers to herself as special kinds of woman: *siccha warmi* (*siccha* woman), *kindi warmi* (hummingbird-woman), *suyuguna warmi* (suyu birds–woman), a "heaven-woman," and a duck. The use of these constructions (commonly employed to denote human-animal transformations in Quichua) and the constant use of the first person express the embodiment of the birds' perspectives by the performer—a transformation that is mimetically experienced by the singer.

The main musical feature is a high-pitched, ascending-descending voice that evokes the quick and agile nature of the hummingbird darting from flower to flower as it feeds. By creating a detailed image of the bird-woman, the singer shamanistically taps into the perceived power of these beautiful creatures; her body becomes what she sings. A poetic and ontological "equivalence" is established between humans and birds; like birds, the songs travel far and wide to reach the souls of their targets.

Scenes are marked by transformations into different kinds of birds. Stanzas begin with high-pitched tones and end with softer, low-pitched and drawn-out vowels, which in turn fade into pauses. Verses are often coupled, the second repeating the previous one with a slight variation in syntax, tone, or length. The phrase *shayauni* (I am standing) often signals the end of a stanza. "Standing" here is a kind of power image with connotations of strength and resilience (Harrison 1988). Almost every line ends in *a* or *i,* usually drawn out to produce the vocal effect of descent. In certain words that end in *–in,* such as *wamburin,* the *n* is only barely audible, mimicking the bird's descent. Lines tend to end with three-syllable words, and these micro-relations of three may resonate with the idea of an intervening relation created through twinning, or the transformation of opposites by a third entity, which is power.

BIRDS AND FLOWERS BY SERAFINA SHIGUANGO AND VICENTE CALAPUCHA

i/A upon MY FLOWERRRRR
  is flyinnnnng
  flyinnnng
  upon my flower
  is flyinnng   5

B	a fire sikchA flies
	a fire sikchA flies
	fire sikcha flies
ii / A	hUMMINGBIRD
	womannnn
	from far awAYYY hummingbird womannn
	I am standinnnng
	with plumes I am standinnng
B	upon EACH floWERRRR
	upon EACH floWERRRR
	I descennnnnd
	upon each floweeeeer
	I descennnnnd
	little husbannnnd
C	waiT FOR ME
	little husbannnd
	upon each FLOWEEEER
	I descEnnnnnd
	hummingbird womannnn descendsssss
	little husband
iii / A	suyUGUna woMAnnnnnn
	IIIIIII
	hEAVAN Heavannnnnn
	I am standinnnnng
	in the cloudsssss flyer
B	hEAVAN womannnnnnn
	hEAVAN hEAVAN I am standing
	suyu bird woman
iv / A	SNOW MOUNTAIN dUCKKKKK
	likkkkke a womannnnn
	duckssss duckssss
B	SNOWWWWW MOUNTAIN
	fliesssss
	I am standinnng duckssss
	in my slow waterrrrr
	duck flyinnnng womannnn
C	BEAUTIFUL WHITE MOTHERRR
	BEAUTIFUL WHITE WOMANNN
	I am standinnnng
	I am standinnnng

Line numbers in right margin: 10, 15, 20, 25, 30, 35, 40, 45

Part 2. The second song, Huallaga, is an example of Hill's (1995:xi) assertion "that music and history are closely intertwined throughout lowland South America" (see also Whitehead 2003). The Huallaga is a river in Peru to which the Napo Runa used to travel, first with the Jesuits and later by themselves to obtain salt (Reeve 1993; Muratorio 1991).[1] Chapter 6 also contains a story that refers to this area of northern Peru, which was an important zone during the rubber boom (see Muratorio 1991). The singer Serafina Shiguango was a member of the last generation of Napo Runa to have traveled to the Huallaga. Her song shows the complementary nature of upriver and downriver ecological zones in the indigenous view. She sings to her husband, asking him to take her with him on the long, arduous journey.

This song presents a marked contrast with the first one. The pattern here is four rather than three syllables in each line. The structure of verses also follows this pattern, with generally two line-couplets making up a verse. The first line is sung in the high pitch while the second is lower pitched. The phrase *rigra, rigra* ("arming, arming") provides the central image, conveying the body movement involved in poling a canoe upriver. Because in Quichua *rigra* means "wing" as well as "arm," this phrase could also be translated as "winging, winging," also reinforced by the singers' reference to a bird in lines 17–18.

One of the defining characteristics of birds is that they are masters of movement and travel, and this is also a notion associated with shamanic power in the Upper Amazon. As Descola (1996b:323) has noted, Achuar shamans employ rhetorical structures in their songs that are "a reaffirmation of the shaman's membership to a vaster community . . . even if he has not traveled much physically, a shaman is by nature a cosmopolitan creature." Indeed, these songs show that *ushay* is linked to movement and transformation, implicit characteristics of the power of birds and other shamanic beings.[2]

HUALLAGA BY SERAFINA SHIGUANGO AND VICENTE CALAPUCHA

i/A	GUAllAGALLAAA		
	up riverrrrr		
	near the deep WATERSSS		
	I am standinnnnnng		
B	GUAllAgAllAAA		5
	up riverrrrr?????		
	lead MEEEEEEEEE TO YOU		
	my little husbannnnnd		
ii/A	WHICHEVER RIVER		
	upstream to thereeee		10
	carry ME TO YOUUUUU		
	little husbannnnnd		
B	ARMING ARMING		
	I am standiiiing		

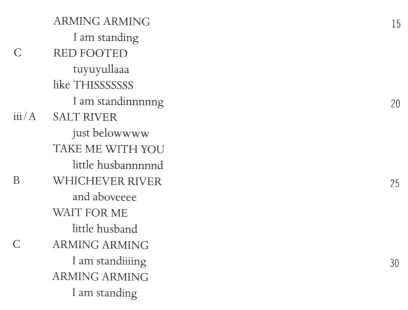

```
                 ARMING ARMING                                          15
                     I am standing
    C            RED FOOTED
                     tuyuyullaaa
                 like THISSSSSSS
                     I am standinnnnng                                  20
  iii / A        SALT RIVER
                     just belowwww
                 TAKE ME WITH YOU
                     little husbannnnnd
    B            WHICHEVER RIVER                                         25
                     and aboveeee
                 WAIT FOR ME
                     little husband
    C            ARMING ARMING
                     I am standiiiing                                    30
                 ARMING ARMING
                     I am standing
```

Part 3. The second song, Fish, according to the singer, was formerly sung during drinking parties among *auya,* relatives linked by the marriage of their children. In the song in-laws try to make the woman drunk, and she likens her ability to resist drunkenness to a *chinlus* fish's ability to resist poison (*barbasco*). The *chinlus* is a small fish that is unique to the fast-moving currents of the Upper Napo region. While it is sometimes caught with a net or a hook, it has an extraordinary ability to elude capture. The song calls upon the power of the *chinlus,* elicited through mimesis of the fish's movements to make the woman strong. It makes reference to the time when Runa used to work gathering gold, and it also locates the singer within the landscape of her home, with references to the Sapo Rumi petroglyph and the Yanayacu River. It also defines the singer in terms of her kinship identities: she is among *auya* (relatives related by marriage) and her name, Shiguango, identifies her as a woman of a particular *ayllu* (kinship group). The song thus combines the animal and historical perspectives of the first two songs with identities of kinship.

Like the first song, this one shows a preference for three-syllable ending words. Again, beginning phrases are sung at high pitch. In contrast to the previous two songs, this one has longer verses—many lines strung together and sung in a more rapid and low-pitched voice. One theme of these repetitions is the assertion of various identities of the singer: "siren," "money mother," "*saporumi* woman," "gold woman," "*yanayacu* woman," "Shiguango woman," and eventually "*chinlus* woman" (29). The historical identities, like the animal alters, are implicitly linked to the singer's power.

One of the central images of this song is the use of the ideophone (Nuckolls 1996, 2000) *kuskalla,* which indicates standing firm within a current against a powerful resistant force, to describe the fish woman as resisting her in-laws' efforts to make her drunk. She is also said to be escaping like the "wind" in the current, a construction that draws a figurative connection between the movement of the fish and that of birds and also highlights the fish's ability to move with currents that carry it to safety. Thus, like the bird, the fish is likened to a master of movement that is intelligent, agile, and powerful.

Vilaça (2002:349) has shown that transformations of kinship and identity and relationships with animals are both structured by the implicit principles of perspectivism in that "humanity is conceived of as a position, essentially transitory, which is continuously produced out of a wide universe of subjectivities that includes animals." The above songs define the singer's soul potency through multiple identities (acquired over time) linked to animal subjectivity, kinship, and historical experiences and through the features (rivers and the Sapo Rumi petroglyph) and history of her place of residence.

FISH BY SERAFINA SHIGUANGO AND VICENTE CALAPUCHA

i/A   A SIREN I AM STANDINNNNG
         a siren I am standinnnng
         one hannnnd
B   A HAND WITH MONEY BILLS
         one hannnnnd   5
         a hand with money in change
             saporumiii
             womannn
                 I am standinnnng
                     a little gold womannn   10
C   yanayacUUU womaNNN
         saporumi mamaaaaa
             I am beinnnng
             I am beinnnng
D   shiwangULLA womannn   15
         a flat piece of goLD WOMANNN
             I am beinnnng
ii/A   IIIIIIII
         a lot of poison
             defeating   20
                 standing womannnnn
                     I am standinnnnng
B   YANA YACU CHINLUSSSSS
         not yet FALLINnnnnng
             I am standinnnnng   25
                 very firm [kuskalla] and straight I am standinnnng
                     lots of poison

```
                    defeating womannnn
                    chinlus womannnn
                        I am standinnnng                    30
C       YOU WILL NOT MAKE ME FALLLLL
            aFflnnnnnnes
iii / A  WHEN YOU COME TO GET ME
         from the back I swim like the wind
            taking me away                                 35
            taking me away
B       FROM THE FRONT I SWIM LIKE THE WIND
            taking me awaaaay
            taking me awaaaay
C       YOU WILL NOT THROW MEEEE                           40
            affinnnnnnes
            affinnnnes
```

The Humanity of Birds

These six women's songs feature mimetic transformations as central images and draw on the ability of the feminine body to fly through space and time as a defining characteristic of its power. The rhetorical patterning of these relations emerges not only in relation to nature but also to kinship, residence, and history. Birds are the core theme; in three of the six songs (Dove Woman, Hummingbird Woman, and Hullaga) the singer explicitly becomes various birds, and in another she becomes a *chinlus* fish, which, like a bird, is associated with movement and flight. The Breast Song and Rubber Tapping Woman implicitly involve references to "flight" through tropes of travel and movement whereby the song as the woman "travels" to its intended target, or in the latter song where the woman herself is a "traveling woman," moving through history via the axis mundi of the Quichua world.

This centrality of birds as objects of metaphor, power, and mimesis is found in other sources that deal with the Ecuadorian Amazon (N. Whitten 1976, 1985; D. Whitten and N. Whitten 1988; Karsten 1998). Norman Whitten (1976:44) proposes that birds are associated with mastery of vertical space and travel and carry women's songs (and their sexualized power to influence others) to faraway places. The implication here is that the songs are transformations of bird-human *samay*, a feminine shamanistic power.

This idea of birds and women's combining corporeal essences becomes even clearer when one looks at Napo Runa myths, whose culture heroes are the twins Cuillurguna (see chapter 5). As discussed in a previous chapter, the mother of the twins is Iluku (the common potoo [*Nyctibiu grisens*, Nyctibiidae]), and every time the moon comes out, it is said, one can hear Iluku calling out to her lover, "luuu, luuu, luuu, luuu," a verse structure that is also present in feminine ritual wailing (Orr and Hudelson 1971:4) and the qualities of women's songs. However, unlike Iluku, whose song does not succeed in restoring her relations with her lost husband, the women's songs featured here show that human singers have learned to improve upon Iluku's art. They become birds and move like birds, but they also draw on the power of the human voice and the spoken word. As the Breast Song shows, women who use these power songs are thought to attract their husbands back to them. These relations have changed, because unlike Iluku, the women today are not *killa* (lazy or morally loose). They are *sinzhi* (strong), *yachak* (knowing), and *kutsi* (quick), all terms used to describe women who sing beautiful songs and who have the character to back them up.

There are other relations as well. The Iluku bird's song (see chapter 3) resonates with the verse structure, melodic contour, tone, and pauses of women's voices in these songs. Like women's songs, the "voice" of Iluku is structured by lines and verses. The call usually has three "lines" but sometimes four or even five and is then repeated, but with variation that makes it both patterned and random, a feature of women's songs. Furthermore, what ethnomusicologists would call the melodic contour of women's and Iluku songs are strikingly similar, as the general motion of both songs is downward at the end of lines. As the Iluku's song descends, the volume of the sound drops. This "tone painting" resonates with the poetic movements of birds as agents of movement. The rendering of the tones in the women's songs and the Iluku's call are also similar in the way individual tones are approached, held, and left. Although we are not trained in ethnomusicology, and more work needs to be done on the relationship of bird music to human poetics, one does not need to be a specialist to hear and feel the parallelism created by women singers with the common potoo's song. The social power of these equivalences connotes the interrelatedness of human and bird *samay*, and the power of birds to make powerful, socially transforming music, music that travels and attracts.

This similarity of patterning between bird calls and song shows the usefulness of ethnopoetic and ethnomusicological analysis in anthropological research, especially among Amazonian peoples that define sociality in terms of complex aesthetic forms and practices (Overing and Passes 2000:8). Our findings resonate with those of a groundbreaking study by Steven Feld (1982:217), who draws on the work of Robert Armstrong (1981) in showing that in the theory of music of the Kaluli (of Papua New Guinea) "becoming a bird" is the core aesthetic metaphor. The sounds of nature are also the sounds of humanity, and vocal art evokes an affective presence of mythological truths that are located in somatic transformations (birth and death). Feld's insights highlight the intimate relationship between vocal art, myth, presence, and the sounds of ecology.

Conclusions

In this chapter we have discussed the social power and aesthetics of six women's songs from the Napo Runa of Ecuador. These songs employ complex principles of the spoken word that, in the Native view, mimetically create relations of feminine attraction and embodiment with masculine complements and natural nonhuman beings—mainly birds. Although birds are a main theme in the songs at which we have looked, we do not think that women are limited to the sphere of avian relationality in creating relationships of power and transformation.

The people featured here use feminine songs to imagine ways of organizing and relating experiences of human-animal relations, corporeal essences, gender, history, and subjectivities. The singers also participate in acts of shamanism achieved through the feminine spoken word, which, when intensified with musicality, becomes a powerful means of altering and changing social relations. Whether it is Gervacio teaching women how to attract men with the "breast song" or Serafina becoming a hummingbird, these singers masterfully employ principles of creation, dissolution, transformation, mimesis, and shape-shifting. The competency displaced here shows a poetics of the body as defined via the imaginative worlds and mythical contours of a reality where many people act shamanically in creative ways. Feminine shamanistic competencies, however, usually have different qualities from the shamanistic arts dominated by men, and these feminine arts have been underappreciated by professional researchers (see B. Tedlock 2005). This lack of appreciation is perhaps because feminine shamanism is more secretive and intimate, and its power derives from women being able to act upon their husbands and others without them knowing what hit them. The Breast Song is a good example of how Quichua women shamanize with their songs.

Let us now move on to discuss the mythological contours created by the culture heroes of the Napo Runa, the twins, or Cuillurguna. Now that we have established the relations surrounding their mother, Iluku (who was not a strongwoman but who birthed strong sons), we are able to appreciate the "miracles" and powers that the twins bring into the world.

CHAPTER 5
THE TWINS AND THE JAGUARS

I n this chapter we employ the verse analysis method developed by Dell Hymes (1981, 1985, 1992, 1994) in analyzing an Amazonian Quichua myth-narrative, "The Twins and the Jaguars," from the province of Napo.¹ The discussion involves two principal themes. First, we provide a more detailed discussion of verse analysis and the aesthetics of grammar in Quichua storytelling. Second, we translate one of the core stories of Napo Quichua mythology—the beginning of the twins cycle—and relate it to the ritual experience drinking the plant *puma yuyu* (*Teliostacha lanceolata*).

The fieldwork for this project was done by Michael while he was living in Campo-Cocha with the Shiguango family, before he met Edith. After we got married (1995) and made another trip for fieldwork to Ecuador (1996–1997), we moved back in with Michael's parents in Omaha, Nebraska, to (re)adjust to life in the United States and for Michael to begin work on the dissertation. In 1998 we made it back to Charlottesville, Virginia, with support from the University of Virginia for dissertation write-up. One afternoon we had the opportunity to sit down with Dell and Virginia Hymes to work on the project and to ask questions about the method. Using a tape recorder, we listened to the narrative and tried to hear the patterning of lines and verses in the narrative. After some months of additional work, reading, thinking, and revisions, the paper was finally published in *Anthropological Linguistics*. This was the first Amazonian Quichua story we translated.

The present chapter is an updated and expanded version of the original article, which contained only a transcription and translation of Act III of the story. Here, we provide the whole narrative with a fresh translation. The Quichua transcription and translation of the story can be found in appendix 1 at the end of this chapter, and readers mainly interested in the story might wish to read it first. Readers who visit book's website can also listen to original audio recording of the story with an accompanying English translation.

In discussing verse analysis, which is our first theme, we begin by examining the organizational and grammatical features that distinguish lines. We then detail how lines are configured into larger blocks of meaning. Initial words set off verses, stanzas, and scenes. The quotative, constructions that cite speech (*nin*, or "they say"), is a principal marker of verses. Features of syntax such as aspect, parallelism, verb tense, and repetition all play a part in the total poetic structure. The narrator achieves rhyme and rhythm from the synchronic artistry of multidimensional vocal and grammatical features. Ideophones also work as a key element of aspect and meaning (see Nuckolls 1996, 2010).

The narrative's theme, "becoming a jaguar," is expressed through a rhetorical logic of onset, ongoing, and outcome that unfolds as a structural transformation relation between humans and mythical jaguars. This structural transformation relation is mediated by a third element, the twins, who not only lend movement to structure but also advance the development of drama by obviating previous relations as a dynamic synecdoche. This chapter demonstrates the major contours of performative complexity involved in Amazonian Quichua narration of traditional mythical knowledge and the importance of the jaguar as an active and dominant symbolic "sign" of "becoming" in Napo Runa cosmology and culture (Brightman 1993; Reichel-Dolmatoff 1975; Sullivan 1988). Narrative performance, as we show, emerges as an important artistic, cultural, and religious tool for experiencing the "transcendence" of everyday human form.

The Ethnographic Setting

All Quechua languages are divided into two groups, but several sets of terms are used to describe them. Ecuadorian Quichua belongs to the peripheral Quechua grouping (Mannheim 1991), also termed Quechua A (Parker 1969:7) or Quechua II (Torero 1974). The other major grouping, which corresponds to Central Quechua (Mannheim 1991), is also termed Quechua B (Parker 1969) or Quechua I (Torero 1974). While it was before assumed that Cuzco or Central Quechua was the original Quechua (Stark 1985), today most scholars view Quechua more heterogeneously and historically complex than previously thought (Durston 2007), and the origins of many dialects of Quecha are unknown or disputed. Quichua (more recently spelled "Kichwa") is the term used to refer to Ecuadorian Quechua dialects, but speakers of Quichua refer to their language as Runa Shimi, or "human speech."

There is evidence that this language was used as a lingua franca and a trade language in the Amazon region in pre-Columbian times (Stark 1985; Oberum 1980), but Quichua gained prominence throughout Amazonia in the colonial era (Stark 1985; Steward and Métraux 1948). Muysken (2000, 2009) doubts that large populations of Quichua speakers could have existed in pre-Hispanic times and attributes the rise of Amazonian Quichua populations to demographic collapse due to the diseases and abuses of colonialism. Colonialism caused the population to decline anywhere from 75 to 90 percent, and "groups which were separate before were forced to mix and reorganize" (Muysken 2009:84). The population decline in Upper Napo after the failed Jumandy revolt in 1578 is well documented (Newson 1995; Ospina 1992).

While in 1985 Stark reported approximately 10,000 Amazonian Quichua speakers, Ruiz (1993) estimated 60,000 Quichua speakers in the Ecuadorian Amazon. Today, there are hundreds of thousands of Amazonian Quichua speakers. Once a fast-growing language that subsumed other indigenous languages in Amazonian Ecuador and Peru (Stark 1985), the Amazonian Quichua dialects are now contracting in some places, especially in or near urban areas, as younger speakers, who are the majority of the population now, are becoming Spanish dominant or Spanish monolingual.

Orr and Wrisley (1981) classify three dialects of Amazonian Quichua: Tena, Loreto-Avila, and Bobonaza-Puyo. Amazonian Quichua dialects are mutually intelligible and closely related in terms of vocabulary and grammar. While Amazonian Quichua designates a linguistic and cultural group, there are various cultural entities and ethnic designations within this classification. The major cultural designations are the Pastaza Quichua, who occupy the region near Puyo toward the south and southeast that includes the Bobonaza and Curaray Rivers (see N. Whitten 1976, 1985; Reeve 1985), and the Napo Quichua, who occupy the "triangle" region formed by the foothills of the Andes and the Coca and Napo Rivers (see Oberum 1980). Quichua speakers who live in Lower Napo speak the Avila-Loreto dialect, but both groups are referred to as Napo Quichua. There is also a large group of Quichua speakers to the North that inhabit the region of Aguarico along the rivers of Aguarico, San Miguel, and Putumayo (Foletti-Castegnaro 1993).[2] There are countless other "micro" identities that flow into the major dialectical groupings, each with its own linguistic and cultural peculiarities in relation to others (e.g., Pano Runa, Sara Yaku). These designations are further broken down into smaller-scale settlements (e.g., *comunidad* or *comuna*), extended families (e.g., *muntun* or *ayllu*), and households.

The narrative under consideration here is by Verna Grefa, who is from Ongota-Dos Ríos, a community on the Misahualli River just a few kilometers from Tena. The narrative is inscribed within the regional geography of the Upper Napo River, and the humanity and communicative capacity of jaguars is its salient theme. The narrator describes the path of the twins along the major rivers that flow through the Tena region, the Pano, Tena, and Napo Rivers. The myth is connected to specific petroglyphs found on large rocks in or near these rivers. Two of these rocks have jaguar-like "footprints" on them (Porras 1985), and the other is a "painting" of frogs (Sapo Rumi) that people say was completed by the twins during their encounters on the Pano River with the mythical jaguars. Chapter 7 provides more in-depth discussion of these petroglyphs and their relationship to the twins.

Fieldwork, *Puma Yuyu*, and "Becoming" Jaguars

While Michael was living in the Upper Napo community of Campo-Cocha, he was interested in collecting stories about the mythical past. Fermin Shiguango, his mentor, was familiar with these stories but insisted that for a good telling we would have to visit his uncle, Verna Grefa, who lived near Tena. We also were going to visit Fermin's mother, who knew about *puma yuyu*, a plant that, if taken regularly, is said to make one turn into a jaguar. Fermin's sons, Galo and Alex, had said that their grandmother had taken this plant often, and now, in her old age, she had gained the ability to turn into a jaguar.

Upon arriving at Fermin's mother's house, we were greeted with bowls of *aswa*, or manioc beer, as we sat to talk. Fermin asked his mother about *puma yuyu*. Fermin and his sons were just as interested in learning about it as was Michael; they felt that there was a mystique about this plant, which represented an ancient knowledge of the Amazonian forest. Samuel, Fermin's nephew, commented that he had taken *puma yuyu* in training to be a boxer. "It makes you stronger," he said. At the time, Michael did not realize he was making a conceptual link between *puma yuyu*, experiences of strength and agility, and the Napo Runa concept of the jaguar (Brightman 1993). Michael would later discover the jaguar "concept" within the narrative not yet heard.

Fermin's mother had some plants hidden in her garden and offered to let us take them. The plant, she told us, takes a whole lifetime to achieve its effect. It gives you the strength of the jaguar and augments your shamanistic power, power that increases with age. Fermin and his mother explained that the plant needed time to ferment inside your body. "Only in very old age could you possibly turn into jaguar form," Fermin said, "But when you die you'll become one forever." These seemed very strange propositions to Michael. While he had read about such ideas in Amazonian cultures, until this point he did not think his host family had knowledge of such practices. At the time, Michael, like many scholars before him, did not realize that perspectivist propositions such as people turning into jaguars were not reified doctrines in the way that Westerners set our beliefs out in the category of "religion." The proposition of humans turning into jaguars is a salient manifestation of the "animistic" philosophy of Native Amazonians in which, according to Descola, "the common point of reference for all beings of nature is not humans as a species but rather humanity as a condition" (Viveiros de Castro 1998:472). Mythical transformations among men and animals reveal not so much a culture/nature distinction as an original state of shared humanity (472).

We then visited Verna's house. We observed proper etiquette, and during the drinking of manioc brew Fermin explained that Michael was an anthropologist who was interested in taping some stories about *ñawpa timpu*, or "the before times." Verna agreed. We propped up the tape recorder, and Verna began telling stories about spirits of the forest, about *supay* (spirit beings) and *aya* (ghosts). After recording a few stories he asked if we had any requests. Michael asked Verna if he could tell a story about the twins, the Cuillurguna. This essay is the academic product of that telling.

After the narrative performance we all felt excited about having taken *puma yuyu* and the connectedness of the narrative to the plant, a point Michael did not catch at first. Fermin, who was helping transcribe the story from the tape a few days later, commented, "you see, these stories just aren't tales. They are real sources of power for us." For Fermin and his sons, the two events connected them to "becoming" jaguars in a deeply personal way.

Verse Analysis Method

The verse analysis method has been well described by Dell Hymes (1981, 1985, 1992, 1994) in a number of pieces. While we discuss our translation methodology in the introduction, it is worth repeating that verse analysis is a method that seeks to translate what is essentially untranslatable, and is but one of a variety of techniques used in the field of ethnopoetics (see, among others, Basso 1985, 1987; Hendricks 1993; Salomon and Urioste 1991; Sherzer 1983; Swann 1992; D. Tedlock 1983; Urban 1991). As we state earlier, although verse analysis cannot convey the experience of listening to oral narrative, it does provide the reader with a glimpse into the artistry from the perspective of the Native language. This is no small achievement, for it challenges us to recognize the poetic complexity present within oral cultural traditions overshadowed by the literary ideologies of our dominant cultures. As the

Hymeses have emphasized, there is vast world of poetry waiting to be released by scholars with some knowledge of languages with oral traditions.

We now present the narrative in brief. A translation and Quichua transcription of the full narrative appear in appendix 1, and the audio file of this performance, as well as some associated images and maps, can be accessed online on the companion website.

Act I. We understand that we are in *ñawpa timpu*, the "before times" and that this is a distinct mythical period from the present. We learn that in the "before times" there were two little ones, twins, that were born. We learn that there were lots of human-eating jaguars that were on the verge of finishing off human life. The narrator points out that God had created and planned the lives of these two little ones.

We learn that the mother of the twins had become pregnant without having sexual intercourse. Feeling afraid she goes to the house of the jaguars to die.[3] Entering the house the woman meets the jaguar grandmother. The grandmother tells her of the danger of her sons and hides her on a shelf, so that her sons will not find the woman when they come home. The jaguar sons come home hungry, and the grandmother jaguar tells them that there is nothing to eat in the house. The jaguar sons smell something, but the grandmother lies to them in hopes that they will not find the woman.

The jaguar sons realize that there is food in the house. They find the woman, kill her, and throw her out onto the floor for consumption. The jaguar sons give the entrails to the grandmother jaguar because they are "soft" and will not damage her sore tooth. The jaguar sons then eat the woman. The grandmother jaguar takes the entrails, with the two babies inside, and hides them.

Act II. The next day the grandmother finds that the twins are alive, having given birth to themselves. She nurtures them and breastfeeds them while her jaguar sons are not looking. The jaguar grandmother thus becomes the adoptive mother of the twins. The twins learn to walk in three days. They are cared for by the jaguar grandmother and make animal and bird traps to catch food. They show the jaguars their knowledge. The grandmother jaguar is protective ("stingy") of the twins in the face of threats from the jaguar sons.

Act III begins with the twins gaining "heart" or strength. Humans come and ask for their help against the jaguars, and the twins agree to put an end to the jaguars. The narrator tells us the names of the twins, Cuillur and Dociru. The narrator reiterates that they were sent by God, and that they are *ushakkuna*, or "powerful." The twins ask the jaguar sons if their hunting trail needs work. The twins follow the jaguars to the forest on their hunting trips and construct bridge traps at the Tena and Pano Rivers. At both locations the jaguars sense danger and avoid the traps. The twins follow the jaguars even further to the Napo River. There, the jaguars tell the twins that this is the most dangerous river to cross. The twins decide to stay behind and build a bridge for the jaguars while they go hunting. The twins build the bridge. With vines and rocks, they construct a large bridge that is secure.

The jaguars come back from hunting, and one of them has killed a human. The twins are positioned at both ends of the bridge and try to convince the jaguars to cross. The jaguar sons are afraid, but by whistling and playing instruments, the twins convince one jaguar to try out the bridge. Feeling that it is secure, the jaguar calls the others. When they are all halfway across, the twins undo the knots at both ends, and the jaguars fall into the water and die. The narrator interjects that on "judgment day" (*izhu punzha*) the jaguars will come back to life. The narrator comments that these events gave human beings "space" to live and to reproduce. One pregnant jaguar female escapes into the forest, and from her there still exist jaguars today.

Organization of Lines and Verses

Following Virginia Hymes (1992), we generally assign one line to each predication, but other features, such as pauses (see D. Tedlock 1983), also define lines. Subordinate clauses also take a line when the subordinate verb phrase ends in a marker that sets it apart from the main predicate. Subordinate verb phrases end in a "same subject" marker, *sha*, a "switch subject" marker, *kpi*, or a past perfect marker, *shkay*. Switch subject endings are often translated as "while," "if," "when," and "as." When these subordinate verb phrases stand as a separate entity, they are represented as a line (some examples are lines 25, 30, 51, 161, and 239). Also, same subject markers can convey a series or sequence of actions that take place one after another (lines 63–66, 266–268) or can work as an adverb, showing how the main action was done (lines 80, 111–114, 269). These phrases generally do not take a separate line.

Phrases that introduce quotations with the perfective *nisha*, "saying" (lines 27, 42, 62, 75, 127, 135, 169, 175, 197), or the switch subject marked version *nikpi*, "upon saying" (lines 124, 173, 193) take a line. The narrator also signals the end of a line by a falling or rising in his voice, rate of speech change (the narrator tends to speed up toward the end of a line), or a pause. Thus, in setting out lines the narrator employs various features: initial words, predication, subordinate phrase relational markers, and vocal qualities. These configurations do not work in isolation but rather in relation to other features that organize lines into larger units of meaning.

Lines are grouped into verses (indicated in the transcription by indentation of all but the first line of the verse) and verses into stanzas (indicated by capital A, B, C, etc.). Stanzas, in turn, are grouped into scenes (indicated by lowercase roman numerals), and scenes into acts (indicated by uppercase roman numerals). Dell Hymes (1992) has noted the importance of the quotative in Hopi narrative as either a marker of verse or of a stanza. Similarly, in this Quichua narrative, the quotative emerges as a marker of verses and, sometimes, stanzas. Often a verse will consist of a subordinate phrase, or a series of subordinate phrases, followed by the main verb phrase and punctuated by the quotative *nin*, "they say" (lines 120–122, 204–205, 209–213, 236–237, etc.). Variations on this pattern abound (lines 86–87, 98–101, 111–114, 131–136). Other features, such as parallelism, repetition, or initial words work in tandem with quotative constructs, so one cannot say for certain what any phrase or feature means in isolation from the others.

Initial words work together with other features to group lines. The initial word *chi* (that) and derivatives such as *chibiga* (in that) or *chita* (that [object]) usually signal a verse; sometimes they signal a stanza. The initial word *shinakpi* (and so being), and its abbreviated form *nakpi* usually signal a stanza or a scene, but they also can signal a verse. Initial words work with features such as repetition, aspect parallelism, quotative, and change of focus in the patterning of lines into verses, stanzas, and scenes.

The narrator uses syntactic parallelism and repetition in cohering lines. For example, in lines 199–208, the narrator consistently uses the plural marker *kuna* in separate verses in the stanza. This predication is in contrast to the more common past tense marker *shka* (*shka* indicates that information is passed-on knowledge). Similarly lines 262, 268, 274, 284, and 293 contain the preterit marker *nawka* (third-person plural preterit), also in contrast to *shka*.

In lines 90–95 the repetition of the word *tuwasha* (to cover with something), in combination with the quotative, helps define the stanza. In lines 110–114 the repetition of domestic actions—gathering firewood, water, and food for the grandmother jaguar—patterns the stanza. Also, the quotative is used repetitively, and *shka* is employed consistently. Parallelism and repetition features, which can be found in almost every stanza, stand out when the next unit is marked by a change in the pattern or set apart by an initial word. See the profile and the narrative in verse form (below) for more examples of parallelism and repetition.

In scene iv of Act III Verna uses the ending *shkawa* twice within stanza C. Each usage marks a separate verse (see lines 263–284), but the parallelism patterns the verses into a stanza. The construction *shkawa* relates actions of one subject to another, much like the switch subject marker *kpi*. In the first example *nishkawa* (and with having said) is used to link what the jaguar brother has just said to the action of his brothers following him onto the bridge. In the second example Verna uses *tukushkallawa* (and just with having happened),[4] to freeze the jaguars on the bridge (*chawpi yakuy* [in the middle of the water]) to continue the action with the twins in the next verse. In both examples the ending *shkawa* creates a past progressive effect that sets up an opposition between two acting subjects.

This stanza, made up of six verses, is one of the most beautiful in the narrative and is pivotal to the action and drama: the twins finally lure the jaguars onto the bridge. The first verse signals the stanza and marks a new unit of lines (*shinakpi*). In the second verse the twins "tempt" the jaguars and get one to enter onto the bridge. In the third verse the jaguar says that the bridge is "ok" and calls his brothers (*nishkawa*). In the fourth verse his twenty brothers enter onto the bridge. In the fifth verse they all decide that it is "ok" and go out to the middle (*tukushkallawa*). In the last verse the twins, in strategic position on either side of the river, then whistle. The action moves between subjects like this:

Verse 1—transition (*shinakpi*)
Verse 2—twins
Verse 3—lone jaguar (*nishkawa*)
Verse 4—jaguar brothers
Verse 5—jaguar brothers (*tukushkallawa*)
Verse 6—twins[5]

Vocal qualities also emerge. After playing back the tape of the narrative over and over, Michael realized that most of the time the pauses corresponded to the ending of lines. But sometimes pauses seem to define the lines themselves, as there are times when lines stand out as just one word, especially when it is a subject change. As Dennis Tedlock's (1983) work has shown, vocal qualities such as pause can create a different patterning of lines distinct from that of a verse analysis, which is focused on the structural and grammatical relations of speech. But we have found that both the sound and structural relations work together in a way in which narrators possess competencies in both sound and structure, in prosody and grammatical "equivalence." As well, Verna's use of ideophones, rhythm, and vocal emphases enrich the texture and flow of the stories.

In this Quichua story, features of repetition and parallelism work grammatically and vocally in the narrative, resulting in rhythm and "rhyme." We are not sure if "rhyme" is a good way of describing this phenomenon, because such occurrences are so common in everyday Quichua speech as well, which tends to favor sound overlap and repetition in general. But ending-sound equivalence is a salient feature of Quichua aesthetics and often the result of grammatical parallelism and repetition.

For example, in our story, the frequency of the ending vowels *a* and *i*—represented through a variety of markers—creates endless situations of final vowel correspondence. Salient examples are lines 90–95, 110–114, 193–196, 253–259, and 294–304. Equivalence is accented by rhythm that puts the emphasis on the last word of a line, often as a punctuated quotative *nin* or a word that features repetition or parallelism. A good example of these relations is in scene iii of Act II (lines 120–128). Here the three stanzas are marked by the presence of the quotative and aspect parallelism. Stanza A ends with the line, *mamaga yapa llakikmi nin* (mama loved them, so they say). Stanza B ends in *mamaga mitsakmi nin* (mama defended them, they say). Stanza C ends with *mitsasha iñachikmi nin* (she defended them and made them grow, they say). In all three stanzas the quotative on the ending line contributes to both sound and grammatical parallelism, cohering not only each individual stanza but also setting them apart as a scene. Verb parallelism contributes to rhyme and rhythm with the sound *kmi* to describe the qualities of the jaguar grandmother as each "loving, defending, and as nourishing." Pauses mark the end of a verse, stanza, or act.

The use of ideophones (Nuckolls 1996, 2010) adds vocal emphasis to important actions in the narrative and gives shape to happenings. Ideophones are analogous to the use of onomatopoeic words such as "thump" and "whack" in English, but in English use of such conventions is very poorly developed compared to Quichua (Nuckolls 2010). Ideophones are central to Amazonian Quichua discursive practice (Nuckolls 1996:4).

Many of the key actions of the narrative are marked by ideophones or sound symbolism. The building of the bridge (lines 215–240) employs repetitive sound symbolism, which imitates the action of the twins tying knots and stringing together sections of the rope bridge (implying duration). In line 283 the twins whistle to signal the undoing of the knots, which is communicated using an ideophone, repeated twice, that conveys doing something rapidly: *dzas, dzas* (line 289).[6] The jaguars fall, *kushnin* (line 291), and are ultimately entrapped by the twins' incantation of "stone, stone, stone, stone, stone, stone" (lines 296–301). The narrator weaves together verses punctuated by the quotative with actions that are expressed as sound symbolism. The result is a series of images giving shape to both durational and rapid events.

In the making of the bridge (Act III, scene iii) the twins weave the rope (*alingasha alingasha*), tie the rope (*day wascama watasha*), and then test the tightness of the bridge (*lunllas mana kuyuk*). The first two images are achieved through repetition of the action, the last through the ideophone *lunllas*, meaning that something is unmoving and still. However, in this scene the narrator repeats the verbs *alingasha* and *watasha* several times to convey the experience of creating the bridge as well as a sense of aspect duration.

In the undoing of the bridge (scene iv, stanzas D, E) knots come untied and the jaguars fall. The sound symbolism, *kushniiiiin*, conveys an image of falling "smoke" as *kushni* means "smoke."[7] The jaguars then convert into "rocks" speeding downward, conveyed by the twins' repetition of *rumi, rumi, rumi, rumi*. The final movement is one of the transformation of jaguar substance to "smoke" (the duration of falling) and back to substance (rocks). The substance change is significant as stones are not only heavy but also conceptualized as containers of vital energy or power.[8]

Other ideophones are *tsiu* (line 82), *pus* (line 195), and *tias* (line 247). *Tsiu* connotes a slippery sliding action and is used to describe the unborn twins' extraction from their mother's womb in Act II. *Pus* normally conveys an image of penetration in Napo Runa usage, but in the context of water it conveys the image of a whirlpool. The use of this word highlights the conditions under which the jaguars cross the Napo River "almost almost dying" (line 194) and explains why they would find a bridge useful. *Tias* describes a clean slicing action, and in line 247 it brings to life the mental picture of sharp jaguar claws having cut up Runa flesh for transport home, imagery that serves as the background for the twins' final encounter with the jaguars.

Time words are used to signal an act or scene but can signal stanzas or verses also. The word *ñawpa* signals the beginning and end of the narrative and also serves to divide the first scene into three main sections (lines 1, 9, 17). In line 17 *Puma timpu* (jaguar times) is used as an analog to *ñawpa timpu* (beginning times). The second act begins with *tutamanta*, meaning "morning" (line 96). The third act begins with *ña washaga*, meaning "now later" (line 129). *Ña*, meaning "now," can signal groupings of lines as a verse (see line 98) or can be used with other time words like *punzhama* (meaning "now . . . days later") or *chishira* (meaning "now in the afternoon") to signal scenes (see lines 106 and 241).

A quick summary of features is in order. The quotative stands out as a marker of verse. Initial words *chi* (those) generally mark verses. The initial words *shinakpi* and *nakpi* (and so being) tend to mark stanzas or scenes. Time words, although they mark a verse and a stanza, primarily mark scenes or acts. Parallelism and repetition occur in stanzas, in verses, and within lines (as a couplet or a triplet). Rhyme rarely stands as a factor unrelated to verb parallelism or repetition. Other narrative features such as change of focus, change of topic, or changes in aspect or tense—similar in function to an initial word—are ways of giving shape to narrative forms.

The Profile

A profile is a summary of the verse relations. It moves stanza by stanza highlighting the poetic and grammatical features found to be salient to the organization of the narrative. The profile also gives an "incident" summary of each stanza that highlights the major action present. We have divided the profile into four tables. The first and second tables correspond to Acts I and II. Because of length, Act III is represented by two tables. The third table contains scenes i, ii, and iii, and the fourth table contains scenes iv and v (see appendix).

Rhetorical Patterning

Dell Hymes, influenced by the philosopher Kenneth Burke (1973 [1941], noticed that Chinookan-speaking peoples of the Columbia River structured narratives according to an onset, ongoing, and outcome pattern (see Hymes 1992:92–99). This pattern was later found to be present in other traditions. Narrators usually mark an onset, ongoing, and outcome pattern via the use of threes and fives (both represent an onset, ongoing, and outcome, pattern; fives have an "interlocking" transition between two sets of threes). Other traditions, in contrast, correspond to an "initiation" and "resolution" patterning, characterized by twos and fours. Hymes argues that a predilection for twos and fours or threes and fives reflects a cultural competence, a "rhetorical" logic to narrative event (Hymes 1992). It is "rhetorical" in that it arouses and satisfies expectation and "accommodates relations of larger scope (e.g., among stanzas, scenes, and acts)."

While numerical patterning is salient among many storytelling traditions,[9] one must be careful in over-interpreting such relations, especially because the expectation of a pattern can be a powerful psychological influence during translation. The numerical patterning, at least in Amazonian Quichua narratives, relates to storytellers using form to create complex relations that define good storytelling. For example, twos and fours derive from oppositions and complements. Threes and fives, which are often built up from dynamic twos and fours, emerge from transformations and process. When combined in a story, these patterns communicate through form the cosmological and social notions of cyclicity and interpenetration. They are not "formulas" (which are tight and restrictive) but rather patterns (which are open ended and moving).

In the narrative, the story is structured as an onset, ongoing, and outcome pattern. In Act I the jaguars consume the twins' mother; in Act II the twins survive and grow up under care of the jaguar grandmother; in Act III the twins fulfill their "destiny" and kill the jaguars. Act I reflects death, Act II life, and Act III death again. This progression of events—onset, ongoing, and outcome—leads to a situation more favorable for human life. Furthermore, the rhetorical logic of onset, ongoing, and outcome entails a structural transformation relation. In the introduction, the narrative brings jaguars and humans together as two opposing groups. The jaguar house is dominant over the humans; human death and jaguar fertility are synonymous. We might represent Act I like this:

jaguar fertility	+	jaguar death	–
human fertility	–	human death	+

At the end of the story, however, the inverse is true. The situation is one of human dominance and fertility at the expense of the jaguars. The "structure" has transformed, but the principle of an underlying unity remains. Act III can be represented as follows:

human fertility	+	human death	–
jaguar fertility	–	jaguar death	+

Act III ends with the death of the jaguars, but the narrator comments that on judgment day (*izhu punzha*) the jaguars will rise up again to reverse the order back to jaguar dominance (lines 302–303). In the narrator's conceptual arrangement of things, the mythical jaguars described in the narrative are never gone but rather are separated to inhabit the "mythical" world.[10] This is outcome.

The human-jaguar opposition reflects a dualism-unity relation. Despite being rivals, neither jaguars nor humans would be fully "human" without the other.[11] The structural transformation relation keeps humans and jaguars—the real world and the mythical world—inextricably interdependent and circular. This is the basic metonymic configuration, which is later submitted to the contingency of later events in the story.

The prime mover of the story is the asymmetric intervention of the twins upon the metonymic system. This intervention is facilitated by the metaphoric relation between the twins and jaguars, a different level of relation that gives the twins a new kind of subjectivity and transformative role. The twins begin as vulnerable humans that are nearly consumed by jaguars (Act I), but they transform into jaguar-like beings themselves in Act II. The narrator conveys this in a variety of ways. The twins were raised on jaguar milk (lines 102–105); they are referred to as "just like jaguar sons" (line 171); they become hunters and "show" the jaguars how to trap animals (lines 115–119). The twins' new subjectivity becomes apparent. They are said to be powerful, *"ushakuna"* (line 163, 164). They are also described as impeccable, *"mana pandakkuna"* (line 165–167). The twins' power is reflected in the intervening aspect of their relation to the human-jaguar system. The twins, in "becoming" jaguars, are able to defeat them and reverse the cosmic balance of things to favor human fertility. The twins, thus, by interceding upon the metonymic system, cause it to operationally "transform."

It is here that the narrative, as a whole, brings into being a new level of meaning. Act I reflects death (onset), Act II reflects life (ongoing), and Act III reverts back to a situation of death again (outcome). Act I reflects the killing of the humans (consumption), focusing specifically on the twins' mother. Act II reflects the conversion of death into the life of the twins and the "becoming" of powerful beings. Act III continues the process engendered by Act II but as dénouement. The twins kill the jaguars (revenge). Acts I and III, although both characterized as death, are inversions of each other. Act I is detrimental to humans; Act III is detrimental to jaguars. Act II occupies an intervening position and represents the conversion of death into life through the "becoming" of something new.

While the metaphoric relation of twins and jaguars creates a new figurative association between source and target domains, it does more because the relation (i.e., the "intervening" relation) returns to the system as metonymy (T. Turner 1991a:150) as the twins embody all of the relations. The return of the metaphorical relation to the system conveys the "new" subjectivity of the twins and acts as the source of the inversion of jaguar-human relations in Act III. These relations assume the character of synecdoche in that the parts (the twins) come to stand for the whole and re-create the whole in their image (see T. Turner 1991a:149).

The synecdoche structure is further recursively represented in the idea of twins. In Act I Verna refers to the twins by the Spanish word *gimelos* meaning "twins" (line 4) as well as by the simple description of "two" babies or sons (lines 3, 5, 7, 15, 20, 22, etc.). They are less than human. In Act II the twins undergo the transformations that cause the jaguar mother to give them names in Act III. In Act III she names firstborn twin Dociru and the other Cuillur (lines 148–159). In the penultimate scene (iv) Verna begins to refer to the twins as the plural of the younger brother, "Cuillurguna" (line 295). This is a synecdoche relation in that one brother represents the whole while being also just a "part." It is no coincidence that the more complex "whole/part" naming relation appears at the key juncture of narrative action, when the Cuillurguna turn the jaguars into stone (lines 295–301). The use of naming in the final scenes replicates and enriches further the synecdoche structure.

Conclusion

This chapter discusses mythical narrative relations of verse and structure as they contribute to the unfolding of drama and theme in an Amazonian Quichua myth-narrative. The quotative emerges as a major organizational feature in marking verses, working in tandem with other features that mark verses, stanzas, scenes, or acts. Other features we discuss are the presence of initial words, parallelism, repetition, and sound similarity. Sound symbolism is essential to verb aspect and action. The narrative, as we argue, follows a rhetorical logic of onset, ongoing, and outcome. This sequencing effects a structural transformation relation between mythical jaguars and humans. This relation is mediated by the intervening Cuillurguna.[12] The poetic organization of the myth not only reveals the conceptual unity of jaguars from *ñawpa timpu* (before times) to humans from *kunan timpu* (nowadays) but also creates a higher order relation between mythical jaguars and humans. This higher order of complexity is represented as a synecdoche relation personified in the twins.

This essay shows some of the complex narrative techniques and sets of propositions involved in communicating how the Napo Quichua view the jaguar as a "sign," that is, the a priori conceptualization of what jaguars are and do, and to which experiences of jaguars are assimilated (Brightman 1993:32). As "signs" in Napo Quichua socioculture, the jaguar sits atop the symbolic hierarchy of animals. However, it is viewed ambivalently, as predator and prey of humans. The jaguar is admired, imitated, and respected, as well as loathed, hunted, and feared. Despite the ambivalence toward jaguars, people seek connection to the power of mythical jaguars by ritually drinking *puma yuyu*, in the same way the twins "became" jaguars in Act II. In this sense the narrative's message is not about "being" but rather "becoming" a master predator of influence. It is no coincidence that synecdoche structures are often employed by those in dominant social positions in order to symbolically subsume "the whole" of society (T. Turner 1991a:156). While it would seem contradictory to want to become something you fear, the narrative demonstrates the point that it is often necessary to become a jaguar in order to avoid being devoured by them.

Appendix 1. The Narrative in Verse Form

What follows is the story in verse form in English translation with the Quichua transcription on the facing page. We provide the Quichua transcription here because this chapter deals with a much more detailed discussion of Quichua grammar than we have previously given. Readers, by looking at the Quichua, will be able to see the grammatical patterns that are defining of this and other narratives.

THE TWINS AND THE JAGUARS BY VERNA GREFA

English

I/i/A   life in the before times
there was they say
a pair of little ones
now days we call them twins
    and so being there was a pair of little ones they say   5
a mama gave birth they say
    to two babies
      she gave birth to two babies they say

B   in those before times
the jaguars ate too many people they say   10
    the jaguars
as the jaguars ate too many people
God had everything ready they say
    for that woman's
    two babies' upbringing   15

C   and so being
in jaguar times too many humans died
    they were getting scarce
      in that time
so two babies were born from a woman they say   20
    they came they say
      those two sons

ii/A   and with that
    that woman
      getting pregnant   25
        being a virgin and getting pregnant got scared

"better to go to the jaguar house to die" saying
    "there they will eat me and I will die" she entered they say

B   and so being
when she entered that crowded jaguar house   30
a grandmother jaguar mama lived there they say
    a grandmother
that jaguar mama said
    "my sons aren't here"
    "if they were here they would have eaten you long ago"   35
"why did you come?" when she [grandmother] asked
    "I came here for a quick death grandmother" she spoke
    they say

C   and so being [grandmother] said "no"
putting up a ladder [to the attic in the house, she said]

Quichua

I / i / A   ñawpa timpu kawsaybimi
tiak nin
shuk ishkipura iñakuna
kunan timpu gimilos ninchi
    shina ishkipura iñakuna tiakunami nin   5
shuk mama pagarichishka nin
    ishki wawara
      ishki wawara pagarichishka nin

B   chiga ñawpa timpu
pumami yapa mikuk nin   10
    puma
puma yapa mikukpimi
Dios charishina purutuka nin
    chi warmi
      ishki wawa iñanara   15

C   shinakpiga
puma timpui yapa runa wañusha
    tukuriusha
      chi timpui
shina chi ishki wawara tupak warmimanda nin   20
    tuparik nin
      chi ishki churi

ii / A   chiwaska
    chi warmiga
      iksayuk tukusha   25
        mana piwas takarikllayra iksayuk tukusha
        manzharisha
"shu ray puma wasima risha wañusha" nisha
    "chibi mikui tukusha wañusha" ikuriushka nin

B   shinakpiga
chi jinti puma wasi ikuriukpiga   30
shuk ruku puma mama kawsashkami nin
    rukumama
chi puma apama
    "churiuna illanaunmi"
      "tiawshkasha unay kanda apisha mikunaun maka"   35
"imarasha shamukangui" nikpi
    "shu ray wañungák shamukani rukumama"
    rimashkami nin

C   nakpiga "mana"
chakanara churasha awapatama

	"climb"	40
	"lie down there"	
	"if not in no time **dzas** they will kill you" saying	
	putting the ladder up top	
	she made her climb up there they say	
	that pregnant woman	45
iii/A	and so being while she was hiding	
	the whole bunch of grandmother's sons trampled inside	
	they say	
	in that [they said]	
	"we didn't eat too much meat mama"	
	"we only got a little, little bit"	50
B	coming	
	they went through the whole house smelling they say	
	"mama what do you have?" [said the sons]	
	"it smells so yummmmie!"	
	they went smelling the house they say	55
C	"what could there be?" [responded grandmother]	
	"you are only smelling my farts" saying	
	said that mama they say	
iv/A	and so being [the sons said]	
	"no, mama"	60
	"we smell it"	
	"it smells so yummmmmie!" saying	
	smelling	
	and smelling	
	one looked above	65
	jumped	
	he climbed up to the attic they say	
	one jaguar	
	one son	
	climbing	70
	there she was lying	
	that pregnant woman	
	he [the jaguar] found her they say	
B	"like that keeping [food from us]" [the jaguar said]	
	"hiding food you deceived us mama" saying	75
	he cut her throat **tias** and threw her to the ground	
	they say	
	one jaguar	
	and so doing throwing her down	
	the whole group	
	[came] tearing eating [the pregnant woman]	80

"sikay" 40
"chibi sirijuy"
"mana akpiga **dzas** wañuchinawnga" nisha
chakanara churasha awama
sikachishkami nin
chi chichu warmira 45
iii / A shinakpi pay pakasha chariungama
ña churi muntun tawkarimunawshka nin ukuman

chibimi
"aychara mana yapa mikunchichu mama"
"ansa ansalla apisha purinchi" 50
B shamusha
intiru wasira muktisha rikukunami nin
"mama imara charingui"
"gustora ñuka mikilla asnanga"
muktisha rikukuna nin 55
C "imara tiangayri"
"ñuka supillara asnangaga" nisha
mama nikmi nin
iv / A shinakpi
"mana mama" 60
"asnanmi ñukanchira"
"gustu ñuka mikilla asnan" nisha
muktiusha
muktiushkay
awaman rikusha 65
saltasha
pata awaman sikakunami nin
shu puma
shu churi
sikasha 70
chibi sirik
iksayuk warmira
tupayrishkami nin
B "kasna wakachisha"
"charishami ñukanchira umashkangui mama" nishami 75
kungara "**tias**" pitisha alpama kachamuka nin

shuk puma
shina rasha kachamushkara
tukuy tandarisha
chilpisha mikusha 80

C	that baby inside the womb	
	they took the whole womb out **tsiu**	
	"mama eat this soft baby with your sore tooth"	
	"you'll miss out" [saying] they gave her [the baby]	
	they say	
v/A	upon looking	85
	there had been two babies they say	
	inside the womb	
B	looking taking and running off with [the babies]	
	[grandmother said] "I'm saving this to eat later" saying	
C	running around	90
	while they were eating like crazy	
	[grandmother] turned over a pot in the back of the house	
	in there she put the babies they say	
	in the upside-down pot	
	and so she kept them	95
II/i/A	waking up in the morning [grandmother thought]	
	"could they be alive in there?"	
	those babies were moving as she looked	
B	now the little clever babies gave birth to themselves they say	
	they had much life	
	they probably shouldn't have lived	100
	but they were very strong and brave	
C	[grandmother] breastfed those two babies	
	while her sons weren't looking	
	breastfeeding	
	keeping them safe she reared them they say	105
ii/A	now in three days the little ones could walk they say	
	not taking long	
	they were growing up they say	
	like so [grandmother] took good care of them	
B	later they did things to help out they say	110
	they helped out their mama, accompanying her,	
	in many things they say	
	they brought firewood they say	
	they fetched water	
	they caught food and fed her they say	
C	they [the twins] became teachers they say	115
	[they showed the jaguars how] to catch the birds with	
	a **lisan** berry trap	
	to make a **tikta** [fence] trap	
	and also to make the **pangwa** [falling log] trap	
	they taught them many things they say	

C	chi iksa ukuy tiak wawara
	intiru wawa wangura "**tziu**" llukchisha
	"mama kan nanashka kiru kay wawara mikuy"
	"kishpingami raunguy" kunushkami nin

v/A	rikukpi	85
	ishki wawa tiyawshka nin	
	chi wawa wasi ukuy	
B	chita rikusha apasha kalpasha	
	"kayta ñuka mikungákmi wakachini" nisha	
C	raykachau	90
	payguna mikusha nuspuringama	
	luntuk ukuy shayak mangara tuwasha	
	chi ukuy wakachishkami nin	
	manga ukuy tuwasha	
	shina wakachishkarama	95
II/i/A	tutamanta jatarisha "imana kawsak sirinaun manzhu"	

	chi kuyuk wawauna akaga nisha rikukpi	
B	ña iyayyuk shituwauna pagarinawshka nin	
	ali kawsarishka	
	mana kawsana mashka	100
	kariashami	
C	chi ishkindi wawaunara chuchisha	
	churiuna mana rikushkallay	
	chuchuchisha	
	wakachisha charisha iñachishaka nin	105
ii/A	ña kimsa punzhama purik shituwauna tukunawshka nin	
	mana unayasha	
	iñakunami nin	
	shina kwuyrasha iñachisha	
B	washaga payta yanapakta rashkami nin	110
	imamas mamara katisha risha yanapanawshka nin	

	yandara aparisha kunawshka nin	
	yakura astasha kunawshka	
	mikunara apigrisha karanawshka nin	
C	paygunami rikuchikuna nin	115
	lisan muyuy mikuk pishkukunara tugllasha japina	

	may tikta rana	
	maypi pangua nisha trampauna rana	
	tukuyra rikuchinawshkami nin	

iii/A	so doing	120
	because they caught food and gave it to mama	
	their mama loved them so they say	
B	those jaguars lived in the house	
	if they wanted to eat [the twins]	
	their mama defended them they say	125
	getting angry	
C	"I will live with whomever I want" saying	
	"elders know what is best" she defended and reared them	
	they say	
III/i/A	now later	
	when they were stronger	130
	the humans [came] and spoke [to them] they say	
	"who will kill those human-eating jaguars?"	
	"how will that jaguar house disappear?"	
	"in that us . . .	
	they are eating finishing us off" saying	135
	they spoke they say	
B	and so being	
	while they [the humans] were complaining and crying	
	[the twins responded] "no"	
	"we are going to see"	140
	"wait"	
	"pray to God"	
	"we think we can do it"	
	saying	
	they spoke they say	145
	[one day the twins asked the jaguars] "is your hunting trail	
	in good shape?"	
	those younglings asked them they say	
C	mama named them they say	
	one	
	Cuillur	150
	one	
	Dociru	
	she named them they say	
D	and so being	
	Dociru was the first brother they say	155
	being that mama first named him	
	Dociru	
	Cuillur	
	was the later brother they say	

shina rasha   120
        japisha mamara karakpiga
          mamaga yapa llakikmi nin
B   chi ukuy tiak churiuna
          mikushun nikpis
        mamaga mitsakmi nin   125
          piñasha
C   "ñuka piwara kawsasha" nisha
        "ruku yachinami" mitsasha iñachikmi nin

III/i/A ña washaga
        payna ali shunguyashakay   130
        runa rimanawshkami nin
            "pita chi runa mikuk pumaunara wañchinga"
            "imasna chingaringa chi puma wasi"
              "chibimi ñukanchira . . .
                mikusha tukuchin" nisha   135
                rimanawshkami nin
B   shinakpi
          nanasha quejasha wakanaukpimi
        "mana"
        "ñukanchi rikungami raunchi"   140
          "chapaychi"
            "Diosta mañaychi"
              "ñukanchillara ushashunmi"
                nishami
                  rimanawshka nin   145
        "kanguna puriushka nambi alichu?"

          chi wawauna tapunawshkami nin
C   mama shutira churashka nin
          shuktaga
            Cuillur   150
              shuktaga
                Dociru nishkara
        shutichishka nin
D   nakpiga
        Docirumi ñawpa punda wawki tukushka nin   155
          mama ñawpa punda shutichishka asha
            Dociru
        Cuillurga
          jipa wawki tukushkami nin.

E in that 160
knowing [the story] well
God had sent those children we say
they were powerful they say
powerful ones
wherever they went 165
they never made mistakes
and they always got the job done
ii/A when they asked [the jaguars about their trail] like so
"our trail is horrible for walking" saying

those jaguar brothers spoke they say 170
like brothers [the twins] became with them
they say
later [the jaguars]didn't try to eat them
anymore they say
when they told [the jaguars that] "we want to fix your
walking trail"
"lead us
to it to see what it is like" saying 175
they [the twins] followed them they say
B going with them up to the headwaters of the Tena River
there is a famous name
[of the] jaguar rock
the rock trap 180
there is where they [the twins] made a trap and waited
[but the jaguars] detected it
[and] one [by]
one
they passed over [it] they say 185
the jaguars
C there not being able [to kill them]
[the twins] went to the Pano River and set another trap
and just like before they waited
there they also got away they say 190
D therefore following they went
now to the headwaters of the Napo River they arrived they say
"how do you cross the Napo River?" [the twins] asked them
[the jaguars]
[they responded] "almost, almost dying . . .
"there is a big whirlpool **pus** . . . 195
we cross by jumping on the tops of the rocks" they say
"it is very scary" saying
they spoke they say

E	chitami	160
	ali yachakpiga	
	Dios shina mandashka wawagunachari aka ninchi	
	ushakuna akmi nin	
	ushakuna	
	mayman rishas	165
	mana pandakguna	
	ali paktachisha purikguna	
ii/A	shina tapukpiga	
	"ñukanchi purina nambiga tormentus akta purinchi"	
	nisha	
	chi puma wawkiguna rimanawshkami nin	170
	wawki kuentami tukunawshka nin	

mana washa piñanawkachu nin mikungák
    nisha
"kanguna purina nambira alichinara munanchi" nikpi

	"pushariway	
	rikungak" nisha	175
	katisha rikunami nin	
B	Tuna yaku umara katisha risha	
	chibi kunagama shuti sirin	
	puma rumi	
	tuglla rumi nishka	180
	chibi tuglla rasha chapakpiga	
	riparasha	
	shukpi	
	shukpi	
	pasakunami nin	185
	pumauna	
C	chibi mana ushasha	
	Pano yakuy risha chibis tuglla rasha	
	shina chapakpi	
	chibis kishpinushkami nin	190
D	chimanda katisha rikuna	
	ña uma napo yakuy paktamushkami nin	
	"Napo yakuy imayra chimbanguichi" nikpiga	

"ñalla ñalla wañushami"
    "shu 'pus' pambaymi . . .   195
      rumi pundallay saltasha pasanchi" nin
        "chibimi yapa jatun manzhay sirin" nisha
          rimanawshkami nin

E	and so being	
	saying that they would help their jaguar brothers	200
	the two brothers	
	stayed right there they say	
	after they [the jaguars] crossed [the river]	
	and went hunting	
	they [the jaguars] would go far they say	205
	hunting until the afternoon	
	and again returning in the late afternoon they say	
	like that [they] suffered	

iii/A   and so being

    [the twins told the jaguars] "now just go"   210

      "when you come back we will have a nice bridge"

        saying

          they spoke they say

    "if you can then do it" [the jaguars] told them as they went they say

B   and so being one brother [of the twins] crossed the river

      they say   215

  and the other waited on this side they say

    [they took] a rope

      each one had an end

        on each side

          about two meters wide   220

            they made a tight, narrow bridge they say

              with that rope

    [with] that rope [they worked]

      lashing

        lashing   225

          lashing

          lashing

  to the other side they got it all ready

    and above

  with what looked like pot shards   230

  they put down layers of thin rock

      tying tightly the rope **day**

        tying tightly the rope **day**

          sewing [it all together]

            they bridged the river they say   235

C   so doing

    walking they tried it out they say

  it was a sturdy **lunllas** bridge they say

    and with the rope above

E	shinakpi	
	chi puma wawkiunara yanapashun nisha	200
	ishkindi wawki rikuna	
	chillay sakirinawshka nin	
	payguna chimbasha rikpi	
	aychara japingák nisha	
	karuma rikunami nin	205
	chishakta purisha	
	kuti chishira tigrakunami nin	
	shinallara tormentarisha	
iii / A	shinakpi	
	"kunaka richilla"	210
	"kanguna shamungama gusto chakara nukanchi charishun"	
	nishami	
	rimanawshka nin	
	"kanguna ushasha ranguychi" nisha sakisha rinawshkami nin	
B	nakpi shuk chimbara pasashka nin	215

shina shuk kay partimanda chapashkami nin
shuk piola waskara
    shuk shuk charikuna
      karan partira
        shuk ishki metro tupulla   220
          ñañu chakara tinglanawshkami nin
            piola waskara
chita waskara
    alingasha
      alingasha   225
        alingasha
          alingasha
chimbakta puruntusha
    chi awayga
shuk manga pakisna rikurik   230
rumi tapagunara mandasha
    day waskama watasha
      day waskama watasha
        sirasha
          chimbakta chakanawshka nin   235

C	shina rasha	
	puriusha kamanawshka nin	
	lunllas mana kuyuk chaka tukushka nin	
	chi piola waska away rakpi	

	they prepared a strong bridge and waited	240
iv/A	now in the afternoon they [the jaguars] arrived they say
	those hunters who went away into the forest [came back]
	and one of them
	had hunted a person
	he was totally dead they say	245

```
            they prepared a strong bridge and waited                   240
iv/A        now in the afternoon they [the jaguars] arrived they say
                those hunters who went away into the forest [came back]
            and one of them
                had hunted a person
            he was totally dead they say                               245
            in the middle [of this body]
                    he was chopped in half tias tias
                        carrying human meat
                            they [the jaguars] came they say
            one [of the twins] was on the other side [of the river}    250
                and one was on this side
                    they waited they say
B           and so being
            [the twins said] "look at this nice bridge we made"
                    whistling                                          255
                        singing
                            playing the harmonica
                                they ran up and down it they say
                                    across the whole bridge
            [but] they [the jaguars] didn't want to go on the bridge   260
                    thinking it might break
                        afraid they didn't want to they say
C           and so being
            [the twins said] "now try it out" saying
                    "with us two walking like this it doesn't even move" saying  265
                        speaking
                            tempting
                                they got one to try it they say
            stepping trying it out to half way
                    [the jaguar said] "hey it's good . . .              270
                        come on" saying
            those twenty jaguars
                    carrying all that meat
                        they all followed him [on the bridge] and tried it out they say
            "it is pretty good" saying                                 275
                    when they [the jaguars] got half way across the river
                        when the whole group was right there
            one brother [was]
                    on one side
                        [and] one brother [was]                        280
                            on the other side standing
```

	sinzhi chakara puruntusha payna chapawshkay	240
iv / A	ña chishira paktamunawshka nin	
	sachama aychara japingák rikuna	
	shukpi	
	runara tupayrisha	
	illakta wañuchinawshka nin	245
	chawpi	
	tias tias pitishka	
	runa aychara kuna aparishka	
	shamanawshkami nin	
	shuk chimbapurama	250
	shuk kay partima	
	chaparishkami nin	
B	shina asha	
	"kasna gusto chakara ranchi"	
	silabasha	255
	kantasha	
	rondinda tokasha	
	kalpay cachanawshkami nin	
	entero chakara	
	mana munanawka ikusha chimbangák	260
	pakaringami nisha	
	manzhasha mana munanawka nin	
C	shinakpi	
	"kunan kamay" nisha	
	"ishkindi kasna purikpi mana kuyunga" nin	265
	rimasha	
	temptasha	
	ikuchinawkami nin shukta	
	chawpigama aytasha kamasha	
	"alimi . . .	270
	shamichi" nishkawa	
	chi ishki chunga pumauna	
	aycha apashka akuna	
	tukuy ikushka kamanawka nin	
	"ali mashka" nisha	275
	payguna chawpi yakuy	
	chi muntun tukashkallawa	
	shuk wawki	
	shuk chimbaman	
	shuk wawki	280
	shuk chimbaman shayawka	

together
   "**wheeeeeeewheeeeeeee . . .**"
  they whistled they say

D   And as they whistled   285
  had the knots ready **dzas** to pull apart
    the knots that held the bridge up
where the rope was tied
  dzas! dzas!
    they undid them they say   290
they [the jaguars] fell **kushniiiiiiiiiiiiiin**
    you could see them spilling [into the water]
    they died they say

E   when they had been falling
the Cuillurguna spoke   295
  "**stone . . .**
    stone . . .
      stone . . .
        stone . . .
          stone . . .   300
            stone . . ."
on *izhu* day they say
  they will rise up again saying
    they yelled they say

v/A   doing so they [the jaguars] disappeared   305
  not coming back too soon they say

B   after that
  now human life got its space [to thrive] they say
  not too much . . .
there we totally killed them   310
  when they [the twins] spoke

C   a pregnant woman
  a jaguar woman
    doubled back
      near the bank falling and then swimming   315
      she caught hold they say

D   because she climbed out and went into the forest
  jaguars later reproduced they say
if it were not so
  all would have been lost they say   320

E   such stories
  of what the Cuillurguna did do exist
    about how in the before times they helped us humans

parijulla
　　"**wheewheeeeeeeeee**"
　　silabanawkami nin
D　Silbakunaga　　　　　　　　　　　　　　　　285
　　chi waska muku "dzas" aysanaylla
　　watashka chaka mukura
waska watariayta
　　"**dzas! dzas!**"
　　lushpichinawshka nin　　　　　　　　　290
"**kuuuushniiiiiiiiiiiin!**"
　　rikushkallay chibi talirisha
　　wañunawka nin
E　urmashka aka
　　Cuillurguna rimanawshka　　　　　　295
　　　"**rumi** . . .
　　　　rumi . . .
　　　　　rumi . . .
　　　　　　rumi . . .
　　　　　　　rumi . . .　　　　　300
　　　　　　　　rumi"
izhu punzha nin
　　payguna jatarinaungami nisha
　　kaparinawshkami nin
v/A　shina rasha chingachisha　　　　　　305
　　mana ukta shamukuna nin
B　chi washami
　　ña runa kawsana hasta lugar tuku nin
　　(mana yapa . . .)
chibi illakta wañuchinchi　　　　　　310
　　payna niushkay
C　shuk chichu warmimi
　　puma warmi
　　　katimuka
　　　　mayangllaway urmasha waytasha　　315
　　　　　apirishka nin
D　chi sachaman sikasha rishkamantami
　　puma washa mirak nin
mana akpiga
　　tukuy chingarina ashka nin　　　　　320
E　shina kwintumi
　　　Cuillurguna rashka samiguna tiyan
　　　ñawpa timpu runara payguna yanapashka

Table 1. Profile of Act I

Act	Scene	Stanza	Verse	Lines	Incident	Salient Features
I	i	A	a b c d e	1, 2, 3, 4–5, 6–8	Introduction	Time word, repetition, quotative
		B	a b c d	9, 10–11, 12, 13–15	Jaguar times	Time word, repetition, quotative
		C	a b c	16, 17–19, 20–22	Death to Life	Time word, initial word, repetition, quotative
	ii	A	a b	23–26, 27–28	Going	Initial word, repetition, quotative
		B	a b c d e	29, 30, 31–32, 33–35, 36–37	Entering	Initial word, change of focus, quotative
		C	a b c	38, 39–42, 43–45	Hiding	Initial word (+ga), quotative, sound symbolism, turn of talk
	iii	A	a b	46–47, 48–50	Danger	Initial word, quotative, topic change (ngama)
		B	a b	51, 52–55	Smelling	Pause, quotative, repetition
		C	a	56–58	Farting	Turn of talk, quotative
	iv	A	a b	59–62, 63–73	Searching	Initial word, turn of talk, quotative
		B	a b	74–77, 78–80	Killing	Change of focus, initial phrase (shina rasha), quotative
		C	a b	81, 82–84	Eating	Initial word, sound symbolism, quotative
	v	A	a b	85, 86–87	Survivors	Switch subject marker (kpi), quotative
		B	a	88–89	Saving	Initial word, repetition, quotative
		C	a b	90, 91–95	Covering	Change of focus, quotative, action phrase (raykachau)

Table 2. Profile of Act II

Act	Scene	Stanza	Verse	Lines	Incident	Salient Features
II	i	A	a b	96, 97	Morning	Time word, switch subject marker, quotative
		B	a	98–101	Birth	Time word (*ña*), parallelism (*scha* ending), change of focus
		C	a	102–105	Nurturing	Initial word, repetition, parallelism, quotative
	ii	A	a	106–109	Growing	Time word, quotative, initial word
		B	a b	110, 111–114	Helping	Time word (*washa*), quotative, parallelism (3 items)
		C	a b	115, 116–119	Teaching	Change of focus, quotative, parallelism
	iii	A	a	120–122	Hunting	Initial word, switch subject particle, quotative
		B	a b	123–124, 125–126	Motherly love	Switch subject marker, quotative, parallelism (*Ilakikmi, mitsakmi, iñachikmi*)
		C	a b	127, 128	Elder	Quotative, parallelism (see above stanzas A, B)

Table 3. Profile of Act III, scenes i–ii

Act	Scene	Stanza	Verse	Lines	Incident	Salient Features
III	i	A	a b c	129, 130, 131–136	Help	Time word, quotative, repetition
		B	a b c d	137–138, 139, 140–145, 146–147	Commitment	Initial word, switch subject marker, rhyme (*raunchi, chapaychi, mañaychi*), quotative
		C	a b	148–152, 153	Naming	Change of topic, quotative, parallelism
		D	a b c	154, 155–157, 158–159	Brothers	Initial word, repetition, parallelism
		E	a b c	160, 161–164, 165–167	Power	Initial word, switch subject marker, parallelism, repetition, rhyme (*-kuna*)
	ii	A	a b	168–172, 173–176	Helping	Switch subject marker, quotative, repetition (*-ami nin*)
		B	a b	177–180, 181–186	Tena	Quotative, switch subject marker, initial word, repetition
		C	a b c	187–188, 189, 190	Pano	Initial word, change of location, quotative
		D	a b c	191, 192, 193, 194–198	Napo	Initial word, change of location, quotative, sound symbolism, switch subject marker, rhyme (*wañushami, pamaibmi, pasanchi*)
		C	a b c d e f g	199, 200, 201, 202, 203, 204, 205–208	Jaguars hunting	Initial word, quotative, change of focus, time word, switch subject marker, parallelism (*rikuna, rikunami, tigrakunami*)

Table 4. Profile of Act III, scenes iii–v

Act	Scene	Stanza	Verse	Lines	Incident	Salient Features
iii		A	a b c	209, 210–213, 214	Bridge 1	Initial word, quotative, rhyme (-*awshkami nin*)
		B	a b c d e f g	215, 216, 217–222, 223–227, 228–229, 230, 231–235	Bridge 2	Initial word, parallelism, repetition, quotative
	iv	C	a b c	236–237, 238–239, 240	Bridge 3	Initial phrase, sound symbolism, quotative
		A	a b c d e	241–242, 243–244, 245, 246–249, 250–252	Arrival	Time phrase, quotative, change of focus, sound symbolism, rhyme (-*shka*)
		B	a b c	253, 254–259, 260–262	Temptation	Initial phrase, parallelism, aspect change, quotative
		C	a b c d e f g	263, 264–268, 269–271, 272–274, 275–277, 278–281, 282–284	Crossing over	Initial word, quotative, switch subject marker, parallelism, rhyme
	v	D	a b c	285–287, 288–290, 291–293	Dying	Change of focus, sound symbolism, quotative
		E	a b c	294, 295–301, 302–304	Judgment	Change of tense, repetition, sound symbolism, quotative
		A	a	305–306	Lost	Initial phrase, quotative, change of focus
		B	a b	307–309, 310–311	Space	Change of focus, change of tense, quotative
		C	a	312–316	Survival	Change of focus, quotative
		D	a b	317–318, 319–320	Reproduction	Initial word, change of location, quotative
		E	a	321–323	End	Initial word, change of focus

CHAPTER 6

THE CUILLURGUNA

World-Making

The Cuillurguna or "twins" narratives are the most extensive and defining stories in Napo Quichua mythology. Culture heroes, the twins effect the "miracles" and transformations that came to define this *pacha*, or "world." Here, we expand the discussion of the twins by looking at three additional narratives, the bird-of-prey tale and two tellings of the mundopuma, or "world jaguar," story. As we have seen in previous chapters, the Cuillurguna, the sons of the union of the moon and the Iluku bird, were adopted and raised by a jaguar grandmother, usually referred to as a puma *abuela* or *rukumama* (grandmother). Transformers and civilizers, the Cuillurguna are the Napo Quichua culture heroes and mythological ancestors of all living people. Like their father, the moon man, the twins are celestial beings, the Venus star, that can be seen in the early morning or evening sky.

Unlike their mother Iluku, however, who was *killa* (lazy, easy, careless), the Cuillurguna are often described as being "wise" as well as "crazy." But the root quality that defines the twins is *ushay*, a spiritual power that drives their other heroic traits: hard work, intelligence, generosity, shamanic powers, poetic and musical abilities, geographical expansiveness, joking, and mastery of trickery, secrecy, and violence. These are all qualities that can be found in people who are described as *sinzhi*, or "strong," especially young men, who, like the twins, are often a bit "loco" or "crazy" (see mundopuma stories below).

As we argue in this chapter, the recurrent pattern in the cycle of the Cuil-lurguna stories is their role as creative and artful world makers. The Cuillur-guna are not only *ushayuk*, or "powerful," but they are also the mythological founders of Runa self-determination, the ability of a people to create and control their own destiny, and to adapt to changing historical and environmental conditions (Hill 1996; N. Whitten 1996; N. Whitten and D. Whitten 2008). As we show, the Cuillurguna overthrow the oppressive regimes of the jaguars and the birds of prey. They create a new "space" (*pacha* or *lugar* in Quichua) in which Runa people can reproduce and thrive. And the Cuillur-guna always achieve the making of "space" through creativity and artfulness. This mythological message has been a part of indigenous life in this region for centuries, and it has helped the Napo Quichua people to adapt to various oppressive regimes throughout their history, a history that has been defined by adaptation to new circumstances as well as violence and struggle.

There are various stories associated with the Cuillurguna, each story being a different "espisode" or "miracle" of their heroic, and sometimes comical, transformations. Instead of trying to present all of the Cuillurguna tales, we have chosen to present a few of the most significant ones. What in one telling could be an act or even a scene could be told as an entire story at a different time. The Cuillurguna stories as a whole could never be told in one sitting, and no two storytellers will tell them the same way, although there is a holistic logic to the tales and a few rhetorical phrases that define crucial scenes in them. Usually, the Cuillurguna cycle starts with their mother Iluku being devoured by the jaguars (in the jaguar house, despite the help of the grandmother jaguar to save her; see chapter 5) and ends with the two broth-ers ascending into the sky. In between, there are many different adventures (see Orr and Hudelson 1971; Foletti-Castegnaro 1993; Goldáraz 2005). The Cuillurguna stories are told in parts, in chunks, over a long stretch of time, and within a social context of family intimacy and elders teaching younger people about the world in general. Each telling, depending on the listeners, context, and setting, varies.

The Cuillurguna and the Birds of Prey

This story was told by Verna Grefa to Michael in the same session (1994) as "The Twins and the Jaguars" narrative of chapter 5. Like the previous nar-rative, this story relates to the twins creating "space" for humans to live, but the spatial geography of this story is vast; the path taken by the Cuillurguna begins somewhere in a garden near Archidona and takes them to a faraway place to the lair of the birds of prey.[1] After they kill the birds of prey the Cuillurguna are lost and have no way of getting home. So, in Act II, they hitch a ride with the vulture man, who has visited the coast, Quito, as well as the Marañon River, a large river in Peru that was part of the Huallaga route to gather salt (see chapter 4).

The vulture man allows the Cuillurguna to ride on his shoulders while he flies back to Archidona (pronounced *Alchiruna* in Quichua). The vulture's pathway, as vulture man says in the story, extends from the coast to Quito, through Archidona, and into the Marañón/Huallaga area of northern Peru.[2] The Cuillurguna, in gratitude to the vulture man for giving them a ride, transform him into a carrion-eating bird, a transformation that suits his extreme desire for food. Like Iluku, the vulture man possesses a moral quirk, that of being *illu* (gluttonous/without control of one's desires), which is at the root of his transformation from being a fully human being into a different species. Like *killa*, *illu* is a negative, undesirable quality in humans.

In Act I, the Cuillurguna are able to kill the man-eating birds of prey by constructing a large rubber ball in which they enter and hide. The rubber shell proves to be impenetrable to the claws and sharp beaks of the attackers, and while the birds of prey are sleeping, the twins sneak out and kill them with clubs called *makana*, ancient fighting weapons made from the *chonta* palm. As in the previous story with the jaguars, the transformative moment is not physical, but it is the spoken phrase "stone, stone, stone, stone, stone" that converts the birds of prey into rock. And as in the jaguar story, Verna comments that on judgment day that the birds of prey will rise up again.

Like his other stories, Verna here uses parallelism, repetition, quotations, and some key ideophones to create a story of considerable poetic quality and beauty. The image of the birds of prey, for example, sleeping inside a *matapalo* tree upside down and with their eyes glowing, is a portrait unforgettable to those familiar with the sublime beauty of the forest at night. Also, the scenes of the Cuillurguna killing the birds of prey reflect the poetics of sound that define death and killing. To the hunter, these sounds, the poetics of death and the spilling of blood with one's own hands, are fundamental aspects of experience.

BIRDS OF PREY BY VERNA GREFA

I/i/A	after they had made a space
	there was a Runa eating bird of prey they say
	in the beginning times
B	despite killing the pumas
	those eating [birds of prey] really
	made things bad they say

5

	right from your own gardens	
	screaming they would carry you away they say	
	the bird of prey	
	coming	10
C	taking alive and going	
	putting you wherever on the Tena River	
	on top of a big rock tearing you apart eating you they say	
ii / A	like that eating	
	they were finishing off [all the people]	15
B	The people begged saying "can't you	
	get rid of them" saying	
	"not just kill them"	
	"we have killed the stronger pumas" they spoke [the Cuillurguna]	
	they say	
C	when they were begging like that	20
	in the garden	
	where they were working	
	they laid down there	
	on top of a bag made out of rubber	
D	when they lay down	25
	dzas (quickly)	
	it was easy to close the bag	
	entering in there	
	both brothers stood up they say	
E	the weapon named *makana*	30
	it was a club made out of the *chonta* palm	
	they took with them	
	they say each brother had one	
	had one	
	all together there inside the bag	35
	entering they stood in there they say	
iii / A	now when they heard the bird of prey was coming	
	dzas (quickly) closing [the rubber bag] up	
	they stood there they say	
B	when they [the birds of prey] saw the **movement, movement**	
	[of the brothers in the bag]	40
	one swooped down and **hiiiiiiiiit** them	
	he flew off **carrrrrrrrrrrrrrrying** the bag behind him they say	
	the bird of prey	
C	carrying it off	
	to the headwaters of the river	45
	[the bird of prey] put [the bag] on top of a rock	
	when (s)he tried to eat it	

it was a very **tooooooough** bag for sure they say
    (s)he couldn't pierce it
when (s)he tried biting it even harder   50
it still wouldn't rip they say

II/i/A and after some time like that clawing (s)he couldn't [rip it]
so (s)he gave up
and ate the old meat from before
while eating   55
the Cuillur brothers were still alive in that bag
(s)he threw it aside
and went inside to hang and sleep they say
inside a huge *matapalo* tree

B two together they [the birds of prey] travel they say   60
    a man and woman
    those birds of prey

C hanging like bats with their heads down
their eyes shining bright **chiuuuu** they sleep they say

ii/A and so while they were sleeping   65
realizing and seeing
from inside that bag
they opened it and came out they say
Cuillur Duciru
    each person   70
    carrying that *makana* weapon with him

B and with that *makana* weapon
while they were getting out they talked they say

C "you, what are you going to do" when one asked
[the other answered] "I am going to cut his head off **tias**" saying   75
he said they say
    "when I swing"

D the other one said they say
"I will break his chest open
    with one blow!"   80

E and like so talking they got ready they say
[to kill] the sleeping, hanging birds of prey

iii/A together talking they stood there
jiuuuuuuuu they whistled
tuuuuk   85
    tuuuk hmm
      they struck blows they say at the same time

B and so being
just like they said they would
one cut off their heads **tias** they say   90

C   the other broke their chests **caaallii** in half
and at that moment
plurplurplurplurplur
    plurplur
       flopping around   95

D   while they were dying
"stone
    stone
       stone
          stone   100
            stone
              stone" [the Cuillurguna said]
"here on *izhu punzha* [judgment day] they will rise up"
saying

E   and while they were speaking and shouting   105
they turned into stones
those birds of prey
    and on that day we became free of the birds of prey

III/i/A oh wait!
after they killed the birds of prey   110
thinking, "where should we go now?"
    "after the bird of prey has taken us so far away"

B   and so being abandoned there
without being able to get home
to the edge of the river   115
those young boys came they say
    they were sad

C   when they came
down the beach they encountered they say
the vulture man   120
God had made vultures into people in that time they say
they had not yet converted into birds

D   he [vulture man] was going upriver they say
encountering
"where are you going?"   125
he asked the two brothers
"we were carried off by the *supay* [spirit] birds of prey
we were inside a bag and the bird of prey brought us here
although (s)he brought us, (s)he couldn't eat us
they then left us alone   130
and we put them to sleep
tranquilizing and making them sleep
then we killed them off and being free we now are trying to
    figure out where to go"

E   they asked "man, where are you coming from?"
        "from our city   135
        coming I am arriving here" [said the vulture]
F   "where is our town of Archidona?" they [Cuillurguna] asked
        [the vulture responded] "it's just over here, not far
        I for sure am familiar with all of the Marañon River [in Peru]
        with the coast   140
        and all of Quito I know these places"
        that is what he said they say that man
            the vulture man
ii/A   and so saying
        "can you take us home man" when [the Cuilluguna] asked   145
        [vulture responded] "wait
        I was going to eat
        I was hungry and was going to eat my meat" he went they say
B   right there they were waiting for a long time
        then washing out his mouth   150
        gargling and washing out his mouth he came they say
            the vulture man
            had eaten
C   and so coming
        "now let's go" [the vulture man said]   155
        "now each of you sit down on one shoulder" saying
        sit down **tsan** [not moving] he instructed them they say
            on his shoulder
D   and so being
        they got on and held fast to his shoulders   160
        when they did that
        [vulture man said] "don't open your eyes
        if you open your eyes I will leave halfway to nowhere"
        saying he told them
        that vulture man   165
E   and so saying
        they shut their eyes tight and held on they say
        now turning into a bird he rose up they say
        blum
            blum   170
               blum
                   blum
                       blum
                       up and away
        taking those young boys with him   175
        he came they say
        hogarrrrr flying

into the wind
huit ohhhhhlla
flying and flying   180
tszan he finally landed they say

iii / A   "ok we are now in Archidona city
now open your eyes" he spoke they say
when they looked
now they were standing at the edge of what looked like a city they say
185

from there coming
to this place after killing the birds of prey they say
there being led [by the vulture man]

B   to that vulture man [the Cuillurguna said]
"now   190
now you don't have to go far suffering to look for food
only God's given meat
eating
all the time being a vulture you will travel high in the air
your whole life   195
like that God's given rotten food you have to eat" saying
and in saying that
right there the man turned into a vulture and took off into
the sky they say
never to return again
that is the story of the bird of prey   200

The Mundopuma Story Told by Lucas Tapuy with Carmela Calapucha

We now present another episode in the "twins" series, the trapping of the mundopuma in the mountain of Galera. *Mundopuma*, which means "world jaguar," refers to the notion of the cacique or dominant jaguar. In Lucas's notion of time and space, the "twins" stories followed the great flood. Lucas also affirmed that his "father" and "father's fathers," the metaphorical extension of his soul substance, "knew" the twins personally.

The version presented here was told to us sometime in 1996 in the house of Lucas and Carmela. The mood was informal, and what we present is only a small part of a considerably longer conversation that involved also the flood story (see chapter 2) and other episodes and experiences related to the twins. Toward the end of the telling Lucas begins drinking manioc beer, and so Carmela has to finish up some of the crucial details of the story. Their style of overlapping during storytelling was always a feature of our conversations with them, and as the night went on the storytelling became a general conversation about places, people, mythology, experience, and personal histories.

We like this version because Lucas's telling involves episodes that are sometimes left out of the "twins" stories, and the mundopuma story is linked back to the origins of their mother being devoured by the sons of the grandmother jaguar (see chapter 5). Stanza E of scene i, when the jaguar sons come home and smell the mother of the twins hiding, features turns of talk and even phrases that are almost identical to those used in Verna's more elaborate telling of these same events (see chapter 5). The sons, for example, in smelling the woman, say *mikilla asnan*, or "it smells good," a phrase not often heard in everyday speech.

Lucas's telling, however, provides more details about the period of time when the twins lived in the jaguar house under the protection of the grandmother. Here, in Act I, there are three key scenes (ii, iii, and iv) of the twins planting a corn garden (which, in the Napo Quichua world, is often a masculine activity while planting manioc is always feminine), fetching firewood, and bringing drinking and cooking water to the house. All of these scenes show the productivity and wisdom of the twins to produce the essential ingredients of a hearth—agricultural products, firewood, and water. However, in each of these scenes the twins' overproductivity and trickery result in practical jokes played upon their grandmother. First, they cause her to get lost in the enormous corn garden that they plant. Next, they build a huge pile of firewood that falls on top of the grandmother. And lastly, they fetch so much water that they create a small "lake" that floods and knocks grandmother down when she opens the tap. After each trick, however, the twins help the grandmother up and have a good laugh.

The playful and controlled "craziness" of the twins is a marked feature of their personality and character. The experiences of whacking out a corn garden and getting firewood or water are normally tedious and physically draining exercises. That the twins' approach them with vigor and humor is the spirit in which such work becomes socially and emotionally "fun" rather than unpleasant. In *mingas* (collective work parties), for example, people engage in moments of "controlled craziness" to provide relief from potential tediousness. Setting harmless "traps," getting people wet or lost, or causing them to trip are all fun ways of enjoying the sociality and aesthetics of working.

The twins, as in chapter 5, come to a moment of "getting their heads and hearts" when they realize they must kill the jaguars. The bridge trap over Napo River was the means toward eliminating the jaguar sons, but the mundopuma is the jaguar father, the granddaddy of predatory beings. In order to get rid of the mundopuma the twins devise an ingenious plan of trapping him within the mountain of Galera. In Act II, they dig a huge cave, and inside the cave they make a "store" with chairs and a musical machine—distractions that are designed to lure the mundopuma into the hole. The mundopuma does not trust the twins and scolds them for being *uyari wawaguna* (heard-about or legendary children). The word is the reflexive form of *uyana*, "to hear," and in this context it refers to the general idea of something or someone being heard about, as in "one hears about those children" but the word, which is not common speech, implies someone with shamanic power. *Uyari wawaguna* is also used in Anibal's telling of Act II of the same story to describe the twins (see below). Not coincidentally, a similar future-tense form, *uyaringa runa* (will hear about or will be legendary person), was used in Chuyaki's shamanic song to describe his shamanic self (see chapter 1).

The twins use shamanism and music to lure the mundopuma into the cave. Once he is inside, they shut the door. The mundopuma is so strong he almost turns over the entire mountain and growls very loudly. Again, another rhetorical phrase is used by the twins to seal off the stone entrance: *pikista, pikitsa, pikitsa*. This phrase makes no sense in normal Quichua speech, but in the mythological genre, it conveys the idea of turning something into stone. "*Pikitsa*," as Anibal explained to us, resonates with *peñas*, or "boulders" in Spanish. And like the other episodes we have presented (see chapter 5 and the "Birds of Prey" story above), the twins turn a master predator into stone. The predators, in death or entrapment, become the landscape. But they are not gone forever; as in all the stories, the predators will rise up again on *izhu punzha*, or judgment day (chapter 2), a circular series of relations. *Izhu*, a past-future happening, is both the beginning and end of the storytelling cycle.

While Lucas, or Chuyaki as he was known, was drinking his manioc beer, he left out this rhetorical phrase so crucial to the end of the story. Without the invocation of *pikitsa, pikitsa, pikitsa* the story is incomplete, not as it should be. This is why Carmela broke in and finished this entire scene for Lucas. She knew it was crucial to the genre. Lucas, after drinking his manioc beer, then ends the story by affirming the validity (*ñay* or *shiñay*) of Carmela's spoken words. This telling, which can be listened to on the website, shows more than the other examples the dialogic nature of many storytelling sessions, sessions that do not necessarily have just one storyteller or interlocutor.

The dialogic nature of such sessions allows for more details and follow-up questions and related stories to be told. After this telling, Michael, a novice of Napo Quichua mythology at the time, asked, "Where was this famous mountain of Galera?" Lucas and Carmela said that it was "right out in the open, from the road you can see it," although the mountain, located some distance to the north, is quite far and not normally visible from Lucas and Carmela's home. They then described how some years ago when the "company" was working near the mountain, on one side the *mundopuma* would growl and howl at night. They also could see him taunting them and sticking out his tongue. Here is the story in verse form.

THE MUNDOPUMA STORY TOLD BY LUCAS TAPUY (CHUYAKI) WITH CARMELA CALAPUCHA

I/i/A	and so being	
	with that being over [the great flood or *izhu punzha*]	
	later now later the forests came back	
	these forests	
B	and so being now these forests coming back and getting bigger	5
	the jaguars reproduced more	
	the jaguars were a menace they say	
	a thatched leaf house like this one [points to his house]	
	with just one hand	
	chin [sound of the jaguars clawing through the walls]	10
	a person	
	chin	
	getting on top they killed them they say	
	and then ate them [the people] those jaguars	
	from house to house	15
C	and so being in the forest	
	there was a grandmother	
	an *abuela* [refers to the jaguar grandmother]	
	I think she was like a person	
	she must have been a person	20
D	and so being	
	being a person she spoke	
	she spoke didn't she?	
	the ladder in this house	
	going up to a platform	25
	there was a ladder they say	
	a ladder standing there to upstairs	
	that child	
	two children [the Cuillurguna] were hidden by that grandmother	
	hiding them upstairs underneath a pot she covered them	30
	those Cuillurguna	
E	one was called Cuillur	
	the other Dociru	
	and while they were hidden	

the jaguar(s) came   35
"grandmother
    something smells good [*mikilla asnan*]!
smells good [*mikilla asnan*]!"
"ay
ay   40
    what food could there be?
    is there nothing in the forest?
        or is there something there?" she got angry they say
F   they [the jaguars] could not climb up [the ladder] they say
            if they would have climbed up   45
                and eaten them [the Cuillurguna]
                    who would have gotten rid of those terrible jaguars?
                        nobody would have gotten rid of them!
ii/A   now they grew up they say
            and became real people   50
        becoming men
            and when they became men
        that jaguar grandmother gave them chores
            "plant some corn" saying
                make a corn garden right now   55
                    what will we eat?
                        make a lot of corn"
B   and when she sent them
        they did what she said they say
        making **luyu** [many fields, patches of garden] cornfields   60
            everywhere
        and when they planted [the corn]
        it was ripe in no time!
C   and now it was ready [the corn]
        "mama" saying
            "you asked us to make a garden and plant corn now   65
                go look
                    go harvest it
                        the corn is now ready"
                            those children followed her [to the garden]
                                she called them "children" of course   70
D   like that following her
            following
        and as they were arriving [to the garden]
        wow!
            a hell of a lot of corn!   75

just corn everywhere the eye could see!
she got lost in the fields and cried they say
    that grandmother [crying out]
      "ooooohhhhooohhooo
      ooooohhhhooohhooo"   80

E   those children who planted the corn
    were laughing their asses off!
      when their mom got lost and cried out
F   they ran to her they did
    they ran to their grandmother right away   85
[grandmother said] "crooked children" saying
    [the jaguar grandmother]
      "why did you plant so much?
      and make me scream like this?
        and make me cry?" she got angry they say

iii/A and so being   90
    doing that
      trying that
        being told that
she sent them to get firewood
    that grandmother   95
      "make firewood" saying
      "what will we light a fire with?" she said
B   so they made firewood
making the firewood [the children said]
      "mama now go get the firewood"   100
      "it is all ready" when they said that
C   "go get the firewood" [telling her]
and when she [grandmother] pulled out just one piece of it
    a huge pile fell on top of grandmother they say
      the whole pile   105
D   and so doing
    she again screamed
      and like before
        they [Cuillurguna] helped her up
        their grandmother   110
iv/A and so doing and experiencing
again later
she asked them to get water
when she asked them to get water
    grandmother went to get it they say   115
      no those children got it and made a lake those crazy kids

B   making a lake for their grandmother
             "go get your water mama" [those kids said]
             it was ready to open [like a faucet]
                  "go get me some water" [when she told them]   120
             and when grandmother opened the faucet
             it came out like crazy!
             and it [the water] took the poor lady for a ride
               the water
C   and so doing   125
             so doing
                  "what kind of crooked children are you? " saying she said
                they say
II/i/A and so doing
             experiencing all those things
             there they got their heads together   130
               and grew up
B   they started to dig out Galera Mountain
             Galera Mountain
             finishing that and doing everything
               painting it and making it beautiful   135
                  then putting in a store and chairs
                     painting it real nice they finished it they say
ii/A   and then later
             the jaguar father
             arrives there they say   140
             when he arrived
              "hey man" saying [the Cuillurguna] "enjoy it!"
               "it's real nice for your enjoyment" saying
B   today's kids are crazy and they do crazy stuff [like
               the Cuillurguna]
             and when they said that [to the jaguar]   145
             [the jaguar said] "ay you are *uyari* children [famous]
              uyari children you are" [famous]
                 he did not want to enter in there they say
                     "no" saying
C   "this is for you this house   150
                  for you all to enjoy it" [said the Cuillurguna]
             "now listen"
             the harp was playing and he [the jaguar] loved it they say
               they had set it up in there
             "you sneaky children" [said the jaguar]   155
CARMELA—they were first dancing and jumping around they say!

D   not yet that jaguar man
        no, that jaguar man was inside just listening to that music
           so that he could hear [the music]
              so that he could hear   160
                 [the Cuillurguna said]
                   "now you play" it was there ready to play
                      [the harp]
                   that machine was playing itself they say
MICHAEL—Uh huh
iii/A   and like that!   165
        the jaguar father didn't want to get close
           refusing
CARMELA—they were jumping
        "let's go have some fun" [said the Cuillurguna]
        they took him up to a platform [inside the mountain]   170
           in the corner supported by columns [gestures to a
              similar structure]
           and got him to sit down
CARMELA—they had him sit down they say but were dancing!
B   yes of course
        they sat down   175
        but there was glue
        when he sat down like this [gestures sitting down]
        they made it sticky they say
           right on the chair
MICHAEL—is that so?   180
              when his bottom touched the chair **tas** he couldn't
              get up
C   and so when that happened
        those dancing brothers spoke
        "you take that door"
           tas paw   185
              the door **tak**
                 tas [gestures closing doors]
D   now and so doing and dancing
        they made the father [jaguar] sit down
        when he sat down   190
           the glue was ready
               and so doing they did
        I will now finish this [bowl of manioc beer]
        [The tape stops and starts again while a new cassette is put in]
CARMELA (tells the whole scene here)   195

iv/A   from each door dancing
        they ran dancing and went there
        they jumped outside
        the door **tas** they shut it
            one brother on one side   200
                the other brother on the other
                    they jumped out!
                    "**pikitsa**
                        pikitsa   205
                            pikitsa" [boulder]
                      saying
        they stomped [the door down] they say
B   he almost knocked down the mountain that mean jaguar father!
LUCAS—he almost toppled it over, yes   210
[The conversation continues about the Galera Mountain]

The Mundopuma Story Told by Anibal Andy (El Ductur) during an Open-Mike Storytelling Contest

This second version of the mundopuma story was told by Anibal Andy, known by nickname as El Ductur, during the fiesta of Sapo Rumi during 2008. Anibal told this story during the cultural presentations of the fiesta, during an open-mike competition that included various genres of Quichua jokes, songs, and storytelling. Anibal's mundopuma story won first prize that night in the field of storytelling.

Anibal's strategy was to use his musical voice to emphasize the musical aesthetics and dialogue of the Cuilluguna trapping the jaguar in the mountain. Anibal, who is also a musician of traditional Napo Quichua genres, is an excellent singer with a powerful voice. His strategy was to emphasize impact over coverage that night, to tell one memorable story rather than a long and complex one.

Act I, which is about the twins growing up and building the music machine in the mountain, is abbreviated, because this act is designed to set up Act II, which is the real focus. In Act II, Anibal uses his voice to mimic the magical sound of the music machine, which he describes as a kind of organ that mesmerizes the mundopuma. Also, Anibal's voice brings to life the emotional poetics of temptation and anger. These musical aspects of the story are represented in bold (which represents an ideophone) and all caps (which represents a loud, emotional way of speaking). However, in order for the reader to appreciate these vocal dynamics, we recommend listening to the recording of the story available online.

Like Lucas and Carmella, Anibal ends his story by reference to experience. And like others who tell the story, Anibal talks about how he has personally heard the howling of the mundopuma coming out of Galera Mountain. Anibal raises the possibility that perhaps the mundopuma has escaped, an interesting and frightening proposition, one that is also brought up in Carlos Alvarado's song Galera Urku (see chapter 8). Also note that Anibal, in this telling, refers to the mundopuma as being an *apamama,* or woman jaguar.

MUNDOPUMA STORY BY ANIBAL ANDY

```
I/i/A   in the beginning times
        many worlds ago
        these jaguars terrorized the world
        from house
        to house                                                    5
            to house
            a child
                or an older person
                they would eat them
                    devour them                                    10
                            living by terminating [us, the people]
B       in those times
        there were two
        young sons that were not yet alive
C       they are                                                   15
            Dociru
                [and] Cuillur
        very smart
            incredibly beautiful
                exceptionally wise children                        20
                    they were people who could do almost anything
                        [and then ] the children grew up
ii/A    so these [sons/people] called Dociru and Cuillur
        one day they thought
            they tried out [different ideas]                       25
B       "why, why can't we get rid of these jaguars?" saying
            "how can we finish them off" saying
                "like this they make life a living hell for our
                    people" saying
C       so they together
            the two of them                                        30
                sat down and talked it out
                    they thought it through
```

iii/A   now nicely even today we still hear
      about the mountain called Galera
B   there these two sons   35
      were working and working for a long time
      the elders used to wonder how they were able to work it out
      I think that they took a long long time
C   at that mountain
      they made a hole   40
        a beautiful big one
          very deep and big
            and long
               in Spanish we would call them caverns right?
D   and like that making a hole   45
      that beautiful hole
  right in the middle
  so after finishing
      an instrument [they installed]
        we might say it was like an organ   50
F   it was a marvelous instrument and how did they find it?
      probably because they were such clever children
        they were beautiful you know
II/i/A   that music machine they set it up
      and told the jaguars   55
      that one jaguar
        the mother, the one called the mother jaguar
B   "look" saying
  "here, if you come into our cave"
      "come and see"   60
        "we found this marvelous instrument" saying
  "you with those long claws will play it so beautifully" saying
      "we don't have long claws like you but it still sounds
        pretty good" saying
ii/A   one [brother] tried it
      the firstborn . . . later son   65
B   entering
      he played like this
  it sounded so **beautiful**
      beautiful
        tiiiiiiin   70
          tiiiiiin
            tiiiiiin
            tiiiiiin

C   and so being
       the brother exited the cave from the other side   75
       the other brother entered
          "now you play" [said his brother]
D   and just the same the music came out beautiful they say
       like this
          tiiiiiiin   80
            tiiiiiin
              tiiiiiiin
iii/A   and so playing like that
       the jaguar
          the big jaguar was listening from afar   85
            being outside
B   the big jaguar stood up
       "they sure are playing great
          it sure sounds nice to me " saying
            saying   90
C   "look this is how we make it play" saying
       but the big jaguar did not fall for it they say
       "no you are *uyarik* [famous] children
          you are wise children
            you are tricking me" saying   95
D   "no way" saying [the Cuillurguna]
       "it just sounds real nice
          we don't even have claws like you
            and without claws like you we make it sound
              pretty good" saying
       "YOU have great BIG claws   100
          SIT DOWN on that nice chair and you'll see everything
            is inside" saying
              "it is so NICE" while they [the Cuillurguna] were talking
iv/A   from afar
       "yes it is true" [said the jaguar]
       in order to tempt her [the jaguar], they had really tempted her   105
          "ok ok ok"
       they [the Cuillurguna] went in again
          and played again
B   "now you try"
       "we did it, now you   110
       we will listen from outside" saying
       "ok" [said the jaguar]

C   and although not really waaaaaaaannntttting tooooooo
      being tempted
        that jaguar mother entered   115
          that great big jaguar
            that jaguar strong woman

D   and so doing
    upon entering
      they [said] "now that sounds soooo good"   120
    "now I am going to play" [more]
    [said] that jaguar strong woman
      playing
    "that soooouuuuunds sooooo goooood" [the Cuillurguna said]
    together the two of them   125

E   and at one door there was Cuillur
      at the other door was Dociru
    they stood there
    they kept saying
      "that plaaaaying is sooo good"   130
    the two of them SAID
      pikitsa [stones]
        pikitsa [stones]
          pikitsa [stones]
            pikitsa [stones]   135
    and they stomped down on that hole
      taasss taaasss [sound of two doors closing]

F   and when they shut the door
    that BIG old jaguar
    roared out   140
    hmmmmmm
      hmmmmmmm
    growling
    she almost knocked over they say
      the whole mountain   145

v/A   and so doing
      doing
    they left just one little hole
      for the jaguar to [reach out and] eat mushrooms
        her food would be mushrooms   150

B   and even today that mountain
    makes lots of noise that one
    Galera [mountain]
      the Galera jaguar growls

	sometimes	155
	only sometimes [can you hear it]	
C	on that side of the mountain	
	trrrrrrrrrrrrrrrrraaaaaaaaaaa	
	that is how Galera's jaguar cries out	
D	it is true	160
	I have heard, heard it myself	
	sometimes it sounds out like that	
	[when that happens] the elders say that the Galera jaguar	
	is roaring they say	
	inside of Galera Mountain	
E	and in that	165
	and for that reason	
	that	
	like so because the Cuillurguna trapped [the jaguar]	
	the termination of Runa people	
	the eating of children	170
	the eating of dogs	
	has been absent	
	and so being	
	you don't see so many [jaguar attacks] anymore	
F	and so being	175
	at that Galera Mountain base	
	some say the jaguar isn't there anymore	
	if he gets out again	
	she sure has been there for a long time	
	even just the other day I was wondering	180
	that perhaps he is out there terrorizing like they say	
G	like this	
	and so this is the story	
	of this Galera	
	of the mountain	185
	thank you very much	

Conclusion

In this chapter we have looked at three stories: the birds of prey, and two versions of the mundopuma story. As we have discussed, the Cuillurguna transformed the world into relations favorable to human life. These relations are perceived and felt in daily experiences in the forest, rivers, and gardens, places where people continually use knowledge, cleverness, controlled "craziness," and artistry to create the necessary things for life. As culture heroes, the twins define these basic qualities of Amazonian strength, but the root source of these competencies is spiritual. Possessors of *ushay*, that inner spiritual power that allows one to transform and mediate relations in the world, the twins are social actors on multiple planes of existence.

The first story, about the birds of prey, is about the twins killing the birds of prey by hiding inside a giant rubber ball, which cannot be pierced by the claws or beak of the predator. The bird of prey takes the twins to its lair, but it cannot get into the ball so it throws the ball aside. When the birds of prey are asleep, the twins exit the ball and beat the birds to death with clubs. They then meet up with the vulture man, who takes them back to Archidona, and, in fitting with his nature as someone with an insatiable hunger or *illu* (gluttonous), the twins transform him from a person into his vulture state.

The next two stories are about the mundopuma, and both tell of the twins digging a cavern in the mountain of Galera and making a beautiful music room. They lure the mundopuma or jaguar father into the space and then close the door. In Lucas's version they put glue on a chair, and he sits down on it and gets stuck. In Anibal's version, the twins use dialogue and music to lure the jaguar into the cavern. In both versions, magical words and music help dupe the jaguar and lure him into the trap. The mundopuma, trapped in the mountain, howls furiously. To this day one can hear him on the side of the mountain where he is trapped.

The Cuillurguna have taught humanity many crucial lessons. They have taught us to be hardworking, to be clever, to use magic, to be musical, and to set traps for our enemies and prey, who one day will set traps for us. They taught us that no world order lasts forever and that one day we will all die and move on to another state of existence. They have also taught us the value of kinship, love, laughing, and shared experience. And like the storytellers featured here, the twins were poets. Their words, which they used decisively, had power and beauty. These stories, which are part of Quichua poetic perception and experience, express the mystery of the relationality among all things—human, nonhuman, plant, animal, and geographical—in the Amazonian world.

CHAPTER 7

THE PETROGLYPHS AND THE TWINS' ASCENT

In this chapter we share with the reader two stories about the twins, a story about the petroglyphs they left here on the earth and their conversion into stars. Both of these stories reveal the inscribed textuality of transformations embodied in the "twins" stories. Our examples show how Quichua speakers "read" their stories from experience within a living landscape that is rich with the presence of mythological beings and transformations.

This chapter, as well, is an axis mundi of the book. The presentation of the final episode of the twins cycle, their ascent into the sky, also forces us to confront the question "What is to be done once all the myths have been told?" For myths force one to ask, "Who am I?" and "What is my relation to the world?" This stirring of the soul is the hidden power of the story, as its textuality is in one's relation to the world, within what the philosopher William James (1967:135) has described as "the crudity of experience." Cuillur taught us this lesson, one morning, as we walked out to the river near our home in Ecuador. But first let us share with the reader the stories of the petroglyphs and the ascent.

The Petroglyphs

One day in 1996 we were visited by Verna Grefa at Sapo Rumi, and he asked if we wanted to tape any stories. We asked him if there was a story about the petroglyph Sapo Rumi, or "Frog Rock," from which our community gets its name. Verna responded, "Yes, there is," and then proceeded to tell us this story. At the time we didn't know that the Cuillurguna had "painted" these ancient designs into this very large stone, as well as other well-known petroglyphs in the Tena-Napo region.

Verna's telling that day was an example of the intertextuality of storytelling, for Verna focused on the petroglyph sites, and especially Sapo Rumi, left by the Cuillurguna. His story, however, refers to the events of "The Twins and the Jaguars" story presented in chapter 5, where the twins are raised by jaguars and finally kill the jaguars with a bridge trap over the Napo River. The petroglyphs, which are the focus of this telling, are places where the twins made traps for the jaguars, but the jaguars, being clever, sensed the danger and took a different path.

In the community of Sapo Rumi the petroglyph, which features carvings of seven distinct frogs, is considered to be a living being, an ancient source of power and life that "watches" over the community. Federico, the president of the community, agrees that the rock was originally painted by the Cuillurguna, but Federico tells other stories about this rock that emphasize the connectedness of his family to the life force of the rock. For reasons of space, we do not include the full stories here, but several generations back a spirit woman from this petroglyph kidnapped and married a boy who was one of Federico's father's uncles or great-uncles. Underneath this petroglyph is a portal to the spirit world that leads to an immense city. It is there that Federico's ancestor resides, still living with his spirit wife and their many children.

In Quichua, for example, it is not unusual to make statements of kinship to features of the landscape. For example, one can say that *"Chi rumimanda samayuk ani,"* or "From that stone, my soul substance derives." Stones that are alive also make people dream and send them fish to eat. They have communicative power and are part of the social community of living beings that inhabit the local landscape. Through the story, Federico and his *ayllu* (family) feel kinship with the landscape that defines them. Their relative, who lives underneath the rock, is watching over them and is now part of the land that they inhabit.

We can also read from Verna's story that day a subtle critique of the younger generation of Napo Quichua people, who, unlike the generation of his father, uncles, and aunts, are educated in schools, are Spanish-Quichua bilingual, and participate in the Ecuadorian world of literacy, bureaucracy, and "development." Verna, at the end of the story, refers to the power the elders had in telling stories and the beauty within their vision of the world. Like the Yekuana's critique of Venezuelan literacy (see the introduction), Verna here implies that the youth have forgotten their own forms of textuality embodied within the petroglyphs. He says that "people today only hear the name" without actually knowing the story, and true "power," behind the name. It is interesting that this loss of traditional Quichua textual knowledge is accompanied by general loss of fluency in Quichua and language shift to Spanish, despite over 15 years of intercultural, bilingual education in many Quichua communities (see Uzendoski 2009). And Verna is not alone in his critique. Almost all of the elder storytellers featured in this book have expressed similar ambivalence about the value of contemporary education and its emphasis on alphabetic literacy, which, for them, has deceived younger people by cutting them off from the wisdom and beauty of the storytelling world.

Here is the story. It is not long, but it ties together three of the defining petroglyphs of the Tena-Pano region that are implied in "The Twins and the Jaguars" story. For a more complete understanding of the story, readers should first consult the story as presented in chapter 5.

THE PETROGLYPHS BY VERNA GREFA

i/A	and so being	
	now let's tell a story	
	about how people lived in the beginning times	
	I first want to tell about	
	the rock named Puma Rumi [the jaguar rock]	5
	about its life (*kawsay*)	
B	in the beginning times	
	they [the jaguars] were just like people	
	although they were people	
	they would grab people and eat them	10
	with long claws	
	those jaguar people lived they say	
	the jaguar people	
C	they	
	would go far	15
	they went hunting to eat runa people	
	they [the Cuillurguna] had an adoptive [jaguar] mother	
	those two sons the Cuillurguna grew up with them [the jaguars]	
	Dociru and Cuillur	
ii/A	those young men wanted	20
	to get rid of those terrorizing jaguars	
	to make them disappear	
	and so being however	
	they didn't have a good chance	
B	and so being	25
	at the headwaters of the Tena River	
	it is still there today	

	the rock named pumi rumi	
	right there	
	they [the Cuillurguna] made a trap and waited they say	30
	from the forest	
	so that the jaguars would get caught	
	and they could kill them	
iii / A	and so being however	
	they [the jaguars] didn't take the same trail [where the trap was]	35
	on top of each rock	
	jumping	
	jumping	
	they crossed [the river] they say	
B	on top of that rock [Puma Rumi] there was a trap they say	
	[left by the Cuillurguna]	40
	they didn't get caught they say	
	being too clever	
iv / A	and from there later	
	straight ahead	
	they passed they say	45
	to Pano	
	going to Pano	
	just below the Puma Yacu River	
	today we still call that place Puma Rumi (the jaguar rock)	
	and there	50
	they waited they say	
	doing the same [putting in a trap]	
B	waiting [the Cuillurguna]	
	on the trail just behind	
	they [the jaguars] didn't	55
	step there again they say	
	being afraid	
	they took a different trail they say	
	through the forest	
	they passed over the ridge of the mountains they say	60
	hiding	
v / A	and so when that happened	
	from there later	
	they went to Achi Yacu River they say	
	right where it meets with the Yana Yaku River	65
B	and there just the same	
	waiting	
	until the afternoon	
	until the afternoon	

	they stayed they say	70
C	when the jaguars didn't show	
	they [the Cuillurguna]	
	on the whole rock	
	they painted it with frogs they say	
D	painting	75
	painting	
	painting	
	they were there the whole afternoon they say	
vi/A	and from there	
	the name of Sapo Rumi rock	80
	is still with us	
B	those three places	
	at the headwaters of the Tena River	
	Puma Rumi rock	
C	Pano	85
	below the headwaters of the Puma Yacu River there is also	
	Puma Rumi rock	
	it lies there	
D	and from there upriver	
	on Achi Yacu River	90
	the Sapo Rumi rock	
	is still there	
	it has not disappeared	
vii/A	these are the stories of the beginning times elders	
	they knew them	95
	and told them well	
	we younger people have to listen and learn	
	however now	
	I	
	I have told you what I can	100
	about the beginning times life	
	about that life	
B	so it is known up until now	
	but people today only hear the name [not the story]	
	Sapo Rumi rock	105
	Puma Rumi rock	
	there are two Puma Rumi rocks that are named	
	up through today	
viii/A	it is not known where those names came from	
	who named them?	110
	nobody knows	
	and so being	

```
            now
            we want to get out in the open
            the storytelling word                                    115
            out in the open
B           all the stories
            have been told here
            in those beginning times
C           they [Cuillurguna] created                               120
            tugla (trap) rock
                at the headwaters of the Tena River
            Puma Rumi rock
            in Pano
            and Sapo Rumi rock                                       125
            at Achi Yacu River
D           that now
            we wanted to tell a story about
```

The Twins' Ascent

After the twins perform all their "miracles" here on the earth, they decide that their work is done and take leave of each other. They ascend into the sky and turn into stars, with each brother taking a different path. One brother turns into the morning star (Venus), and the other brother turns into the evening star (also Venus).

Here is how we tell this story: the end of the cycle, the end of a new beginning.

THE TWINS' ASCENT

English

i/A   the Cuillurguna
       sons of the Moon
         Dociru
         the firstborn brother
         Cuillur
            the younger of the two
            angels of the Amazonian world
            raised by jaguars

B   all the miracles
       having finished
       they declared
         "our work
           on earth
             is done" saying

C   they thought
       "where should we go now?"
       "what should we do?"

ii/A   and so being
       they decided
       "let's go to heaven
         above . . .
         we have nothing left to do
          here on this world"

B   and so doing
       they gathered a lot of tobacco
         a huge pile of tobacco they made they say
         they wrapped it in a plantain leaf
     and lit the tobacco on fire **chiiiissssss**
     after some time
       smokiiiiiiiiiiing
         smokiiiiiiiiiiiing

C   it became a big ladder they say to above
         a ladder that touched heaven
         a nice long ladder it was they say
     and so being they climbed above

D   climbing
       climbing
       climbing
       they climbed **very high** they say

Quicha, Ciluman Sikanaun

i / A   Cuillurguna
      killa churiuna
        Dociru
        nawpa punda wawkimi
        Cuillur
          kipa wawkimi
          Amazoniamanda angelkuna
            pumakunawa iñakkunami
B   tukuy tarabanara
      tukuchisha
      rimanawshka
         "ñukanchi tarabana
            kay pachay
              tukuchishkanchi" nisha
C   iyarinawka
       "cuna mayman rishun"
       "imara rashun"
ii / A shinakpi
      iyarinawka
      "aku ciluman
        awaman
        mana imas tiyanzhu rangák
          kay pachay"
B   shina rasha
      ashka tabaku tandachisha
        atun tabaku ranawshka nin
        shuk palanda pangawa piluchisha
    chi tabacu apichinawka **chiiiiiiissssss**
    ña unayllay
      kushniiiiin
        kushniiiiin
C   chi kushni atun chakana tukushka nin awaman
          cilukaman llutakta chakana
           gustu suni chakana ashkami nin
    shinakpi payguna sikanawshka awaman
D   sikasha
      sikasha
      sikasha
      awaaaaaaay sikanawshkami nin

E   and so doing
       the smoke divided into two
          two trails it became they say
          one trail went this way
             one trail went that way

iii/A   and so doing
       it was time to say goodbye
     Dociru spoke first
        "Cuillur, you take that path and go down
       where the sun comes out
          I will take this path and go toward the head
          where the sun sets."

B   then Cuillur said
     saddened
   "brother"
     he said
     "we are the sons of the moon
        the children of the jaguars
        the saviors of humanity
          the makers of miracles."

C   "we worked planting gardens
     we danced
     we built bridges
        and music halls inside of mountains
       we made traps
         and sang magical songs"
           [such as] pikitsa pikitsa pikitsa pikitsa
           rumi rumi rumi rumi rumi"

D   and so doing
     "we killed the jaguars
       the mundopuma
         the birds of prey
         the anaconda
          making a world
          to peacefully
            live well."
          they reflected

iv/A   to that Dociru replied
         "we have passed our time well together brother
         and so being it is time to go
           we are brothers eternal
         we will meet again
           on judgment day"

E   shina rasha
        chi kushni ishki ñambi tukushka
            ishki ñambi tukushkami nin
               shuk ñambi kayman
                  shuk ñambi chayman
iii / A   shina rakpi
            puchukay rimanara rimanawshka
        Dociru ñawpa rimashka
           "Cuillur, kan urayma ringui
           inti llukshishka punguy
           ñuka umama risha
              inti ikuna partima."
B   Cuillur rimashka
        llakirisha
      "wawki"
        nisha
           "ñukanchi killa churiuna anchi
              puma wawaguna anchi
              karan tunu
                 tukuy tunura rurakanchi wawkichu" nisha
C   "tarabakanchi chagrara rasha
        baylakanchi
        chakagunara rurakanchi
           wasi urku ukuy rurakanchi
           karan tunu tuglla rurakanchi
              yachay takinagunara takikanchi
                 pikitsa pikitsa pikitsa pikitsa nisha
                   rumi rumi rumi rumi rumi" nisha
D   shina asha
           "pumagunara chingachikanchi
        mundopumaras
           angagunaras
           amaruntas
             lugar
             sumaklla
               kawsangák'"
              iyarinawka payguna
iv / A   Dociru kuti rimashka
           "yapa sumak sumaklla pasakanchi wawki
        shinakpi rina uras tukunmi
           wiñay wawkigna anchi
        kuti tuparishun
           izhu punzhay"

B   and so they left
                each taking his path
                each brother
                        shedding a tear
C   in the morning sky
                Cuillur can be seen
                        as he took that path
                        the path where the sun rises
D   Dociru on the other hand
                in the evening sky
                appears
                        as he took that path
                                the path where the sun sets
v/A   this is our story
                of all the miracles they did, the Cuillurguna
                        sons of the moon
                        children of jaguars
                                Amazonian angels

B   rinawkami nin
            karan partima
            karan dueño
                iki talichisha
C   tutamanda
            Cuillur rikurin
                chi ñambi apishkamanda
                inti llukshishka punguy
D   Dociru randi
            tuta
            rikurin
                chi shuk ñambi apishkamanda
                    inti ikuna partima
v/A   kay kwintu tiyanmi
            Cuillurguna karran tunura rashkamanda
                killa churiuna
                puma wawaguna
                    ñukanchi Amazoniamanda angelkunami

The Crudity of Experience

Poetic-mythical engagements help us to feel "the crudity of experience" that "remains an eternal element thereof" and for which "there is no possible point of view from which the world can appear an absolutely single fact" (James 1967:135). The crudity of experience is the basis of what William James has termed "radical empiricism," a way of appreciating the infinity and diversity of the world by not reducing things to "determined systems of knowledge" (Jackson 1995:160). More than anyone else, the anthropologist Michael Jackson (1995) has helped us to see the usefulness of William James's work for anthropology, which has helped us to learn many things about human consciousness and the richness of human experiences, especially religion, but also poetry and its engagement with the world.

Being in relationality with all things in existence, somatic poetry is also part of the perspectivism of daily life. In knowing myth, and the truths that myths convey, one can come to see the relations and nuances of myth within the world of experience. Myths tell us who we are, where we came from, and where we will go. But the beauty of myth and somatic poetry is that we are not trapped within ourselves. "I" is but one of many perspectives in the flow of relations that defines who one is, where one is going, and where the journey of life will end. In mythical poetry, there are no individuals (people trapped within themselves and ruled by their egos), no absolutes, no finalities to the world. Each day is a new life of transformation into something else, a shedding of a skin, a new power, a new loss, a new journey, a new "I."

We wake up early in the morning after a hard rain. We walk outside our house and head toward the river. The dull roar of the river is melodious. As we approach, the sound of the river intensifies. The sun's rays are just beginning to stimulate the day. We look up.

> Cuillur Sings [Cuillur takinmi]
> the river [yaku]
>   has become angry [piñarishka]
> the sun [inti]
>   makes the flowers happy [sisagunara kushiyachin]
> the hummingbirds [kindiguna]
>   descend [urmamunawn]
>   sucking the sweetness [mishkira tsunganawn]
> the savage ants [awka añanguguna]
>   pursue [katinawn]
>   their prey [paywa aycha]

the red chuku tree [chuku yura]
tempts the parrots [ichilugunara timptiryan]
    with its flowerbuds [paywa sisa waytawa]
        which fall like rain upon us [tamya shina urmanawn]
it is all within us [tukuy ñukanchi ukuy tiyan]
  it is us [tukuy nukanchimi an]
      we came from this world [kay pachamanda shamukanchi]
      we will return to this world [kay pachama tigramunga raunchi]

Conclusion

In this chapter we discuss the petroglyphs and the twins' ascent into the sky. The petroglyphs show the intimacy of relations between inscribed rock art and the Napo Quichua storytelling tradition, as well as revealing the communicative power of the landscape in Napo Quichua storytelling. In the second story, The Twins' Ascent, the twins climb up to the celestial world, but as the path forks into two directions, each brother must take a different way. As they depart, the brothers discuss their experiences and then say goodbye. Each takes his own path. One brother becomes the morning manifestation of the Venus star, and the other brother becomes the evening appearance.

The twins, in their ascent, create a complex axis mundi of mythological relations. Like Iluku and the Moon and The One-Eyed Anaconda Sun and the Princess, the ascent of the twins creates a multidimensional relationality of axis mundi relations. These relations extend into the rocks, rivers, mountains, and other sites of their actions. The twins are the conduit between the day and the night, the earth and the sky, humanity and divinity, civilization and destruction, and death and life. All is transformation.

Cuillur taught us an important lesson as we walked out by the river in the early morning near our house in Ecuador. We learned from Cuillur that we too are myth and that our destiny, like that of mythological personae, is to transform into something new. All is I and I is All. We are myth.

CHAPTER 8

COSMOLOGICAL COMMUNITAS IN CONTEMPORARY AMAZONIAN MUSIC

Runa Paju or Runa Magic

In the last chapter we explored the notion that myth telling and somatic poetry create a "stirring in the soul" and force one to confront the question "Who am I?" in relation to the crudity of experience. Even in today's world of globalization, myths and mythological truths provide answers to the deep and mysterious questions of life for many Quichua speakers, although today mythological truths are more commonly being expressed through a new genre of music called Runa Paju. Despite its modernistic and technological qualities, Runa Paju conveys deep mythological truths. And like storytelling and the musical practices of the past, Runa Paju is a multimodal mode of expression (Feld and Fox 1994; Finnegan 2007) that emphasizes the power of the human voice, the whole expressive body, and the power of music to elicit social and cosmological action.[1]

During the festivals of indigenous communities, which take place outdoors, Runa Paju performances are experienced as a montage of traditional Quichua symbols and meanings articulated through the modernistic technologies of vocal and instrumental amplification. Runa Paju is music but it can also refer to how people dance when they are filled up with the sounds of the music. The name *Runa Paju*, or "Indigenous Magic," refers to this mysterious and powerful feeling that Quichua speakers experience when Runa Paju music enters their souls.

The music of Runa Paju appears paradoxical to some tourists and outsiders, who often make comments about its inauthenticity. The music, due to its technological nature,[2] is perhaps disappointing to those seeking "the primitive." Indeed, Runa Paju contradicts the stereotypical imagery of the untechnologized Native living in isolation. In this sense, Runa Paju shares qualities with other types of music of the globalized world in that the people making the music are influenced by a diversity of musical styles and instruments, as well as amplification. Nevertheless, when one enters into the semiotics of the music itself, as we show, Runa Paju music "deconstructs" its own forms and conditions of production (Fox 1992), a process of reversal in which Amazonian Quichua cosmology, in becoming musically embodied, obviates Hispanic narratives of modernity and history.

The Runa Paju experience is transformative for those who possess various cultural, musical, and linguistic competencies. Specifically, the five pillars of competency involved in Runa Paju are the sounds of Quichua music, the poetics of the Quichua language, Quichua socioculture and traditions, the kinestheics of indigenous dance mythology, and the ecology of the Amazonian landscape. While Runa Paju is made through modern instruments, the Quichua voice defines it as well as the body. Runa Paju is music made for dancing, and, the total Runa Paju experience creates shared feelings among people that otherwise would not be experienced. As one person commented, Runa Paju music flows from *ñukanchi shungumanda*, or "from our hearts" and "makes us feel happy."

By examining the semiotic meanings of several Runa Paju songs, we show their transformative logics and condensed meanings that emerge through a technique that Quichua speakers use often in storytelling, ritual, and other forms of art: figure-ground reversal or FGR (see Guss 1989; Wagner 1986).[3] We discuss how, in musical events, the structures and realities of "this world" (*kay pacha*) become "opened up" (*paskana*) to the meditative power of spirits, plants, animals, and other unseen forces, a FGR that elicits an "affecting presence" of religious perception and feelings (Armstrong 1971; N. Whitten and D. Whitten 2008). In this sense, we join a host of scholars who "focus on transformative and affecting powers of ritual performance . . . toward a processual symbology and hermeneutics of voice, self, and action" (Feld and Fox 1994:39; see also Basso 1985, 1987; 1995; Seeger 1987; Feld 1982; Bauman and Briggs 1990).

We argue that the affecting presence of Runa Paju is elicited and embodied through outdoor performances where, in nights of discourse, dancing, and making music, people experience a special kind of somatic transformation, *cosmological communitas* (Harvey 2006; Mentore 2007, 2009; E. Turner 2006; V. Turner 1967, 1969) a ritual journey where people feel the Amazonian cosmos as shared destiny.[4] Cosmological communitas, however, is not an idyllic state of affairs, for it is a tenuous moment of experience that sometimes breaks down into social conflict and violence, a noted feature of many Native South American rituals (Allen 1988; Whitehead 2002; Whitehead and Wright 2004). The phenomenon we attempt to describe is how musical experience allows people to cross normal social boundaries and emotions and feel a shared social connectedness to the subjectivities of their cosmological world. The transformation is elicited through a total aesthetic experience, one in which language, music, the body, and all of the senses come together to produce a ritual sociality of emotion and action.

Brief Description of Runa Paju

In Quichua communities throughout Amazonia, Runa Paju has become the dominant mode of indigenous artistic expression since the late 20th century. Quichua speakers say that Runa Paju is *tradicional,* or "traditional," despite the fact that its musicians use electronic keyboards and amplification and have largely abandoned the instruments of the past. The music is stylistically eclectic, and groups borrow features of Sanjuanitos, Huaynos, and even Cumbia and Salsa. The most popular groups tout full-fledged "orchestras" that include electronic organs, guitars (electric and classical), bass guitars, violins, various styles of drums, rattles, and other instruments. The orchestra performances, which are almost always outdoors, sometimes include women stage dancers who are colorfully and provocatively clothed in traditional dress of beadwork, leaf skirts, tops, and jewelry. Orchestra musicians, most often men, also dress in traditional clothing, usually the *kushma,* a blue top and short pants, a style of dress introduced by the Jesuits in previous centuries.

The lyrics of Runa Paju songs are in the Quichua language, although most groups now sing a few Spanish songs. The lyrics, which we examine in more detail below, are poetically and semiotically complex. They share many of the aesthetic principles of traditional music and storytelling, such as parallelism, equivalence, metaphor, and the body's subjectivity and interconnectedness with the landscape. Like myth, ritual, storytelling, and more traditional music, Runa Paju is a genre of somatic poetry, a way of using language creatively to invoke new subjectivities and experiences of the body.

Runa Paju groups have names that usually imply a *samay,* or soul connectedness, to the forest or rivers, and the names are mostly in Quichua, but other groups are simply named after their lead singer or composers. For example, there are two groups named after notable birds, the Chawmangos (Cacique Bird) and the Guacamayos (Guacamayo Parrot). The names Sacha Samay (Forest Breath), Taki Tamya (Musical Rain), Intipak Churi (Son of the Sun), and Sumak Taki (Beautiful Music) imply a spiritual connectedness to the rainforest world. The groups named after people are Patricio Alvarado and his Llaki Shungu (Loving Heart) Orchestra; Carlos Narváez, "el mimado de Orellana" (the spoiled one from Orellana); and Los Jilgueritos, the first group to emerge from the zone of Tálag. Some groups, however, have Spanish names, like the Playeros Quichua (Quichua "Beach Boys"), Agua Azul (Blue Water), the Amaguas (named after the Tupian culture of Omaguas that resided in the Lower Napo region), and Los Primitivos (The Primitives).

Runa Paju musicians are not professionals in the sense that any of them make a living playing and performing Runa Paju, but Runa Paju performers receive some money for live performances and shows. Runa Paju's essence comes from the experience of the Quichua world, and a good Runa Paju performer must live in and relate to Quichua cosmology and culture in the very fiber of his essence; without a knowledge of the forest and rural Quichua life, the music would fall flat. The musicians are not regarded as famous people, nor do they have fans. Musicians are simply members of the community and face the same problems and issues in life as other community members.

Recently there has been an explosion of new Runa Paju groups, and every year more groups appear on the scene, but the origins of Runa Paju go back to the 1980s. A book published by the Association of Native Artists and Groups of Napo (AACTIN 1991) lists only one native musical group existing before 1983, but by 1987 there were 49 groups, with about 30 groups listed for Napo Province in 1983.[5] As well, the book lists upstart groups pertaining to other Amazonian ethnicities, not just Quichua speakers (see below).

With the support of FOIN (Federation of Indigenous Organizations of Napo), the first indigenous federation of Napo Province, as well as government organizations of Tena and Napo Province, the first congress of Native Musicians and Artists was organized in 1983. Other indigenous groups sent delegations of musicians to this congress, including Cofanes, Secoya, Siona, Waorani, Shuar, and Quichua peoples of Pastaza and Lower Napo. The meeting took place in Rukullacta, an indigenous community near Archidona. Rukullacta is significant because it is the home of Carlos Alvarado Narváez, the leader of the group Los Yumbos Chawamangos and the founder of modern Quichua music. We have more to say about Carlos Alvarado below in a section on the origins of Runa Paju.

The most well-known groups in the early 1990s, at least in the region of Tena, were the following: Carlos Alvarado Narváez and his Yumbos

Chawmangos group, the Wakamayos, Patricio Alvarado and his Llaki Shungu group, and Los Jilgueritos. There are perhaps others, but these are the ones that people remember today. These groups formed the essential "corpus" of older songs that all of the groups play today, songs that are the backbone of the genre. However, for a group to make a name for itself today, it must also create newer songs that become popular in the community. Two examples are perhaps worth noting. Some years ago the Playeros Quichua made themselves known through their song Chini Panga, or "Nettles Leaf" (see below)—the Quichua equivalent of a "hit." In 2008, the new group Amaguas became known with their catchy song Chucula, a song about a mashed plantain banana drink consumed for breakfast daily by Quichua speakers. People know that a song is popular when it is played over and over again on the radio but also played during festivals, weddings, and celebrations of schools, occasions when music is required, so that Quichua people can perform traditional dances and experience communitas in a Quichua way.

These points raise the question of how Runa Paju music circulates in the community, for Runa Paju is not regulated nor managed by record companies or recording studios but by the community. The heart and soul of Runa Paju is the live performance, which we describe below in a later section, and for which there is demand during special events. In addition to their performances, Runa Paju groups circulate their music through CDs and increasingly by making MTV-style music videos in Video CD format, although the CD is not as socially important as live performances.

The CDs are purchased by community members who often play them during school celebrations or graduations, weddings, and festivals or at cabañas, outdoor gathering spots where indigenous people congregate to play sports, socialize, dance, drink, and listen to their own music. Runa Paju music is also played on several local radio stations during the early morning hours, between 3 and 6 a.m., a time when Quichua people traditionally would wake up, drink wayusa tea, and play music. Most families have a radio or a boom box, and early risers start their day by listening to the Quichua programs.

The groups that make their own CDs either sell or distribute them to people who ask for them or whom they know. Increasingly, people "rip" Runa Paju and share the files on computers, cell phones, and MP3 players, as well as upload Runa Paju music videos to YouTube. Runa Paju disks are more likely obtained and copied by market vendors who specialize in music and movie pirating. The disks cost between $1.00 and $1.50, and there are several locales in Tena where they are sold. The artists feel somewhat ambiguous about this practice because they don't receive any money for their songs, but on the other hand they do receive promotion from the circulation of the songs; in their music videos, for example, the groups always include subtitles with phone numbers for contracts and invitations. The jacket covers also contain contact information.

Copyright conventions are not followed with Runa Paju, as artists borrow and perform the songs of other groups freely and without legal or social repercussion, although recently the CDs of some of the groups now state that they are protected under law. On the one hand, artists who create songs "own" them in the sense of artistic rights, but people feel that the music also belongs to the community of all Quichua speakers. As mentioned, neither the music nor the musicians are regulated by corporations, the market, or the state; the music is regulated by the community of artists and the Quichua-speaking community. Artists freely use and often change or adapt the songs of other groups to fit their own creative purposes.

Because Runa Paju music is sung in the Quichua language, it is very difficult for mestizo or non-Quichua people to "steal," imitate, or co-opt it. This insulation from co-optation is also due to the fact that apart from the Quichua lyrics and the Quichua voice, the music has already been borrowed from general indigenous-mestizo and Caribbean–Latin American culture—which is one of its defining characteristics. Most Runa Paju is musically similar to a genre of music that is sung in Spanish, *música nacional*, although Runa Paju music as a whole is semiotically defined through Quichua competencies that include culture, language, environment, and mythology. But as one musician commented, to be a good Runa Paju artist, one must not only know Quichua music but also be versed in "Caribbean sounds." We hope that in the future ethnomusicologists will be able to give more precise descriptions and classifications of these eclectic Runa Paju musical styles.

Music in Our Veins: The Birth and Lifeblood of Runa Paju

Runa Paju was born one day in a manioc garden. While walking through the forest one morning, Carlos Alvarado, the founder of Runa Paju, passed by a garden where a woman was working.[6] He paused and listened to her song, as she was singing a *takina*, or magical song, to her manioc plants as she cleaned up the weeds around them. Inspired by this scene, he decided to create a song, titled Lumu Mama, or "Manioc Mother," dedicated to these women who toiled day after day in their gardens to provide food and manioc beer for their families (AACTIN 1991:75). The song's lyrics, which are below, speak to the poetic meanings of manioc gardening and motherhood in the Quichua world.

indimama kantashkaybi	when the indi mama [insect] sings
lumu warmi tarpujunmi	the manioc woman plants
indimalla rikushami	just looking at the sun
chagrawara pichajunmi	she is weeding her garden
lumu sisa rikushami	looking at the flowers of the manioc
siki panga ichurinmi	the leaves fall [to the base]
nishamari takijunga	saying this she is singing [takina]
nishamari bailajunga	saying this she is dancing
kisamanga paskastasha	opening the pot
yaticabi upiachiwan	here she gives me to drink [manioc beer]
yaya mama illanunmi	my parents are gone
nishamari rimakayri	saying this she spoke
malta musu rikushami	looking at a young man
sumak warmi shayarinmi	the beautiful woman stands up
asa mama mani nisha	saying/thinking I am a manioc beer woman
luma mama ani nisha	saying/thinking I am a manioc mother
lumu siki takikami	singing at the base of her manioc plants
lumu siki bailakami	dancing at the base of her manioc plants

As Alvarado mentions in an interview (AACTIN 1991:75), this song came out of a moment of empathy with a woman working in her manioc garden. Inspired by this experience, Alvarado decided to make a song dedicated to all manioc mothers, and in it he told the story of manioc women. In making this song, he created a new genre of Quichua music but followed the traditional Quichua convention of making music out of experience and its constitutedness in human-ecological communicative interactions.

For example, the *indimama*, or cicada, sings in the morning as the sun rises; this is the exact communicative moment when the woman begins working in her garden. This moment of experience and communication is the meaning of the first four lines of the song. The woman looks at the sun, weeds her garden, sings, and gives a young man manioc beer to drink. These, and the other details in the song, represent the poetics of experience and human-ecological communication perceived by Alvarado watching the woman in her garden.[7]

The "tones" or sounds of the song, as Alvarado points out, were derived from the *takina*, or magical song, of the woman working in the garden (AACTIN 1991:75). It is worth quoting this part at length, for it shows how Runa Paju is built up on experience and traditional music. Alvarado describes how he found the tones:

> The tonality came from the woman I mentioned [in the Lumu Mama song], it is to say that I just played the tones of the music. Let's just say I played the

tones of the music. Well, as I am not a musicologist, I just play them. However, I think that the tones and the scales that our elders left run in our blood. And I don't want to lose them. Little by little I went composing the song, fixing it, and changing it until it became music, a song. (AACTIN 1991:75)

What Alvarado says here is that the sounds of his song were patterned upon his experience of hearing the *takina* of the woman singing to her manioc plant. The process of composing he describes, like the traditional music, is "empirical" in that it relies on one's own ear (and feelings) rather than reading music or machine measurement.

Other sounds of Amazonian ecology find their way into Runa Paju, and their presence in the music allows people to feel and recognize a shared cosmovision and sociality with older Quichua music and storytelling (see chapters 1 and 4). For example, in relation to other songs, Alvarado speaks of how he composed his music in relation to these various voices of Amazonian ecology and storytelling:

I go in agreement with the sound, for example, the sound of the birds or sounds of the forest; I go looking for example for the song of the toucans who sing guen, guen, guen, guen, erre, erre, erre, erre. So, using the base of this rhythm, to this beat, I make the music and make the lyrics. There are also times that the grandparents know part of the songs [ancient songs], they know some phrases. . . . The elders that I visit in my travels converse with me, they sing like their grandparents sang, in relationship to the mythology; from this I get the music, I complete the words and the music (AACTIN 1991:77)

As Alvarado states, Quichua music draws on the various subjectivities of the forest—specifically birds, but any aspect of being in the forest, the rivers, or the garden can be a source of musical inspiration. Ecological sounds, which are often circular in their aesthetic shape, are common in many Runa Paju songs. Similar to the poetics of mythology as discussed by Levi-Strauss (1964–1971), Quichua musical composition involves complex and higher-order relations. The pauses, cyclicity, rhythms, and musical contours, for example, invoke the patterns and experiences of living in various and diverse rainforest realities. Just as manioc, for example, grows and is harvested, consumed, and replanted, so too does Runa Paju music elicit patterns of cyclicity and repetition. People mimic these patterns of growth, death, and rebirth in creating musical sounds and lyrics, as well as stories. We see human-ecological musical redundancy in many performances described throughout this book. Salient examples are Federico's manioc poem (chapter 1), Chuyaki's shamanic song (chapter 1), the women's songs (chapter 4), and Verna's Iluku story (chapter 3). We now explore similar aesthetic dimensions in Runa Paju music.

The Poetics of Couplets

Like "The Twins and the Jaguars" story (see chapter 5), which is defined by patterns of diametric and concentric dualisms, transformations, and "mediators," the essence of Quichua poetics is the dynamic play of patterns of twos and threes, patterns that are articulated into wholes, deconstructed, and then rearticulated again. In Napo Runa speech, the moving patterns of twos and threes, wholes and parts, are both linguistic and musical with words and musical features such as melodic patterning and pause working together to create semiotic montages of condensed meanings. Following Mannheim (1998), who was the first to show the importance of couplets in Quechua (Peruvian) poetic speech, we pose as well that the elementary form of Napo Runa poetic play is the dynamic play of couplets. Couplets are varied and then repeated over and over again (creating Jakobson's [1960] "equivalence") so that any one song, as well as the music in general, in the experience of Quichua speakers, is felt to be a circle of complex, interwoven relations.

For example, relations of cyclicity can be discerned in a lullaby that Edith sings to our baby, Rumi, to help him sleep. Edith sings a song that is composed of chains of couplets, in which two couplets (indicated by numbers 1 and 2) are linked to form a "stanza" (indicated by capital letters, A, B, etc.). The song for her contains three basic syllables (marked off with a dash in the Quichua transcription) that are repeated over and over again.[8] Each line is defined by a pause. The song goes like this:

A/1	puñ-un-gui	sleep
	puñ-un-gui	sleep
2	Rumi-ci-to	litle Rumi
	puñ-un-gui	sleep
B/1	puñ-un-gui	sleep
	wa-wi-to	little baby
2	puñ-un-gui	sleep
	puñ-un-gui	sleep
C/1	pa-piwa ña sha-mun-ga	daddy will soon come
	pa-piwa ña sha-mun-ga	daddy will soon come
2	puñ-un-gui	sleep
	wa-wi-to	little baby
D/1	ma-mi-ta kan-wan-mi	mommy is with you
	puñ-un-gui	sleep
2	puñ-un-gui	sleep

[songs repeats until the baby falls asleep]

This very simple song contains within it some basic forms of Quichua prosody—couplets that involve musical and language interpenetration. As in other lyrical arts, the syllables are defining, for the aesthetic patterning of the words is considered to attract power, or *ushay*. Music, as discussed in previous chapters, is social and magical action. In the Quichua world, mothers use musical *ushay* to make babies go to sleep and to soothe them when they are upset. Like the *takina* of the woman in the garden singing to her manioc plants, Edith's song draws on Quichua assumptions that music can influence growth, health, and feelings, feelings that are associated with *kawsay* or vital energy.

The aesthetics and sociality of the song convey redundancy and cyclicity and the dynamic play of twos and threes, redundancy that is also defining of the music of shamanic rituals and shamanic music in general (see Belzner and Whitten 1979). These forms, which could be examined in more detail by music specialists, are the sound-relations, as commented upon by Alvarado above, that "run in the blood" of Amazonian Quichua speakers (AACTIN 1991:75).

Specialists often separate out different domains of analysis, such as the words or song texts, music, dance, gestures, cultural and social significations, experience, and history. Quichua speakers, however, view their musical practices as an inseparable whole, and in this sense the words of songs are simultaneously music, kinesthetics, experience, social process, and culture itself in the making. This point is perhaps not emphasized enough in the ethnopoetics and ethnomusicological literature, which in many ways are two separate discourses existing in methodical tension (see Feld and Fox 1994). The whole expressive body, however, is our point of departure and the axis mundi of the Quichua creative soul, a soul that takes advantage of multiple modes and media of expression in getting out its messages and feelings. There are other, more complex forms of expression, however, that also define Runa Paju and that can be elicited through symbolic analysis.

Chini Panga, or "Nettles Leaf": Whole-Part Analogies

Let us now look at a Runa Paju song by the Playeros Quichua, Chini Panga, or "Nettles Leaf," a song that displays fractal relations,[9] a kind of organization in which self-similar relations create wholes that are the same as the parts—forms that have been shown to be useful in anthropological analysis (Gleik 1987; Mosko and Damon 2005). Self-scaling relations, which are present in many aspects of Native Amazonian thought and practice (Uzendoski 2010a; Kelly 2005) are forms that emerge in complex nonlinear ways. Like a drop of water that suddenly becomes an entire world, or a leaf that becomes a tree, or a body that becomes an entire society, fractal relations allow parts to become wholes, wholes to become parts, and scales to shift from the tiniest to the largest—invoking infinity and poetic complementarity among things not normally linked though linear processes of association. The song Chini Panga is a clear demonstration of the poetry of fractal forms in Napo Quichua cultural thought. While the basic structure of this song is made up of couplets, music and grammar work together in creating an elegant but semiotically complex poetic structure of whole-part similarity.

In the song, *chini* refers to stinging nettles, a plant that is used in Quichua culture to treat certain illnesses, cleanse the body, or punish an unruly child. The verb *chinina* means to "to sting with nettles," and like many of the plants used in Quichua culture, *chini* not only is medicine but also creates a change in bodily subjectivity, one from tranquility or normalcy to one of feeling pain, tingling, and intensity. To *chinina* (cleanse with nettles) someone the healer takes a cutting of the plant and lightly strikes the patient rhythmically, over and over, in the affected area—similar to the way shamans cleanse their patients with *suru panga* leaves. The medicine, which is inside the thorns, enters the skin through the tiny breaks created through the strikes. Patients often wince while they are being "chinied," and the pain lasts for some time after the treatment is done.

In the song Chini Panga, the singer compares himself to a nettles leaf. He sings:

A	**Chini** panga shina	Like a nettles leaf
	Asi**chini**mi	I make laugh
B	**Chini** panga shina	Like a nettles leaf
	Kuyu**chini**mi	I make move
C	**Chini** panga shina	Like a nettles leaf
	Asi**chini**mi	I make laugh
D	**Chini** panga shina	Like a nettles leaf
	Waka**chini**mi	I make cry
E	Kipa ñañawara waka**chini**mi	My older sister, I make cry
	ruku ñañawara asi**chini**mi	My younger sister, I make laugh
F	Kipa ñañawara waka**chini**mi	My older sister, I make cry
	ruku ñañawara asi**chini**mi	My younger sister, I make laugh

The song appears simple but is poetically complex because of its fractal organization. In the above text, the fractal relations are indicated in **bold** and include the forms of grammar in their construction. Let us explain in detail the fractality of this song, which requires a brief discussion of Quichua grammar.

The grammatical particle *china* is a form that Quichua speakers add onto the root of a verb to convey that someone or something else makes the person do the action. An example would be *asichina* (to make laugh), which is a combination of the verb root *asi* (laugh) and *china* (to make). In the first-person the phrase, "I make laugh" would be *asichini*, a construction in which the *chini* at the end of the word refers not to a plant but to making someone laugh. It is the play between the two kinds of *chini,* the plant and the grammatical form, that is at the heart of the song's poetics.

The song Chini Panga refers to the singer making one sister cry (*waka-chinimi*) and one sister laugh (*asichinimi*). The sound of *chini* (the grammatical form) in these phrases invokes the subjectivity and intensity of the *chini* plant itself, which "stings" and "wakes up"; it makes people act differently. The part, the grammatical form **chini** (I make do) replicates the "whole" here, the **chini** plant itself.

The pattern of the song, like Edith's lullaby, is defined by couplets, with one line sending "out" a phrase and the next line bringing it back "in" to form a stanza. There are two main musical couplets to the song, the "like a nettles leaf . . . I make cry/laugh/move" pattern, and the contrasting couplet "My older/younger sister I make laugh/cry . . . my older/younger sister I make laugh/cry." Each couplet is repeated two times (with many possible variations of the words), but at the end of the second singing of the final couplet, the final line ascends in pitch and is held, "Asichini**miiiiiiiiiiiiiiiiii** (I make laughhhhhhhhhhhhhhh). A musical interlude occurs and then the song is started over again, this time with other variations of "making someone move," "making someone carry," or making someone do something else. The singer also improvises in that the song can refer to the "younger sister" or the "older sister" and alternate back and forth between them.

The semiotic patterning of Runa Paju builds upon traditional musical and mythological organization: dualities, triadisms, transformations, cyclicity, fractality, and metaphor. These significations occur at multiple levels: in the melodic contour, the words, the dancing, and the actual subjectivities of experience itself. These "soundscapes" (Brenneis and Feld 2004) are similar to the patterns by which the ancients composed their music and developed the poetics of their stories.

Galera Urku: Myth as Music

The words of Runa Paju songs often invoke the ways of speaking of the elders; Runa Paju, in other words, is a new tradition that is creatively linked to the traditions of the past. It is not the exact words of the elders that define these songs but rather words that invoke how the elders spoke, a kind of quotative relationship in which new music cites the knowledge and experience of the elders as historically situated within a larger narrative of Quichua time-space relations (see chapters 4 and 5). The Runa Paju songs, through music, elicit the knowledge of the past, older ways of speaking and thinking, as well as the richness and varied experiences of living in the Upper Napo world. This varied Quichua music has a special power that allows Quichua speakers to feel, in intense ways, the realities of their cosmovision and their interconnectedness to ecology and the past in deep, spiritual ways. This cosmovision, although explicitly historically situated, transcends history in that all narratives are defined by their link to *kallari,* or the beginning time-space, a reality that interpenetrates all aesthetic forms.

Carlos Alvarado's song, Galera Urku, originally a story of the Cuillurguna, is a good example of how musical storytelling connects people to *kallari,* or beginning time-space. Readers should familiarize themselves with the mundopuma story of chapter 6, which is the myth upon which this song is based. The song goes like this:

Galera urku rikurinmi	you can see Galera Mountain
atun urku ashkamanda	because it is a big mountain
galera urkuy puma tianmi	there is a jaguar inside of Galera Mountain
runa mikuk puma ishkaryan	the man-eating jaguar is trapped
Cuillurguna ishkanushka	the Cuillurguna trapped [him]
mundu puma ishkaryanmi	the mundopuma is trapped
izhu punzha llukshingami	on *izhu punzha* [judgment day] he will get out
kutillara mikungahua	to eat [people] again
manzhanguichi manzhanguichi	are you all afraid? are you all afraid?
churu puma mikungami	the snail jaguar will come to eat [people]
manzhanguichi manzhanguichi	are you all afraid? are you all afraid?
wagra puma micungami	the tapir jaguar will come to eat [people]
bunu yacu llukshimunmi	the Bunu River comes out from
galera urcu nishkamanda	our named Galera Mountain
manzhanguichi manzanguichi	are you all afraid? are you all afraid?
churu pumas mikungami	the little jaguar will eat [people]

In the above song, Alvarado tells the whole mundopuma story through the first stanza, which ends in "the man-eating jaguar is trapped." The second half of the Galera Urku song invokes a future *izhu punzha,* or judgment day, when the jaguars will escape and devour people again. Alvarado poeticizes this moment by asking listeners if they are afraid, "are you all afraid? are you all afraid?" As we saw in chapter 5 in Verna's telling of "The Twins and the Jaguars," the jaguar stories were always linked to the notion of a future *izhu punzha* when they would escape their stone forms and rise up again to eat people. The song Galera Urku is a musical exploration of this very same theme. Alvarado masterfully deploys words that convey enough information and imagery to allow Quichua speakers to feel myth as music and to dance to the transformationality and aesthetics of mythology. The song connects people to beginnings, to *kallari*, which is also a future reality.

Figure-Ground Reversals in Amazonian Musical Expressions

Like storytelling and the more traditional genres of musical expression, Runa Paju songs elicit moving and dynamic imagery of reversal and transformation. Runa Paju composers are masters of this technique, which we describe here as figure-ground reversal (FGR), a perceptual "trick" of oral textuality by which the foreground and background of a system of relations are reversed (Wagner 1986) so that one apparent reality is collapsed into a new set of relations. An example can perhaps clarify what we mean.

When Michael visited the Spurlock Museum at the University of Illinois two years ago, he saw a ceramic vessel with a representation of an oil boss riding an anaconda canoe.[10] This drinking vessel, made by a Quichua-speaking woman of Pastaza Province, shows quite clearly the dynamic tension of modernity and indigenous spiritual power (*ushay*) in indigenous Quichua thought and experience. On the one hand, there is the social and hegemonic power of the state and its extractive processes, notions evoked in the figure of the gringo oil boss. On the other hand, the oil boss is riding in an anaconda canoe, and the anaconda, which evokes a different reality of spiritual power, reverses the paradigm represented by the oil boss.

This ceramic work of art is defined by figure-ground reversal, or FGR. The image of one world is transformed into that of another. In the ceramic vessel, the FGR of the oil boss takes him to the domain of the andaconda, which reverses his power and takes him, unwittingly, on a journey toward death. As in the twins stories, here the power of one dominant "predator" is reversed by that of an unseen transformer. The vessel is metaphoric of the larger forces of modernity in relation to those of the indigenous world; the oil boss stands for "the company," the oil industry in general, while the anaconda invokes the eternal presence of forest subjectivities and powers. Also salient is the canoe, as Amazonian Quichua speakers traditionally buried their dead in canoes, and to dream about a canoe or a river journey is an omen of death. The canoe, the anaconda, and the water all signal the revenge of the unseen world upon the forces of modernity.

The "twins" stories exemplified this kind of FGR movement. The twins, as shown in chapters 5 and 6, were masters of FGR. They were able to create appearances that masked hidden relations and provided favorable outcomes. In the story of Galera Mountain, the twins trapped the mundopuma inside a mountain, and in general, the twins elicited FGR on a massive, forest-wide scale. The twins, unlike Iluku and other personae of mythology, were the ones able to metamorphose the relations of humans as prey into the relations of humans as predator (see chapters 5, 6, and 7). This perspective change, however, is not permanent, for on *izhu punzha*, or judgment day, the relations will be reversed again (see chapter 2). What is in the foreground now will one day be the background again.

FGR, thus, is not just an aesthetic technique. It is also a principle of Amazonian perspectivist cosmologies and the circularity of all things in the Napo Quichua world, a way of eliciting the interpenetrability of axis mundi relationality among different worlds of time and space (see chapters 6 and 7). FGR tells us that no social order, no set of relations, no period of peace and prosperity, will last forever (see chapter 2). New relations of suffering, dominance, and death are likely to arise as new (old) orders take their place. On the other hand, suffering and disharmony will one day end in the transformation into a new set of relations. But the "newness" in these transformations involves evoking a set of relations from the past, relations that also define the future. This is the notion of *izhu punzha,* or judgment day (see chapter 2). While *izhu punzha* is circularity, the pathways of the transformation are the axis mundi(s) of the mythological world. In artistic expressions, FGR implies travel. It evokes a journey from one state of affairs into the relations of the past (future) world of experience.

Figure-Ground Reversal in Runa Paju

These processes of FGR are explicit in several Runa Paju songs and even in the name *Runa Paju. Runa* means "human" or "indigenous person." *Paju* is a complex word that means "power," but magical power, power that emanates from the spirit world. *Runa Paju* is spirit-world-derived music, "our music" that is "traditional" because it continues the flow of relations between people, their ancestors, the spirit world, and the landscape. Despite the technology and apparent inventiveness of the genre, the essence of Runa Paju is circularity and the interpenetrability of all things in the indigenous world. And like storytelling and traditional forms of music, Runa Paju evokes a stirring of the soul in engagement with the crudity of experience. It also conveys the notion that life is a journey, a long journey through the contours of axis mundi pathways and mythological transformations. Runa Paju, like the music of the past, tells the varied and diverse stories behind these journeys, journeys already taken by the ancestors but journeys on which the living are still traveling.

I Have to Die

In one song, for example, Patricio Alvarado sings into being the aesthetic presence and power of death. In Ñukas Wañunami Kani, or "I Have to Die," Alvarado evokes the eternity of rocks, rivers, and clouds. These entities, which are described as *wiñay*, or eternal, are beautiful and powerful entities that stand in contrast to the rest of living things in the world that are going to die and dissolve. Part of songs goes like this:

ñukas wañunami kani	I have to die
kanbas wañunami kangui	you have to die
chay kawsayta yuyarisha	thinking of that life
llakinayami llakinayan	we get/feel sad
yakukunata rikukpiga	looking at the rivers
rumikunata rikupiga	looking at the stones
wiñay wiñaylla sirinawnga	they will lie for eternity
mana ima uras tukuringa	they will never run out
wayrakunta rikupiga	looking at the wind
puyukunata rikupgia	looking at the clouds
wiñay wiñaylla kawsananga	they will live for eternity
mana ima uras tukuringa	they will never run out

In comments during the musical interludes between the verses, Alvarado uses his spoken voice to expresses sadness because he must die, but he affirms that we can live well with the time that we have. This technique is also a kind of FGR, a way of "metaphorizing" the listeners in relationship to the music. The song elicits a heartfelt and powerful relationship to experience that is further intensified through musicalized spoken words, words that cut to the heart of the matter. The words parallel and take further the song's engagement of experience—in this case, the experience and reality of death.

The song has a salient figure-ground reversal that defines its poetics. The song joins death with life in a way that is analogous to the imagery on the oil boss vessel. In the song, the rocks, rivers, and clouds are given subjectivity and animacy, but they are not really "figured out" by the singer. On the contrary, they are very mysterious, powerful, life-giving forces in the world; they are the *paju*—the presence of powers of the unseen world.

If I Die in a Far-Off Forest

Another song, Karu Sachai Wañukpi, or "If I Die in a Far-Off Forest," addresses dying in a far-off forest or river where there are no people. The singer, Alirio Tapuy, who is Edith's cousin and sometimes sings for Patricio Alvarado's Llaki Shungu group, takes the perspective of being dead and asks who will find him. He sings about the crab, the catfish, and the piranhas eating him, biting his flesh. In the forest the vultures eat him and bite his flesh. The song is a beautifully crafted perspective change or FGR on life. Here is how the song goes:

karu yakuy wañunaukpi	if I die in a far-off river
karu yakuy wañunaukpi	if I die in a far- off river
pita rikuwanagayrilla	who will see me?
pita tupawangayrilla	who will find me?
pita rikuwanayrilla	who will see me?
pita tupawangayrilla	who will find me?
aparungachu mikunga	will the crab eat (me)?
aparungachu kaninga	will the crab bite (me)?
bagrewachu mikuwanga	will the little catfish eat me?
pirallawa mikuwanga	will the little piranhas eat me?

As the singer states, death is a process of FGR. In death, people become food for animals, fish, and birds rather than these creatures being food for humans. The journey of life, thus, is one of circularity and reversal of relations, the transformation of predator into prey and vice versa.

These songs addressing death, of which there are many, are the point metaphor—the beginning and ending point of all the journeys defined throughout the whole of the music. Within this field of relations, other kinds of songs take people to different places, experiences, feelings, and realities, but as a whole the music returns people to the flow of analogical relations among the living and dead. This flow of "opening up the world" is also achieved through the ritual processes of the performances, which we discuss below. But first let us discuss other themes of the music, other "places" visited in the journey of experience traveled by the living.

Other Themes in Runa Paju Songs

Runa Paju music is a process of storytelling by which different people become interconnected through threads of the larger narrative of life and death. The music celebrates the Napo Quichua experience of life, in all its richness and complexities; it invokes common feelings experienced in different places and times along the collective journey that will one day require people to face death. In being a commentary on experience, it reminds people that their daily lives are part of a larger cosmological narrative, the same narrative traveled by their ancestors. Although Runa Paju is a different genre of music from the past, its qualities of storytelling and narrative work in the same way as the old-time music.

The music of the elders, for example, addressed themes pertinent to the historical experiences of past generations as well as their experiential engagements with the mythological world. We saw, for example, in the chapter on women's songs (chapter 4), songs that addressed the rubber boom, the hacienda era, and gathering salt from the Huallaga River in Peru. Today's Quichua speakers face a different historical reality, one that is musicalized through Runa Paju, but one that, like the old-time music, articulates history from the perspective of the subjectivities of Amazonian cosmology. In this sense, like myth, Runa Paju is built up from the implicit assumptions of perspectivism (see chapters 1 and 4).

The historical situatedness of Runa Paju involves various social transformations that include the de-articulation of the oppressive hacienda system, the beginning of education for indigenous peoples, the rise of indigenous movements and federations, struggles for land rights, globalization, and environmental degradation. Runa Paju songs address many of these historical themes through the aesthetics of experience and, like the music of the ancients, through figure-ground reversals.

Generally, Runa Paju songs fall into some basic categories, but there really are not limits for what constitutes a good Runa Paju song as long as it engages Quichua experience. In Runa Paju, there are songs about identity and politics, songs about food production and hunting/gardening, songs about kinship and family relations, songs about love and marriage. All the songs, in one way or another, speak to the experiences and feelings of daily life, its problems and challenges, and the way Quichua speakers face these problems along the journey of life. Oftentimes they invoke a range of feelings including everything from love to feeling hunger when there is no food. Sadness and loss are also invoked often, and there are several well-known songs that address death, orphanage, and adoption of orphan children by relatives, a theme also present in the music of the ancients.

A major theme in the music is the Napo Quichua food system as a source of identity, experience, and tradition. Other songs, however, take on themes related to the subjectivity and power of plants and animals, like the Chini

Panga song we described earlier. There are songs about agoutis, turtles, birds (*guacamayos, chawamangos, tapia pishku, suyu pishku, iluku*), bears, and other animals. There are also songs about spirits and shamanism, death and the spirit world, and songs that invoke mythology. For example, there are songs about the spirit women that inhabit rivers, the *yaku warmiguna*, as well as songs dedicated to those who become shamans. Like the oil boss vessel discussed earlier, the music "reverses" the assumptions and powers of Western modernity for the realities and experience of Quichua cosmology and Quichua sociality.

Yet, the individual Runa Paju song is not significant. What is significant is the corpus of songs put together in a performance, the montage of imagery, experience, and feelings created and shared by people during a fiesta or Runa Paju celebration, a *atun tushuna tuta*, or big dancing night. As in storytelling, Runa Paju music is defined by a gathering.

Atun Tushuna Tuta, or Big Dancing Night

Like Amazonian Quichua stories, Runa Paju songs are works of art that are highly metaphorical and which condense and concentrate meaning. In an *atun tushuna tuta*, or "big dancing night," Runa Paju songs are strung together for an all-night dance celebration, one that has ritualistic as well as festive qualities. The *atun tushuna tuta* is a shared journey, a journey that might be described as a social process of "cosmological communitas," an idea borrowed from Victor Turner (1967, 1969) but nuanced to emphasize the cosmological qualities of Runa Paju that are brought into presence through music (see E. Turner 2006; Mentore 2009). The *atun tushuna tuta* allows people to experience somatically the realities and powers of Napo Quichua cosmology, realities upon which cultural and social practices of daily life have been built. Let us describe briefly these dancing events.

During a fiesta or wedding, the Runa Paju musicians take an outdoor stage (in Spanish it is called the *escenario*, or place of the scene), which is always a raised platform, usually made out of wood and bamboo. The stage is a place of social action; on the stage people make speeches and tell stories and jokes, and there might be performances of various genres of Quichua music and storytelling. The stage is "open" rather than closed space, and there are various modes of meaning creation and experience involved, modes that include the spoken voice, song, dance, and co-participation with the people of the community.

In all Quichua celebrations the microphone circulates from musicians to community members, and speakers invite people to dance and send greetings or make jokes targeted at specific people in the crowd. Musicians call out the names of people, invite them onto the stage, or metaphorize them during their songs. Drinks move from community members to musicians, who are socially obligated to accept and consume an offered cup of beer or a bowl of manioc beer. As the evening goes on, the musicians and community members consume manioc beer and other alcoholic drinks, most often bottled beer or trago, through a social pattern of inviting others to consume. People do not consume as individuals but rather in pairs and in groups. As one musician commented when I asked him why he played the keyboard with only his right hand: "I have to keep my left hand free to accept drinks while I am playing."

The stage is always outside in open air and usually located in a cleared area, basketball court, or soccer field. The playing field, in front of the stage, is where people dance, but they also spend time doing a lot of other things including drinking, talking, telling stories, laughing, and passing the time. If it is not cloudy or raining, stars are visible, and the sounds of the locale, such as the flow of a river or stream, can be heard in the background.

Napo Runa people dance in pairs of one man and one woman, and there is a distinct style of dancing Runa Paju that is unique and that the Napo Runa have practiced for centuries. The style involves moving the feet backward and forward repetitively and creating an aesthetic of "lightness," a positive value in Quichua life often described as *kutsi* when referring to women. When women dance, they rotate their heads from one side to another so that their hair, which is always kept long and flowing, falls from one side to the other. Men also must appear "light" and "bouncy," and although the moves are not complicated to learn, they are very difficult to achieve and to master.

Manioc beer, which can be made in several ways in Quichua culture, is always found at celebrations and circulates freely among participants and performers. Traditionally, manioc beer is served upon arrival, and in the old days women would dance while they served it, a practice that is often followed in the festive atmosphere of Runa Paju dancing. Manioc beer, considered the most defining of beverages in Quichua culture, signals the sociality of Quichua culture and evokes viscerally the positive values and themes also echoed in Runa Paju music: strength, the food system, the beauty of Quichua women, masculine-feminine complementarity, and the connectedness of the Quichua community to the earth.

The dancing and drinking goes on all night until the early morning hours, and the performers usually stop when the people have drunk and danced to the point of exhaustion. However, it is at this point that fights, conflicts, and problems sometimes begin to happen. The violence during late night parties is a complex issue, for it usually involves men who have drunk a lot and become overwhelmed by their anger for some perceived lack of respect or transgression against their family or community. As Neil Whitehead's (2007) piece "Violence and the Cultural Order" has shown, violence is not always a simply negative kind of behavior that causes the total breakdown of meaning. Indeed, just a few generations ago it was a common practice in wedding festivals, during the late-night drinking, to have competitions among men to see who was the strongest. As many people told me, these ancients practiced a kind of ritual wrestling that was like fighting but in which using the hands or punching was not allowed.

The violence that characterizes "big dancing nights" is part of the larger social logic of breaking down social barriers. Stimulated by the physiological and mental effects of alcohol, in the ritual space of cosmological communitas, people shed their normal social inhibitions and let feelings, and felt bodily strength, become more dominant. These moments can be liberating, but sometimes violent scenes emerge. Most of the time the conflicts are resolved, and the party goes on without any further repercussions. Over the past few years, however, the violence at social gatherings has diminished, mainly because the government is now enforcing laws against fighting, and people fear possible legal repercussions.

Napo Quichua Evangelicals, who are a minority compared to Catholics and non-Christians, participate in the cosmological communitas created by *atun tushuna tutas*, but in a way that does not break down or collapse all social barriers, just some of them. Evangelicals or *kirikuna* (believers), for example, are expected to follow rules of no dancing, no excessive drinking, no smoking, and no getting angry (Uzendoski 2003). Evangelicals can and do participate in festivals or celebrations where Runa Paju music is present, but they do not normally dance; they watch others dance, tell stories and jokes, and talk about the events going on around them, as well as interact with people who are drinking and dancing. They also consume manioc beer and bottled beer in moderation, but they are careful not to get drunk. Most Evangelicals go home early while other people stay up late drinking and dancing.

Evangelicals do not see Quichua culture as contradictory to their Christian identities; on the contrary, they see themselves as being fully Quichua. In this sense the Evangelicals are the same as the Catholic Runa, who are the majority. While contradictions are present, Evangelicals still retain the communicative patterns of perspectivism and consider animals to have hidden human subjectivities.[11] Like the Inuit described by Laugrand and Oosten (2009), *kirikuna* consider God to be the superior being within their perspectivist cosmos. In this configuration of forces and powers, God is the supreme "master of animals" (Vilaça and Wright 2009:12). For almost all Quichua people, including Evangelicals and the *yachakguna* or shamans, Yaya Dios (Father God) sits atop the hierarchy of perspectivist relations (Shiguango 2006).

Socially and morally, however, there is a constant struggle among Evangelicals, especially men, to avoid *urmana*, or "falling" (Uzendoski 2003). Falling, a Quichua way of describing moving into a status of "sin" within the Evangelical church, usually involves an episode of excessive drinking, accompanied by dancing, smoking, or infidelity. Indeed, social gatherings where Runa Paju is present create potential moral dilemmas for Evangelical men who feel powerful social and cultural expectations to drink, dance, and smoke (Robbins 2004). The situation is complex, however, because modernity, globalization, television, the shift in language, the money-economy, and consumerism are increasingly powerful forces in Quichua communities—"desire" is not as socially tethered to agricultural practices and rooted in interactions connected to the land as it once was (Uzendoski 2005). While these are complex issues for future research, our main point is that Evangelicals view Runa Paju in a positive way, but the morality of their religious system creates a different experience of the music, one that is both contradictory and congruent with the social expectations of communitas.

We have been arguing that the social space created by the *atun tushuna tuta* brings into being cosmological communitas. Cosmological communitas is a ritual transformation where cosmology is experienced collectively as a journey, and the cosmological journeying elicited through Quichua music displaces the master narratives of the nation-state and modernity. Quichua speakers sometimes gloss the emergence of their cosmological world as *paskana*, or "opening up"—a portal or ritual is enacted that "reverses" the perceptive focus from this world to the spirit world (N. Whitten and D. Whitten 2008); D. Whitten and N. Whitten 1988). As the ritual unfolds, the performers sing songs that poeticize the Napo Runa life cycle and take people on a metaphorical journey of life itself. As people dance or clap their hands through this journey, they also take time to tell stories and make their own "poems" about the journeys in their lives and in the lives of others. The process is one whereby the shared experience and cosmological destiny of Napo Runa life, what Quichua speakers refer to as *kawsay* (see Uzendoski 2005; N. Whitten and D. Whitten 2008), fills up one's embodied consciousness. These social events are cosmological and religious, but religious feeling is evoked through techniques of FGR and musical journeying.

The music and the stories that people tell feature FGRs that shift perspectives from this world toward the mysteries and powers of nonhuman natural beings, spirits, and the subjectivities of the landscape. Despite the newness of the music involved, the techniques of cosmological communitas and musical journeying are very old. For example, sources from the 16th century describe people in this area of Amazonian Ecuador using "celebrations" to feel the presence of the spirits by drinking *chicha* all night long until they "lose all sense" (Ortegòn 1989[1577]:260–261). Thus, while Runa Paju is a new genre of music, it still fills the same social function—the creation of communitas in relation to other people and perspectivist subjectivities.

Conclusion

In this chapter we have tried to explain what Napo Runa people do socially and cosmologically with their contemporary music called Runa Paju. We first discussed the origins of Runa Paju music as defined by the aesthetics of historically constituted experience. Like the old-time music, Runa Paju derives from a communicative relationship and redundancy with local and regional ecology in which the poetics of plants, animals, and the landscape become musicalized and experienced as a greater human-ecological sociality. We also described Quichua music as a dynamic play of couplets that involve sound as well as language, a patterning of sound that Quichua speakers identify through metaphors of the body such as music that "runs in the veins." While analysts often look at the words, music, kinesthetics, and sociocultural significations of musical practices as separate domains of analysis, Quichua speakers perceive and feel their music as an inseparable whole that is defined by the simultaneity of these things. We argued that in modern Quichua music, as in stories, people draw experience and history, but the patterns of meaning are configured so that life, as art, reflects the redundancy and cyclicity of all things living and existing.

We then discussed the idea of figure-ground reversal, or FGR, a process in which art invokes and reorganizes relationships among modernity, people, the environment, and the spirit world. These processes create the collective experience of Amazonian cosmology—not as something that is illusory or unreal—but rather as a cosmological journey in which people's lives become interconnected threads of a larger narrative of life and death. These musical stories, which are told through metaphors and music, are not just about "what happened" but how to live and die the Napo Runa way, and how "we" feel in different places and times along the collective journey.

More specifically, we argued that the point metaphor in Runa Paju music is the figure-ground reversal of life and death, a reversal of perception in which people circulate as food and *samay*, or breath, within their rainforest landscapes. As people live out their lives, they move along different paths of history and experience, and like their ancestors before them, they accept that they will one day become part of the cosmological landscape they themselves have lived. These notions are consistent with how storytelling works, and as in storytelling, the power of Runa Paju is its ability to create metaphors and link them together so that cosmology is experienced from multiple perspectives and within the richness of daily practices.

The cosmological communitas involved in the experience of Runa Paju, or "indigenous magic," is emotional and physically and mentally exhausting. The ritual space of such practices breaks down normal social barriers, and sometimes violence and conflicts occur. Cosmological communitas, as we discussed, is a ritual transformation where cosmology is experienced collectively as a journey, and the cosmological journeying elicited through Runa Paju displaces the master narratives of the nation-state and modernity. In this sense, like the music of the elders, Runa Paju is counterpower (Graeber 2004:35–37; see also N. Whitten and D. Whitten 2008:256), a medium of reorienting perception and its relation to social practices that obviates the basic assumptions and values of modernity and Hispanic life. Like storytelling, Runa Paju draws on Amazonian inscriptions of meaning in the landscape and roots people within Amazonian *allpa*, or land. These processes of social and cosmological transcending are features highlighted in the musical practices of other indigenous peoples as well (Campbell 1995; Seeger 1987; Feld 1982).

There are many qualities of Runa Paju music that we have not been able to explain, as the music as a whole is complex and varied, and our focus here has been the sociality of the cosmological communitas in "opening up" the world. We also have not been able to present or analyze any Evangelical Quichua music, which shares features and themes with Runa Paju, especially an aesthetic emphasis on figure-ground reversals of life and death, bodily power and *samay* regeneration, and opening up the world. We hope that future researchers can provide, for example, more details about the history of Quichua music, descriptions of other songs and groups, and more detailed analysis of the musical styles and ways of dancing involved. However, as we argue throughout this book, no analysis of Quichua or other performative practices will be complete, for to analyze the lived realities of others is to emphasize certain aspects of what is a more complex, infinite whole of relations. But we can say with confidence, as the final word on this chapter, following Anthony Seeger (in Campbell 1995:19), that whenever Quichua music is present, the body is doing something socially, culturally, and cosmologically potent, as Runa Paju is modern music of the ancient Quichua storytelling soul.

CONCLUSION

Throughout this book we are concerned with discussing how Quichua speakers use storytelling to make sense of experience and create poetic, spiritual relations among people, ecology, and the larger world they inhabit. We try to convey not just the stories but also the stories behind the stories. We hope that readers can more fully appreciate the complexity and beauty of storytelling as a living, community practice of shared art, experience, and meaning.

In our presentations of the materials, we use a multimodal strategy. Readers can read our ethnopoetic translations in the book; then, by going online, they can also hear digital copies of original Quichua performances and listen to English translations. Although digital media enhances the printed word, it is not a substitute for experiencing storytelling in situ, in the context of the community and the ground, the earth, in which it is located.

We insist that stories in the Amazonian world, unlike books in the West, are considered relational and inalienable. By this we mean that stories, in their original social context, are not meant to be transformed into "things" (such as "Dickens," "Amazonian folklore," or MP3 files) nor canonized. Stories are part of the dynamic process of making and dissolving social relations and engender complex, interwoven meanings that exist among tellers, listeners, and the spirits that inhabit the landscape.

The community of storytellers originates in *kallari pacha*, or the beginning of time and space itself. Storytelling creates relationships with subjects inside the story, such as the mountain Chiuta (see chapter 2) or the Supay Rumi rock (see chapter 1). To tell a story is to invoke a living presence, a world of complex interrelations that define Amazonian reality. The story in this sense opens up a pathway, a "line" of religious thought and experience, one that is traveled spiritually and socially. We saw various pathways come into being through stories that elicited axis mundi relations, relations of interconnection among different planes of existence: the Iluku tale, women's songs, the origin of the sun, the Cuillurguna cycle, and modern Quichua music (see chapters 3, 4, 5, 6, and 8). Stories create relations of social and religious being.

Let us now summarize in detail the stories and different Amazonian Quichua genres presented in this book and their relations, the flow of materials and the story within.

We begin with an analysis of a vapor-bath cleansing that Michael experienced in Campo Cocha with Fermin Shiguango, a *yachak*, or healer, with whom Michael lived during his first fieldwork period in 1994. We also describe the aesthetics of manioc lines in the manioc poem by Edith's brother Federico. Lastly, we present a transcription of a shamanic song of power by Edith's uncle Chuyaki.

These materials reveal the multimodal and multisensory complexity of Quichua storytelling, music, and ritual performances, all of which emphasize the body's central role in the creation of artistic meaning, meaning that is visceral, emotional, and dramatic. In this sense, we describe Quichua storytelling as "somatic poetry," for Quichua storytelling always involves the body and one's experience of the body's various subjectivities, feelings, and hidden powers. Somatic poems, which are defined by experiences and relations as well as language, are basically indescribable and untranslatable, as their full meaning depends upon being able to experience the story holistically through and with the body.

In chapter 2, we present two stories and a song about *izhu punzha*, or judgment day. *Izhu punzha*, as we show, is a primordial story of destruction and remaking of the world. In these stories, the ancestors of today's Amazonian Quichua speakers were saved atop a powerful and magical mountain named Chiuta, a mountain that is the symbolic hearth of Upper Napo Quichua speakers living near the Tena region. The *izhu punzha* stories teach us that the world is constantly in flux and that no order, no state, no state of dominance will last forever. *Izhu punzha* is both a past and future reality, often embedded in the tellings of other stories and songs. For example, in the story of "The Twins and the Jaguars," the storyteller embeds in his story a line about how on *izhu punzha* the mythological jaguars will rise up again (see chapters 5 and 6). *Izhu*, thus, is the beginning and the end of all Quichua stories. Quichua aesthetics are always defined by circularity in the last instance.

We next present two stories about celestial transformations, the Iluku story and the origin of the sun story. As we show, Iluku, the mother of the twins or culture heroes, is the analogical mother of all Quichua-speaking peoples while the sun, which is a one-eyed anaconda, is analogic of masculine potency and the human penis. Both of these stories involve complex aesthetics of experience and ecology; in both stories, axis mundi imagery is central. When it is a full moon, one can sometimes hear Iluku calling out to her lover, "myyy bellllovvved husssband," a mimetic outpouring of her desire and longing to be with her husband, the moon man. Whether it is Iluku or the storyteller, the sounds of Iluku's song, her presence, are real and felt by all. Similarly, the story of the anaconda and the sun show us that celestial bodies, like many plants and animals of mythology, were at one time part of the human domain and integral to cycles of human reproduction. "Nature," which is a meaningless concept in the Quichua world, is a transformed humanity, a somatic interconnectedness in which all things are linked through axis mundi relations.

Chapter 4 is a detailed study of six women's songs, the Breast Song, Dove Woman, Rubber Tapping Woman, Birds and Flowers, Huallaga, and Fish. These songs are defined by feminine shape-shifting relations between birds and women, fish and women, as well as identities located within historical periods, such as the rubber boom. Here we point out the more condensed quality of the musicalized spoken word, which, as in storytelling, allows the voice to evoke principles of form and sound to attract power to the body—women then use that power for social action. These songs, we argue, are manifestations of the shamanic power of Quichua strongwomen to attract men, powers, and abilities necessary for good living. The lesson here is that many people, especially women, who do not officially occupy the office of being a shaman or *yachak* still practice shamanistic arts in their daily lives.

Chapters 5, 6, and 7 discuss the culture heroes of the Napo Quichua world, the Cuillurguna or twins. The sons of the union of the moon man and Iluku, the twins were sent by God to make the world safe for human civilization. Chapter 5's main theme, "becoming a jaguar," shows that the twins are shape-shifting beings, mythical humans infused with jaguar substance and power. This story is analogized by the ritual experience of *puma yuyu*, a plant that connects people to the *ushay*, or power, of mythical jaguars. Chapter 6 looks at the Cuillurguna overthrowing the oppressive regimes of the jaguar father-mother and the birds of prey. The twins created a new "space" (*pacha* or *lugar* in Quichua) in which we people could reproduce and thrive. And, like the storytellers and musicians featured in this book, the Cuillurguna always achieve the making of "space" through creativity, humor, music, and artfulness.

Chapter 7 discusses the way the twins inscribed their presence into the landscape by creating petroglyphs, rock art that connects people to the world of *kallari timpu*, or the beginning times. As living things possessing subjectivity and power, the petroglyphs Puma Rumi (Tena), Puma Rumi (Puma Yacu), and Sapo Rumi (Achi Yacu) are sites of landscape textuality. As sites of axis mundi relationality, the petroglyphs link people and stories socially to the land that the Upper Napo Quichua speakers inhabit. The petroglyphs, for Quichua speakers, continue to be living objects that inspire wonder and sociality with the twins and beginning time-space.

We finish our discussion of the twins with a poem-story of their ascent into the sky. Having finished their work here on earth, the twins decide to go the upper world and thus become part of the celestial world. The twins say goodbye to each other, and each brother takes a different path. They transform into a star, the Venus star, which shines brightly in the early morning hours and the evening. Cuillur is the morning version, and Dociru comes around at night.

The Cuillurguna have taught humanity many things. They taught people to be hardworking, clever, magical, and musical. They showed us how to set traps for enemies and prey, who, as they told us, will also one day will set traps for us. The twins also revealed, as in the *izhu* stories, that no world order lasts forever and that we all must die and move on to another state of being. The twins also taught us about the value of kinship, love, laughter, and shared experience.

Our own journey with storytelling has been inspired by the elders and the Cuillurguna, who helped us comprehend the deeper realities and questions hidden within storytelling practices. As many of our mentors commented, to really know a story is to understand something about the world and the human experience of Amazonian life. What we realized was that stories create a stirring of the soul. This stirring, as discussed in chapter 7, is the hidden power of the story, as its textuality is in one's relation to the world, within what the philosopher William James (1967:135) described as "the crudity of experience."

However, unlike Christianity, the religious qualities of storytelling do not have an accompanying "theology" or discourse that comments about the hidden meanings and mysteries of the stories. People are expected to confront the questions of "Who am I?" and "What is my relation to the world?" directly through their own experiences and in relationship to the problems and issues of life itself. Artistic expressions are how Amazonian peoples confront such issues aesthetically as well as philosophically.

We finish our journey into Quichua storytelling with a discussion of the modern musical genre Runa Paju, a genre that features clever Quichua lyrics, electronic amplification, and eclectic use of instruments and musical styles.

Our argument focuses on the social dynamics of the music and its relationship to Quichua cosmology and mythological thought. We argue that, like other kinds of global music, Runa Paju deconstructs its own conditions of production. It is music made with machines and in modernity, but Runa Paju, or Runa Magic, is music that invokes the *kallari,* or beginning ways, of thinking and feeling. The five pillars of Runa Paju music are the poetics of the Quichua language, Quichua socioculture and traditions, the kinestheics of indigenous dance, mythology, and the ecology of the Amazonian landscape.

The artful techniques of "opening up the world," as we show, are similar for Runa Paju as they are for the other genres. Like the storyteller, the Runa Paju musician uses his or her art to link together stories with the larger narrative of life experience. In this sense, as in the vapor-bath ritual of chapter 1, Runa Paju brings into artistic contour the experiences of life's problems and experiences with a larger narrative of cosmological destiny. To achieve this "work of art," which targets the human soul, however, musicians must "reverse" many of the superficial or apparent relations by which modern life is structured. Using techniques of figure-ground reversals, musicians disentangle the threads of modernity and reconnect them to cosmology. The threads of Quichua life become newly interwoven into musical pathways of cosmological communitas and *kallari.*

The things that Runa Paju musicians do with their art follows upon the traditions of the elders in that Runa Paju musicians create art embedded in history. Like the figures of the mythology itself, the modern artist uses the present to define and enrich the relations of *kallari*, which cannot occur without a contemporary time-space context of experience. In this sense, there is a common thread throughout all of the materials we present in this book, in that they are in and of the body, which, in the Amazonian world, is a complex web of spiritual and social relations that extends through the community of people, through history, through individual lives, into the myriad forms and beings of the landscape and the ancestors.

We argue that somatic poetry is a shared philosophy of life and art that defines all the materials in this book. Somatic poems, we hope to have shown, connect the individual life to the history of a community and its landscape in a way in which experience itself becomes tangled up with the stories and history of the place (see Casey 1993, 1997, 2001). There is no "nature" divorced from "culture" (see Latour 1993; Kohn 2007); nor does there exist an arrogant humanity that considers itself superior to all other living and existing things. This humility, this interconnectedness, this grounding, and the liberation it provides to the soul, are the secret of *kallari* that we learned from our mentors and relatives, the essence of their teachings.

In the general literature about verbal art and oral poetry, the practices of Native Amazonian artists deserve more recognition and discussion in relationship to the Western and Latin American greats, who continue to overshadow the living practices of indigenous peoples (Finnegan 2007). For example, even the comparative approach of Alfred Lord (1960), a major contribution to the field of ethnopoetics, potentially creates tensions with regard to non-Western cultural traditions. We find, for example, the elevation of Homer above poets and singers of all other cultural traditions to be problematic[1]. Homer is indeed a great poet, but he does not transcend culture, history, and society, and there is no reason to build a general model of oral poetry for all of humanity out of one man's contributions. The reason Homer is considered to be a transcendent figure is because he is a crucial part of the Western canon and the importance of the ancient Greeks in Western philosophy. The reason Amazonian storytellers are ignored is because the West does not understand nor embrace the philosophy of perspectivism and the mode of life that defines it (Latour 2009).

We would never label any of the artists or traditions in this book as inferior versions of Homer or Shakespeare or place them into a temporally previous category of "orality." As discussed in the introduction, we reject Walter Ong's and Jack Goody's neo-evolutionary, linear approach that supposes that orality is previous and lesser than alphabetic writing. We begin with perspectivism and the communicative philosophy that defines storytelling and music in the Amazonian world. It is only by grasping the textuality of the landscape and ecology that one can begin to appreciate the stories of many indigenous peoples, peoples who view rootedness in the land as a defining social and textual quality of life (Abram 1996).

As shown in various chapters, in today's era of globalization, oral textuality is one of many kinds of communicative practices circulating in the Amazonian world that is combined with alphabetic writing and other communicative technologies in creative ways to create new, hybrid forms of expression (chapters 4, 7, and 8). These forms of expression are not corruptions but enhancements that still reflect Amazonian communicative values. Specifically, as discussed, Napo Runa expressions, even the hybrid forms, emphasize the power of the human voice to connect the body to place and the cosmos via experience in the world.

In a symmetrical anthropology (Latour 1993), there is no room for implicit or veiled neocolonialisms, as systems of communication are not "modern" versus "pre-modern" but rather different ways of defining, engaging, and experiencing the world. Indeed, we hope that the materials in this book can serve as one example of the diversity of philosophies and practices of communication that are distorted when framed by Western categories and values, especially the modernist project of "alphabetizing" all human thought and action. The power of culture lies in its ability to shape one's very perception of what communication is and how it works, as communication is the very stuff of human thought and action (Handler 2004; Silverstein 2004). One's own communicative practices, which seem so familiar and natural, are not universal, however, when put to the test of immersed ethnographic research. The people of the West, the lettered people, still have much to learn from others about communication and alternate ways of conceptualizing textuality.

The great artists in our lives are those found in this book. They are real people, our relatives, people with whom we share life as well as art. We hope to have shown they are not just good storytellers, musicians, and artists but also amazingly wise people. These people, mostly elders, have taught us that the secret to good living is to live life aesthetically, as if every day, every relation, every word, every action and pause in life were the creation of poetry, poetry in the somatic sense of aesthetic relationality to the world. In a time of globalization, where so many things are defined by alienation, commodification, and manipulation, there is a great need for such practices, for more life poetry, somatic poetry, the poetry of experience and place. For your teachings we thank you, Nachu Yaya, Mama Bicha, Lucas, Carmela, Verna, Gervacio, Camilo, Jacinta, Anibal, Federico, Yaya Santiago, Bolivar, Fermin, our dear compadre Carlos Alvarado, and the rest of the Runa Paju artists.

NOTES

Introduction. What Is Storytelling?

1. The Napo Runa are Amazonian Quichua speakers of which there are perhaps fifty thousand or more speakers. Although they are an ethnicity that was formed in the colonial period (see Uzendoski 2004a; Uzendoski 2005), Napo Runa stories are much older and have their roots in the substrate groups that later became Quichua speakers: the Quijos, Omagua, and Zapara, as well as others. See chapters 2 and 5 for more details on these transculturation processes. Also, the current accepted spelling of the language is "Kichwa" rather than "Quichua." We have decided to go with the spelling "Quichua" (signaling Ecuadorian dialects) so that the language's link to Quechua (Peruvian dialects) is clear.

2. Amazonia has always attracted scientific and anthropological attention, but less known are the contributions of the peoples of this region to the humanities. Indeed, the general public associates Amazonia with a threatened natural paradise and as a repository of valuable plants and animals, but the mythology of this region is as vital to understanding the place as ecology or politics (Slater 2002).

3. To learn about the way Amazonian people organize communication around and through the power and potentialities of the body's expressiveness is an opportunity to learn about the liberating possibilities of a more holistic view of communication. This holistic view contrasts with the Western notion that the pinnacle of human achievement is the "lettered self" (Rotman 2008) and the productive apparatus of printing, circulating, and consuming books and other printed matter.

4. English speakers do not just view Other cultures but also their own through the narrow prism of the alphabetic empire. In the cultural patterning of the English-speaking world, poetry and artful language are domains of practice that are left to specialists, students, musicians, and interest groups, but not defining of how language and communication are perceived and practiced. Poetics, left to the poets, is not part of the master

narrative of the modernistic machine-driven lifestyle. However, as many researchers have shown, there are lots of "poetics" and artful word-use in any language.

5. Walter Ong, "Writing Is a Technology That Restructures Consciousness," Warhaft Lecture, University of Manitoba. Recorded 26 Jan. 1984. (Time: 1:34:07, 86.1 MB). Available at http://cdm.slu.edu/, accessed June 7, 2011.

6. In the scheme of "orality" versus "literacy," which is developed in detail in the written work *Orality and Literacy* (1982), Ong frames the so-called oral cultures as being both previous and less advanced than literate ones. Orality, here, like other classifications of "savagery" in the past, is thought to be a universal state that defines all Others.

7. Ong (1982: 175) writes: "I have never encountered or heard of an oral culture that does not want to achieve literacy as soon as possible. . . . Yet orality is not despicable. . . . Nor is orality ever completely eradicable: reading a text oralizes it. But orality and the growth of literacy out of orality are necessary for the evolution of consciousness."

8. "Stated in the language of oral narrative, a belief emerges that can be compared to the "literacy hypothesis" of Jack Goody, which, simply stated, claims that only with alphabetic literacy was it possible for Western people to develop the critical and logical mental skills that enabled them to achieve the scientific and technological advances of the last several hundred years (1977:37) [Guss 1986: 425].

9. There is also nothing absolute about "nature," which we insist does not really exist. "Nature," as shown by Bruno Latour (2005:110), was an idea, a "collector" or category for classifying reality that was invented (along with "society") by Western peoples in the 17th century.

10. Bruno Latour (2009:2) considers that perspectivism could be considered a "bomb with the potential to explode the whole implicit philosophy so dominant in most ethnographers' interpretations of their material." Perspectivism—a collectively authored philosophy wrought by Amazonian peoples—should have its place in the world's canon of revolutionary discoveries. It is unfortunate, for example, that many people of the ecological movement are unfamiliar with perspectivist philosophies and continue to draw on Western ideas without acknowledging that Amazonian peoples have already "discovered" what ecocritics are searching for.

11. For example, our storytelling world stretches far beyond the Upper Napo Tena/Archidona cultural hearth to also overlap with Quito (the capital of the Northern Inkan empire) and Upper and Lower Napo and extend into the Huallaga and Maroñón Rivers of Peru. The storytelling world, as well, includes petroglyphs, mountains, rivers, and other features of the landscape, features that are implicit to storytelling's semiotic complexity.

12. At this time, the impacts of new technologies, the Internet, and other digital tools upon Napo Quichua culture, however, are still yet to be fully known. Unlike a generation ago, today's Napo Runa youth participate in YouTube, Facebook, and other social networking technologies; these youth are adept at, and enjoy, using cameras, videos, and the latest smart-phone technology.

Chapter 1. Somatic Poetry

1. The "natural" divide between our reality and their reality (Viveiros de Castro 1998) creates a communication barrier, but when this barrier is traversed, one is thrust into religious experiences that involve power, beauty, and danger.

2. When Amazonian Quichua speakers experience and express beauty, they not only use words but also interweave them with images, memory, life experiences, ecology, and social processes. Somatic poetry is not a practice or set of practices that is divorced from life or the daily concerns of social relations (Finnegan 2007). On the contrary, similar to Kohn's notion of the "anthropology of life," somatic poetry is an attitude whereby people approach the animacy and subjectivities of life (in its widest possible sense) through aesthetic practices that involve but are not limited to human expression. These practices are part of defining social and cosmological relationships and "doing things" in the world (Finnegan 2007). Quichua speakers and other native peoples know that "beauty" is a relationship or series of relationships rather than just a stand-alone "object" or a "thing" (Uzendoski 2008; Kohn 2007; Nuckolls 1996, 2000). The term "somatic" refers to the body, but in the Quichua world the body is not exclusively human; the body, as defined by *samay* or soul substance, is interconnected with other bodies, plants, animals, and the surrounding landscape. The body itself implies the perspectivist relations of an intersubjective landscape so that any expression, including poetic ones, implies the body's relationship to other powers, forces, and beings.

3. Barbara Tedlock (2005) prefers the term "shamanic states of consciousness" to "altered states of consciousness" because shamans often combine knowledge gained through altered states with "insights that take place while they are cognitively aware or lucid" (80). The crucial point for us in Tedlock's argument is that there are various ways to use the shamanic "imagination" in order to travel, shape-shift, or perceive the bodies of the sick or afflicted.

4. We thank Norman E. Whitten Jr. for this insight.

5. Mimesis is most often discussed as reflecting the transference of power created through making "copies" (representations) of original things (Benjamin 1979; Callois 1984; Stoller 1995; Taussig 1993), but here, as in many other rituals, mimesis is simultaneously organized around substance embodiment and contact (Taussig 1993:111).

6. The main requirement is to make a sincere and sustained effort to participate in the world of the field, not as an arrogant outsider, but as someone who takes participation, and the critical interpretation of that participation, seriously. Fabian has argued that the process of working through such experiences is a requirement of good ethnography: "critically understood, autobiography is a condition of ethnographic objectivity" (Fabian 2001:7; see also Goulet and Miller 2007:7; B. Tedlock 1991).

7. We say that it is dramatic because of the poetics involved and the drama (action) of bodily healing. We realize that all poetry is not necessarily dramatic, but drama is central to somatic poems of healing.

8. A week later our group went on a camping trip on Wasila Mountain, and all noticed that indeed there was strong odor of "perfume," most likely from some kinds of flowers, up on the mountain. The fragrant qualities of the ecology, thus, are also part of the shamanic poetry of Chuyaki's world.

9. The analogy here is one that is also present in the Cuillurguna, who are also "many things" and embody the qualities and powers of a variety of "substances." The relation here is one of the unity of diversity, a poetics of experience and place that defines the Napo Quichua world (see chapter 6).

10. Sharimiat Shiguango (2006), a sociologist and Napo Quichua leader, has written an insightful book on Napo Quichua shamanism in which he provides an insider's analysis

of shamanic songs. Shiguango mentions that shamanic sounds are ways of harmonizing energies of the spirit world with the body of the patient, and that the repetition of sounds like "ri" and other shamanic "sacred words" open up shamanic consciousness so that the healer "sees" directly into the body of the patient. Shiguango also reports that the shaman does not compose his song. The spirits, who are servants working for God, "possess" the shaman. The shaman, thus, is not singing from a human perspective, but rather from the perspective of the spirits of the lands, the same forces that also give him or her power.

11. Although Napo Quichua shamans do not insert Christian themes or God into their *takina* songs, it is implicit in their religious cosmology that they are working with God instead of against him. Many shamans feel persecuted by Catholics and Evangelical authorities who consider that a *yachak* works with the devil (Shiguango 2006).

Chapter 2. Primordial Floods and the Expressive Body

1. As the Amazonian anthropologist Peter Gow has discussed, there is a methodological flaw in assuming that mythological traditions, like societies, are, in Leach's words, "stable systems geared to self-identical reproduction through time" (Gow 2001: 20).

2. The social theory implicit in flood myths is not an emphasis on controlling or building society upon the "natural," as is the case in the Western world, but of transforming social relations through interactions and co-creation with the forces, powers, subjectivities, and energies of the landscape, what might be termed phenomenological others (Ricoeur 1992), who, like people, have "souls," "culture," and communicative competence within their own existential realities. In the mythological world, all things have sociality, and all processes in life are perceived as social happenings.

Chapter 3. The Iluku Myth, the Sun, and the Anaconda

1. Ecological others should not, as they commonly are, be referred to through the simple abstraction of "nature," for, as the Bruno Latour (2005:110) has showed us, "nature" is not a reality but a "collector" that was invented in the Western world, along with its twin concept of "society," for political reasons in the 17th century. Like society, the "humanity" of nature is all about relationality, a relationality that flows through and defines human existence at every turn of thought and action.

2. In the region of Iquitos this bird is known as the *ayamama*, or "mother of the spirits," by mestizos and ribereños. These stories are distinct from the Iluku ones and often rely on scenes or ideas from European folklore (such as Hansel and Gretel). All of the stories, however, revolve around an axis mundi of sound between the earth and the moon and involve a channel of desire or love among kin.

3. This theory, which was most elegantly expressed in Albert Bates Lord's (1960) *Singer of Tales*, argues that oral performances are categorically distinct from written works and that "orality's" great challenge is memorization. Storytellers, according to this theory, use "formulas" by which to remember epics and stories of great length without the use of writing.

4. The one-eyed anaconda is mimetic of the human penis, an association implicit in other aspects of Amazonian Quichua culture (see Uzendoski 2005; N. Whitten 2009).

Chapter 4. Birds and Humanity

1. These trips ceased with the border war with Peru in 1941, which closed off trade from the Upper Napo region downriver toward Amazonia. Trade upriver (into the Andes) and downriver has been a feature of this area for quite some time and can also be shown to be central to pre-Hispanic dynamics (Uzendoski 2004a).

2. Because Quichua speakers do not separate time from space, this theme of traveling evokes temporal as well as spatial movement; powerful beings are able to move through different *pacha*, or worlds of space-time (see D. Whitten and N. Whitten 1988; N. Whitten and D. Whitten 2008).

Chapter 5. The Twins and the Jaguars

1. "The Twins and the Jaguars" is one of the most important Amazonian Quichua stories. It is a long story with many happenings. In the story, the twins, the sons of Iluku and the culture heroes of the Napo Quichua people, are born, grow up, and go to work ridding the world of its mythological beasts. Thus starts a cycle of predatory "miracles" where the twins make the world safe for humanity (chapter 6). The twins cycle ends when they ascend into the sky and turn into stars (chapter 7).

2. Although they are beyond the scope of this chapter, sizeable numbers of speakers of Amazonian Quichua also exist in Colombia and Peru. For example, Iquitos, Peru, one of the central places of commerce during the rubber boom, also has heavy Amazonian Quichua influence in the Spanish of its urban inhabitants.

3. In other versions of this myth the woman is actually impregnated by her brother, who later goes up into the sky and becomes the moon. In this version you can see that the teller has syncretized his knowledge of the Bible with his knowledge of the mythical world. By likening the twins' mother to the Virgin Mary, the narrator expresses the divine nature of the twins (see Muratorio 1991 for a discussion of the Virgin Mary in Napo Quichua conversations).

4. In this usage the narrator has inserted the marker *lla*, which means "just" in this case. Here the marker is adding to the precise nature of the jaguars being in the middle of the bridge.

5. The stanza begins with the simple opposition of twins and jaguars but later develops into a triad of twins, lone jaguar, and jaguar brothers. As the jaguar brothers enter onto the bridge, they come together forming a whole again. The stanza thus begins with dualism, moves to triadism, and ends in dualism again. It is the narrator's use of the "-shkawa" suffix that moves the action from one party to the next, setting up and obviating structures via ensuing events.

6. See Nuckolls (1996:252–255) for a more detailed discussion of "*dzas.*"

7. *Kushni*, or "smoke," has many symbolic connotations in the narrative and in Napo Runa culture in general. Smoke is essential to shamanic healing, and smoke signals transformations. For example, when the shaman blows smoke over the patient's body, it is said to "open up the body" so that the shaman can see sickness. Smoke also has healing properties in itself, as it carries away pathogens when it is "blown" away as in the case of a "cleansing" event. In the narrative the smoke also conveys the escaping of the jaguars'

vital energy, which signals their transformation from "human" form into stone. Smoke is a vehicle for, and makes visible, energy that is normally unseen.

8. The Napo environment is typically one of relatively fertile, volcanic soils. Rivers are laden with rocks and fast-moving water, in contrast to the ecosystems further east that are characterized by slower-moving rivers with "sand" bottoms (Villavicencio 1984[1858]). The environment makes possible the abundance of stones to make the bridge, as well as speaking to the danger of crossing rivers. Stones of power are said to have *kawsay*, life that you can see if you look into the center.

9. Nancy Hornberger (1992) found that Quechua narratives from the Department of Cusco contain patterning of threes and fives. She writes, "the clear showing of relationships of three and five in this major South American language is of theoretical significance to the verse-analysis approach to narrative, in that it confirms patterns which have already been identified in other oral narrative traditions" (Hornberger 1992:450). We suggest the rhetorical patterning of Hornberger's and our analysis might be linked to the importance of number representations among many South American (Carpenter 1992; Crocker 1969, 1985; Levi-Strauss 1963, 1976; Murra, Watchel, and Revel 1986; Urton 1997; Zuidema 1964, 1990).

10. Theses configurations of death parallel A. C. Taylor's consideration of how Amazonian selves are configured out of two seemingly contradictory views of death, the "naturalistic" versus the "persecutory" (Taylor 1996). On the one hand the death of the twins' mother drives them to commit vengeance homicide against their jaguar relatives. On the other hand, the death of the twins' mother seems part of a larger divine plan by which humankind finds new life through the cycles of death and killing. Just as humans and jaguars are in a duality-unity relation, so too are life and death. "Naturalistic" death is really a consideration of death from the point of view of life.

11. The dualism-unity relation here is similar to the *yanatin* relation common to highland Quechua cultures. Writes Catherine Allen (1988:187), "antagonists automatically paired themselves with their most equal counterpart. Rivals in battle, like lovers, are *yanatin* (a matched pair; helpmates). . . . Any release of energy—whether constructive or destructive—calls for collaboration."

12. The role of the *Cuillurguna* in the narrative—intervention—is analogous to the shamanic role of mediating the "mystical means of reproduction" (see Santos Granero 1986). The shaman, like the *Cuillurguna*, intervenes into the mystical realm in order to effect the reproduction of life.

Chapter 6. The Cuillurguna

1. The story's geography harkens back to a time when the larger Tena area, the current capital and populated city in Napo, was insignificant, and Archidona was the seat of Amazonian civilization. Many Quichua people who now live in Tena or elsewhere, for example, trace their origins to Archidona, and, historically, Archidona was the first "settlement" to be created in this region.

2. Historically, as Muratorio's (1991) and Reeve's (1993) work have shown, this is an area that was once frequented by Quichuas of Napo to gather salt and transport rubber during the rubber boom. But ethnohistorical evidence shows that these long-distance

relations have pre-Hispanic roots predating these colonial epochs (Uzendoski 2004a). The mythology reflects the free-flowing geographical complexity of Amazonian-Andean regional and historical relations, relations that were not in the past constrained by the nation-state borders of Peru and Ecuador as they are today.

Chapter 8. Cosmological Communitas in Contemporary Amazonian Music

1. This is a beginning study, as Runa Paju is a huge and complex emergent cultural phenomenon in the Napo Quichua world. We do not pretend to be able to describe it in all its complexity, nor do we provide classifications of musical styles. To this day there is not a single study that has been done on Runa Paju in English, and there is only one source in Spanish (AACTIN 1991). We hope that future scholars will take interest in this music and provide further insights into its forms, cultural processes, socialities, and characteristics.

2. The Playeros Quichua, for example, sometimes call their music "techno-Quichua."

3. *Figure-ground* is defined by the Apple dictionary as "relating to or denoting the perception of images by the distinction of objects from a background from which they appear to stand out, esp. in contexts where this distinction is ambiguous." Figure-ground reversals are ways of dissolving one set of relations into another, forms that disarticulate what was once in focus as a new "image" or reality emerges. See Roy Wagner (1986) for a sophisticated anthropological account of figure-ground reversals in relationship to symbolic realities and anthropology in general.

4. Communitas is, according to Victor Turner (1967, 1969), a moment in the ritual process where people come together as equals due to the temporary dissolution of social structure (Morris 1987). The notion also refers to shared intimacy and conviviality created in the ritual space of liminality (Mentore 2007). In contradistinction to Victor Turner's emphasis on structural processes and typologies, we follow more recent reconfigurations of communitas that foreground people's experiences and specifically those approaches that include spiritual and unseen subjectivities within the intimacies of ritual action (E. Turner 2006). Edith Turner, who is working on a book on this topic, comments that communitas "is hard to describe in words, ephemeral and ineffable. It can be said to be the great feeling of all being together, and having extraordinary or terrible times together, a feeling that doesn't necessarily last very long" (Mentore 2009:xiv).

5. At this time, the geographical political mapping of Napo Province also included Lower Napo. Today Lower Napo is the province of Orellana.

6. In recounting his life history, Carlos Alvarado points out that when he was a child he would follow his parents, without their permission, to weddings and compadrazgo rituals, as his father was a *pingullo* (bone flute) player (AACTIN 1991). He would wait until everybody became drunk, and then he would pick up the violin that had been left on the ground. He began to play it, but his parents got very upset that he did this. As a punishment, they would rub his face and eyes with hot peppers the next morning for his charade. But during the weddings the people danced to the rudimentary violin music he produced, and sometimes the group of people implored his parents to allow him to keep playing, "so that the drunks would dance instead of fight" (73). So he kept attending the weddings and festivals, and playing the violin, despite the fact that his parents punished him every time by rubbing hot peppers in his eyes the next morning.

7. In the Quichua world, manioc plants and manioc gardening are symbolically conceptualized as a mother-child relationship, and the garden represents an extension of the feminine body (Uzendoski 2005). The Lumu Mama song creatively implies the complexities of these meanings in its imagery and use of poetic phrasings, phrasings that invoke the oral textuality of manioc garden space.

8. William Belzner has also noted the predominance of "threes" in Amazonian Quichua music. He writes in an analysis of a shamanic song, "The tonal materials are essentially tritonic; the three predominant tones being the 'tonic,' and the major third and perfect fifth above this 'tonic,' giving the impression of Western music's major triad" (Belzner and Whitten 1979).

9. The Apple dictionary [Version 2.0.2 (51.4)] defines *fractal* as, "a curve or geometric figure, each part of which has the same statistical character as the whole. Fractals are useful in modeling structures (such as eroded coastlines or snowflakes) in which similar patterns recur at progressively smaller scales, and in describing partly random or chaotic phenomena such as crystal growth, fluid turbulence, and galaxy formation." Please see Mosko and Damon (2005) for a more sophisticated account of the use of fractals and chaos theory in anthropology.

10. The website of the William R. and Clarice V. Spurlock Museum, University of Illinois at Urbana-Champaign, describes the piece in this way: "The vessel's top features a humanoid figure from the torso on up wearing a baseball cap and scratching his head with one raised arm. The aperture of the hollow vessel is directly opposite this figure. The main body of the vessel curves down and then flares out again, forming a bottom bulge that is decorated as the coils of an anaconda. The vessel is decorated with a geometric motif on the main body and a scale motif on the serpentine portion. Light brown, dark orange, dark red, and black make up the coloring of the piece" (http://www.spurlock .illinois.edu/search/details.php?a=1997.15.0063).

11. Many people, however, do not like to talk freely about this Quichua-Christiain hybridity, especially with outsiders, because they think that they will be accused of or judged as being "devil worshippers" by non-Native Christians (Engelke 2007). Indeed, since the early colonial period, the indigenous world has never been allowed to develop their own version(s) of Christianity, and associated communicative styles, without coercion from outside authorities (Durston 2007). We cannot do justice to all of these issues in this chapter, but we anticipate future publications dealing with Napo Runa engagements with Christianity (Uzendoski 2003).

Conclusion

1. Lord (1960:xxxv) writes, "This book is about Homer. He is our Singer of Tales. Yet in a larger sense, he represents all singers of tales from time immemorial and unrecorded to the present. Our book is about these singers as well. Each of them, even the most mediocre, is as much a part of the tradition of oral epic singing as is Homer, its most talented representative." But we agree with Lord (1968:46) when he writes, "we all must be willing to learn from the experience of other oral traditional poetries."

CONTENTS OF THE WEBSITE AND DESCRIPTION OF THE MEDIA

The media files on the book's website, http://spokenwordecology.com, are movies, audio files, and image files.* The website was designed by Malcolm Shackelford (Florida State University Libraries), who provided the technical expertise to embed the video and audio players directly onto the site, as well as embedding an image viewer for the viewing of photographs and illustrations. The media files catalogued below are organized by chapter, and each entry contains metadata concerning the title, format, artist or storyteller, date of the recording, location of the recording, social context, and a short summary of its content. Unless otherwise indicated, the reader should assume that the stories and songs are performed in Quichua. All videos contain English subtitles that correspond to the translations in this book.

* This area of the website will contain additional links and embedded videos of Runa Paju music videos available on YouTube.

Chapter 1. Somatic Poetry: Toward an Embodied Ethnopoetics

Title	File type	Artist/Storyteller	Date	Location	Social context	Summary
Chuyaki's Shamanic Song	Audio-movie	Lucas Calapucha (Chuyaki)	2007	Sapo Rumi	Field School	Lucas sings a *takina*, or shamanic song
Chuyaki Blowing	Audio file	Lucas Calapucha (Chuyaki)	2007	Sapo Rumi	Field School	Lucas does a cleansing of a student using shamanic blowing
Fermin with the *Kiru Pangu*	Photo	Fermin Shiguango	2000	Campo Cocha	Visit	Fermin shows the *kiru panga* plant, used in vapor bath healing
Federico and Esteban in the Garden	Photo	Federico Calapucha and Esteban Calapucha	2001	Sapo Rumi	Gardening	Federico and Esteban are in the garden while Federico explains their family history with an analogy to manioc plants
Supay Rumi Rock	Photo	n/a	2009	Sapo Rumi	Daily life	A photograph showing the Supay Rumi rock that is featured in Lucas's shamanic song
Wasila Mountain	Photo	n/a	2010	Sapo Rumi	Daily life	A photograph showing Wasila Mountain, also featured in Lucas's shamanic song

Chapter 2. Primordial Floods and the Expressive Body

Title	File type	Artist/Storyteller	Date	Location	Social context	Summary
Verna's Great Flood Story	Movie	Verna Grefa	2003	Ongota/Dos Ríos	Visit with Fermín Shiguango	A story about the great flood in the beginning times
Chuyaki's Great Flood Story	Audio movie	Lucas Tapuy (Chuyaki)	1996	Sapo Rumi	Visit to his house with Edith Calapucha and others	Another story about the great flood in the beginning times
Camilo's Great Flood Song	Movie	Camilo Tapuy	2004	Sapo Rumi	Visit by Camilo to Sapo Rumi with Lucas Tapuy and Carmela Calapucha present	A song with violin about the great flood in beginning times
Map of the Mountains	Map	n/a	n/a	n/a	n/a	A map that shows the locations of the three mountains in the great flood story
Child's Drawing of Great Flood Myth (1)	Drawing	Génesis Grefa (10 years old)	2010	Pano	Drawing done in school	A picture done in crayon of the great flood myth
Child's Drawing of the Great Flood Myth (2)	Drawing	Sisa Uzendoski-Calapucha	2010	Pano	Drawing done in school	A picture done in crayon of the great flood myth

Chapter 3. The Iluku Myth, the Sun, and the Anaconda

Title	File type	Artist/Storyteller	Date	Location	Social context	Summary
Iluku's Bird Song	Audio	Taped by Mark Hertica	2002	Venecia	n/a	The call of the common potoo bird (Iluku) at night
Verna's Iluku Story	Movie	Verna Grefa	2006	Ongota/Dos Ríos	Visit to Verna's house by Michael, Edith, and Sisa	Story about the origins of the common potoo bird and her relation with the moon
Bolivar's Origin of the Sun Myth	Movie	Gerarado Andi	2002	Pano	Performance during the annual fiesta of Pano	Story about the origins of the sun and the anaconda
Michael's Performance of Iluku Story (English)	Audio	Verna Grefa/ Michael Uzendoski	2009	Tallahassee, Florida	Folklore Festival at the Florida State University	Michael performs his translation of the Iluku story for an academic audience
Painting of Iluku by Jaime Choclote	Painting	Jaime Choclote	n/a	Iquitos, Peru	n/a	Painting of the common potoo bird
Child's Drawing of the Iluku Myth (1)	Drawing	Unknown 5th grader	2010	Pano	School	Drawing with crayons of Iluku in her human form calling out to the moon, her husband
Child's Drawing of the Iluku Myth (2)	Drawing	Génesis Grefa-Andi, 5th grader	2010	Pano	School	Drawing with crayons of Iluku in her bird form calling out to the moon, her husband

Chapter 4. Birds and Humanity: Women's Songs

Title	File type	Artist/Storyteller	Date	Location	Social context	Summary
The Breast Song by Gervacio	Audio movie	Gervacio Cerda	2002?	Limon Cocha	Visit by Santiago Calapucha and Carola Cerda	Song about how to call one's husband back after he has left
Kids Singing the Breast Song	Movie	Camilo Tapuy and his granddaughters	2010	Sapo Rumi	Practice session for a music group dedicated to old time music	The Breast Song performed by Camilo and the younger generation using alphabetic literacy and digital technology as learning tools
Dove Woman by Jacinta	Movie	Jacinta Andi	2002	Pano	Visit by Michael Uzendoski, Edith Calapucha, and other relatives	A song that describes the travels downriver of the singer and her transformation into a dove
Rubber Tapping Woman Song by Jacinta	Movie	Jacinta Andi	2002	Pano	Visit by Michael Uzendoski, Edith Calapucha, and other relatives	A song that describes the singer and her experience related to the rubber boom
Birds and Flowers Song by Serafina	Audio movie	Serafina Shiguango and Vicente Calapucha [violin]	1980's	Sapo Rumi	Visit by Timoteo Tapuy, grandson	A song that describes the singer transforming into various birds, including a hummingbird
Huallaga Song by Serafina	Audio movie	Serafina Shiguango and Vicente Calapucha [violin]	1980's	Sapo Rumi	Visit by Timoteo Tapuy, grandson	A song that describes the singer's travels to the Huallaga River in Peru
Fish Song by Serafina	Audio movie	Serafina Shiguango and Vicente Calapucha [violin]	1980's	Sapo Rumi	Visit by Timoteo Tapuy, grandson	A song that describes the singer becoming a fish and resisting her in-laws trying to get her drunk

Chapter 5. The Twins and the Jaguars

Title	File type	Artist/Storyteller	Date	Location	Social context	Summary
Verna's Twins and Jaguars Myth	Audio movie	Verna Grefa	1994	Ongota/Dos Ríos	Visit by Michael Uzendoski, Fermin Shiguango, and his two songs	A story about the birth and childhood of the twins (Cuillurguna) and how they defeat the jaguars with a bridge trap
Puma Yuyu	Photograph	n/a	2003	Campo Cocha	Visit by Michael	A photograph of the puma yuyu plant (*Teliostacha lanceolata*)
Map of the Path of the Jaguars	Map	n/a	n/a	n/a	n/a	Map depicting the three petroglyph sites mentioned in the twins and jaguars story
Jaguar Woman	Photograph	n/a	1994	Campo Cocha	Festival	Photograph of Fermin Shiguango's mother, a woman reported to have turned into a jaguar upon her death

Chapter 6. The Cuillurguna

Title	File type	Artist/Storyteller	Date	Location	Social context	Summary
Verna's Birds of Prey Myth	Audio movie	Verna Grefa	1994	Ongota/Dos Ríos	Visit by Michael Uzendoski, Fermin Shiguango, and his two songs	A story about how the twins (Cuillurguna) got rid of the birds of prey and transformed the vulture-man into a vulture
Chuyaki's Mundopuma Myth	Audio movie	Lucas Tapuy (Chuyaki)	1996	Sapo Rumi	Visit to his house with Edith Calapucha and others	A story about the upbringing of the twins (Cuillurguna) and how they trap the mundopuma or Father Jaguar in Galera Mountain
El Ductur's Mundopuma Myth	Audio movie	Anibal Andy (El Ductur)	2008	Sapo Rumi	Annual festival of Sapo Rumi/ storytelling open mike contest	A story about how the Twins trap the mundopuma jaguar in Galera Mountain
Path of the Vulture Man	Map	n/a	n/a	n/a	n/a	Map showing the path of the vulture man in the birds of prey story
Child's Drawing of the Mundopuma Myth (1)	Drawing	Sunzure Shiguango, 5th grader	2010	Pano	School	A drawing with crayons of the mundopuma trapped within Galera Mountain
Child's Drawing of the Mundopuma Myth (2)	Drawing	Unknown 5th grader	2010	Pano	School	A pencil sketch of the mundopuma trapped within Galera Mountain

Chapter 7. The Petroglyphs and the Twins' Ascent

Title	File type	Artist/Storyteller	Date	Location	Social context	Summary
Verna Tells the Story of the Petroglyphs	Audio movie	Verna Grefa	1996	Sapo Rumi	Visit by Verna to Sapo Rumi	A story explaining the names of petroglyphs and their connection to the twins (Cuillurguna)
Edith Reads the Twins' Ascent	Audio movie	Edith Calapucha/ Michael Uzendoski	2010	Sapo Rumi	Living in Sapo Rumi	A Quichua story-poem about the twins (Cuillurguna) ascending to heaven and turning into stars
Michael Performs the Twins' Ascent	Audio	Edith Calapucha/ Michael Uzendoski	2010	Chambira, Napo	Congress of "CONAKINO" (Confederation of Organizations Quichua of Napo and Orellana)	Michael performs "The Twins' Ascent" in Quichua in front of a Quichua audience
Michael Reads the Twins' Ascent (English)	Audio	Michael Uzendoski/ Edith Calapucha	2010	Sapo Rumi	Living in Sapo Rumi	Michael reads the English translation of "The Twins' Ascent"
Puma Rumi Petroglyph	Sketch	Adapted from Porras (1985: 134)	n/a	Tena	n/a	A sketch of the design on the Puma Rumi rock near Tena
Puma Rumi (2) Petroglyph	Sketch	Adapted from Porras (1985: 134)	n/a	Puma Yacu	n/a	A sketch of the design on the second Puma Rumi rock near Puma Yacu
Sapo Rumi Petroglyph	Sketch	n/a	n/a	Sapo Rumi	n/a	A sketch of the design on Sapo Rumi rock
Photograph of Sapo Rumi Petroglyph	Photograph	n/a	n/a	Sapo Rumi	n/a	A photograph of the Sapo Rumi petroglyph with kids from the community playing on top of it

Chapter 8. Cosmological Communitas in Contemporary Amazonian Music

Title	File type	Artist/Storyteller	Date	Location	Social context	Summary
Lumu Mama	Audio	Carlos Alvarado and the Yumbos Chawamangos	n/a	n/a	n/a	The famous Runa Paju song Lumu Mama or Manioc Mother
Galera Urku	Audio	Carlos Alvarado and the Yumbos Chawamangos	n/a	n/a	n/a	The Runa Paju song Galera Urku, about the Mundopuma Myth
Grandmother Jacinta	Photograph	n/a	n/a	n/a	n/a	A photograph of Grandmother Jacinta performing her women's songs during the annual fiesta of Sapo Rumi (2008)
Big Dancing Night at Sapo Rumi	Photograph	n/a	n/a	n/a	n/a	Photograph of people dancing to Runa Paju at the annual festival of Sapo Rumi
Los Yumbos Chawamangos	Photograph	n/a	n/a	n/a	n/a	Photograph of Los Yumbos Chawamangos performing in Tena during a festival (2010)
Michael and Carlos in Tena	Photograph	n/a	n/a	n/a	n/a	Photograph of Michael with Carlos Alvarado after at a festival in Tena (2010)

REFERENCES

Abram, David
   1996   The Spell of the Sensuous: Perception and Language in a More-Than-
          Human World. New York: Vintage Books.
Allen, Catherine
   1988   The Hold Life Has. Washington, DC: Smithsonian Institution Press.
Alvarado Narvaez, Carlos
   1994   Historia de una cultura: La que quieren matar. Quito: Editorial Quipus.
Anderson, Benedict
   1983   Imagined Communities: Reflections on the Origin and Spread of National-
          ism. London: Verso Press.
Århem, Kaj.
   1993   Ecosofía makuna. In La selva humanizada: Ecología alternativa en el trópico
          húmedo colombiano. François Correa, ed. Bogotá: Instituto Colombiano de
          Antropología, Fondo FEN Colombia, Fondo Editorial CEREC.
Armstrong, Robert Plant
   1981   The Powers of Presence: Consciousness, Myth, and Affecting Presence.
          Philadelphia: University of Pennsylvania Press.
Arnold, Denise Y., and Juan de Dios Yapita
   2006   The Metamorphosis of Heads: Textual Struggles, Education, and Land in
          the Andes. Pittsburgh: University of Pittsburgh Press.
Association of Native Artists and Groups of Napo (AACTIN)
   1991   La Cultura Tradicional Indigena en la Provincia de Napo. Quito: Abya-Yala.
Basso, Ellen B.
   1985   A Musical View of the Universe: Kalapalo Myth and Ritual Performances.
          Philadelphia: University of Pennsylvania Press.

1987   In Favor of Deceit: A Study of Tricksters in an Amazonian Society. Tucson: University of Arizona Press.

1995   The Last Cannibals: A South American Oral History. Austin: University of Texas Press.

Bauman, Richard, and Charles L. Briggs

1990   Poetics and Performance as Critical Perspectives on Language and Social Life. Annual Review of Anthropology 19:59–88.

Belzner, William, and Norman Whitten

1979   Soul Vine Shaman. Recording dated November 6, 1976. Booklet published by the Sacha Runa Research Foundation. Occasional Paper, 5. New York: Crawford.

Benjamin, Walter

1979   Doctrine of the Similar. Knut Tarnowski, trans. New German Critique 17(1):65–69.

Brenneis, Donald, and Steven Feld

2004   Doing Anthropology in Sound. American Ethnologist 31(4):461–474.

Brightman, Robert A.

1993   Grateful Prey: Rock Cree Human-Animal Relationships. Berkeley: University of California Press.

Brown, Michael

1985   Tsewa's Gift: Magic and Meaning in an Amazonian Society. Washington, DC: Smithsonian Institution Press.

Burke, Kenneth

1973 [1941] The Philosophy of Literary Form: Studies in Symbolic Action. 3rd edition. Berkeley: University of California Press.

Callois, Roger

1984   Mimicry and Legendary Psychasthenia. John Shepley, trans. October 31 (Winter):16–32.

Campbell, Patricia Shehan

1995   Anthony Seeger on Music of Amazonian Indians. Music Educator's Journal 81(4):17–23.

Carpenter, Edmund

1972   Oh, What a Blow That Phantom Gave Me! Northridge, CA: Media Works.

Carpenter, Lawrence K.

1992   Inside/Outside, Which Side Counts? Duality of Self and Bipartization in Quechua. In Andean Cosmologies through Time. Robert Dover, Katherine Seibold, and John McDowell, eds. Bloomington: Indiana University Press.

Casey, Edward S.

1993   Getting Back into Place: Toward a Renewed Understanding of the Place World. Bloomington: Indiana University Press.

1997   The Fate of Place: A Philosophical History. Berkeley: University of California Press.

2001   Between Geography and Philosophy: What Does It Mean to Be in the Place-World? Annals of the Association of American Geographers 91(4):683–693.

Cassell, Justine, and David McNeill

1991   Gesture and the Poetics of Prose. Poetics Today 12(3): 375–404,

Cipolleti, María Susana.

2007   The Napo Runa of Amazonian Ecuador—By Michael Uzendoski. Anthropos 102:652–653.

Clifford, James

1986   Writing Culture: The Poetics and Politics of Ethnography. James Clifford and George E. Marcus, eds. Berkeley: University of California Press.

Conklin, Beth

2001   Consuming Grief: Compassionate Cannibalism in an Amazonian Society. Austin: University of Texas Press.

Crocker, J. Christopher

1969   Reciprocity and Hierarchy among the Eastern Bororo. Man, n.s., 4(1):44–48.

1985   Vital Souls: Bororo Cosmology, Natural Symbolism and Shamanism. Tucson: University of Arizona Press.

Cruikshank, Julie

2005   Do Glaciers Listen? Local Knowledge, Colonial Encounters, and Social Imagination. Vancouver: University of British Columbia Press.

Csordas Thomas J.

1990   Embodiment as a Paradigm for Anthropology. Ethos 18(1):5–47.

Cuellar, Andrea Maria

2006   The Quijos Chiefdoms: Social Change and Agriculture in the Eastern Andes of Ecuador. Ph.D. dissertation, University of Pittsburgh.

Derrida, Jacques

1967   Of Grammatology. Baltimore: Johns Hopkins University Press.

Descola, Philippe

1992   Societies in Nature and the Nature of Society. In Conceptualizing Society. Adam Kuper, ed. Pp. 107–126. London: Routledge.

1996a   Constructing Nature: Symbolic Ecology and Social Practice. In Nature and Society: Anthropological Perspectives. Philippe Descola and Gisli Pálsson, eds. Pp. 82–102. London: Routledge.

1996b   The Spears of Twilight: Life and Death in the Amazon Jungle. Janet Lloyd, trans. New York: New Press.

Duranti, Allesandro, and Charles Goodwin, eds.

1992   Rethinking Context: Language as an Interactive Phenomenon. Cambridge: Cambridge University Press.

Durston, Alan

2007   Pastoral Quechua: The History of Christian Translation in Colonial Peru, 1550–1650. Notre Dame, IN: University of Notre Dame Press.

Enfield, N. J.

2001   "Lip-Pointing": A Discussion of Form and Function with Reference to Data from Laos. Gesture 1(2):185–212.

Engelke, Matthew

2007   A Problem of Presence: Beyond Scripture in an African Church. Berkeley: University of California Press.

Fabian, Johannes

2001   Anthropology with an Attitude: Critical Essays. Stanford: Stanford University Press.

Farnell, B.
1999   Moving Bodies, Acting Selves. Annual Review of Anthropology. 28:341–373.
Fausto, Carlos
2000   Of Enemies and Pets: Warfare and Shamanism in Amazonia. American Ethnologist 26(4):933–956.
2007   Feasting on People: Eating Animals and Humans in Amazonia. Current Anthropology 48(4):497–530.
Feld, Steven
1982   Sound and Sentiment: Birds, Weeping, Poetics, and Song in Kaluli Expression. Philadelphia: University of Pennsylvania Press.
Feld, Steven, and Aaron A. Fox
1994   Music and Language. Annual Review of Anthropology 23:25–53.
Finnegan, Ruth
2007   The Oral and Beyond: Doing Things with Words in Africa. Chicago: University of Chicago Press.
Foletti-Castegnaro, Alessandra
1993   Quichuas Amazonicos del Aguarico y San Miguel. Los Pueblos Indios en sus mitos 16. Quito: Abya-Yala.
Foley, John Miles
2002   How to Read an Oral Poem. Urbana: University of Illinois Press.
Foucault, Michel
1975   Discipline and Punish: The Birth of the Prison. Alan Sheridan, trans. New York: Random House.
Fox, Aaron A.
1992   The Jukebox of History: Narratives of Loss and Desire in the Discourse of Country Music. Popular Music 11(1):53–72.
Friedrich, Paul
1988   Multiplicity and Pluralism in Anthropological Construction/Synthesis. Anthropological Quarterly 61(3):103–112.
1989   The Language Parallax. Austin: University of Texas Press.
1996   The Culture in Poetry and the Poetry in Culture. In Culture/Contexture: Explorations in Anthropology and Literary Studies. E. Valentine Daniel and Jeffrey M. Peck, eds. Pp. 37–57. Berkeley: University of California Press.
2001   Lyric Epiphany. Language in Society 30(2):217–247.
2006   Maximizing Ethnopoetics: Towards Fine-Tuning (Anthropological) Experience. In Language, Culture and Society: Key Topics in Linguistic Anthropology. Christine Jourdain and Kevin Tuite, eds. Pp. 207–229. New York: Cambridge University Press.
Galeano, Juan Carlos
2000   Amazonia. Bogotá: Editorial Magisterio.
2007   Cuentos Amazónicos. Jalisco, Mexico: Literalia Press.
Gleick, James
1987   Chaos: Making a New Science. New York: Viking.
Goldáraz, José Migual
2005   Napo Mayumanta Runakunapak Sumak Yuyarina Yachaykuna. Quito: Ediciones CICAME.

Goldman, Irving
  2004   Cubeo Hehénewa Religious Thought: Metaphysics of a Northwestern Amazonian People. New York: Columbia University Press.
Goodwin, Charles
  2007   Environmentally Coupled Gestures. *In* Gesture and the Dynamic Dimension of Language. Susan D. Duncan, Justine Cassell, and Elena T. Levy, eds. Pp. 195–212. Amsterdam: John Benjamins.
Goody, Jack
  1977   The Domestication of the Savage Mind. Cambridge: Cambridge University Press.
  2000   The Power of the Written Tradition. Washington, DC: Smithsonian Institution Press.
Goody, Jack, ed.
  1968   Literacy in Traditional Societies. Cambridge: Cambridge University Press.
Goulet, Jean-Guy A., and Bruce Granville Miller
  2007   Embodied Knowledge: Steps toward a Radical Anthropology of Cross-Cultural Encounters. *In* Extraordinary Anthropology: Transformations in the Field. Jean-Guy Goulet and Bruce Miller, eds. Pp. 1–14. Lincoln: University of Nebraska Press.
Gow, Peter
  2001   An Amazonian Myth and Its History. Oxford: Oxford University Press.
Graeber, David
  2004   Fragments of an Anarchist Anthropology. Chicago: Prickly Paradigm Press.
Graham, Laura R.
  1996   Performing Dreams: Discourses of Immortality among the Xavante of Central Brazil. Austin: University of Texas Press.
Guss, David
  1986   Keeping It Oral: A Yekuana Ethnology. American Ethnologist 13(3):413–429.
  1989   To Weave and Sing: Art Symbol, and Narrative in the South American Rain Forest. Berkeley: University of California Press.
Haboud, Marleen
  2004   Quichua Language Vitality: An Ecuadorian Perspective. International Journal of the Sociology of Language 167: 69–82.
Handler, Richard
  2004   Afterword: Mysteries of Culture. American Anthropologist 106(3):488–494.
Hanks, William F.
  1989   Text and Textuality. Annual Review of Anthropology 18:95–127.
Harrison, Regina
  1988   Signs, Songs, and Memory in the Andes: Translating Quechua Language and Culture. Austin: University of Texas Press.
Harvey, Tenibac S.
  2006   Ipseity, Alterity, and Community: The Tri-Unity of Maya Therapeutic Healing. Zygon 41(4):903–914.
Haviland, John B.
  2000   Pointing, Gesture Spaces, and Mental Maps. *In* Language and Gesture. David McNeill, ed. Pp. 13–46. Cambridge: Cambridge University Press.

2004   Gesture. *In* A Companion to Linguistic Anthropology. Alessandro Duranti, ed. Pp. 197–221.

Heidegger, Martin.
1971   Poetry, Language, Thought. Albert Hofstadter, trans. New York: Harper and Row.

Hendricks, Janet Wall
1993   To Drink of Death: The Narrative of a Shuar Warrior. Tucson: University of Arizona Press.

Hill, Jonathan
1993   Keepers of the Sacred Chants. Tucson: University of Arizona Press.
1995   Foreword. *In* The Land without Evil: Tupí Guaraní Prophetism. By Héléne Clastres. Jacqueline Grenez Brovender, trans. Urbana: University of Illinois Press.
1996   Introduction: Ethnogenesis in the Americas: 1492–1992. *In* History, Power, and Identity: Ethnogenesis in the Americas: 1492–1992. Jonathan Hill, ed. Pp. 1–19. Iowa City: University of Iowa Press.

Hornberger, Nancy
1992   Verse Analysis of "The Condor and the Shepherdess." *In* On the Translation of Native American Literatures. Brian Swan, ed. Pp. 441–469. Washington DC: Smithsonian Institution Press.

Hornborg, Alf
2001   The Power of the Machine: Global Inequalities of Economy, Technology, and Environment. Walnut Creek, CA: Altamira Press.

Hurtado de Mendoza, S.
2002   Pramgmatica de la cultura y la lengua Quechua. Quito: Abya-Yala Press.

Hutchins, Frank
2007   Footprints in the Forest: Ecotourism and Altered Meanings in Ecuador's Upper Amazon. Journal of Latin American and Caribbean Anthropology. 12(1):75–103.

Hymes, Dell
1981   In Vain I Tried to Tell You: Essays in Native American Ethnopoetics. Bryan Swann, ed. Philadelphia: University of Pennsylvania Press.
1985   Language, Memory, and Selective Performance: Cultee's "Salmon's Myth" as Twice Told to Boas. Journal of American Folklore 98(390):391–434.
1992   Use All There Is to Use. *In* On the Translation of Native American Literatures. Brian Swann, ed. Pp. 83–124. Washington, DC: Smithsonian Institution Press.
1994   Ethnopoetics, Oral Formulaic Theory, and Editing Texts. Oral Tradition 9(2):330–370.
2003   Now I Know Only So Far: Essays in Ethnopoetics. Lincoln: University of Nebraska Press.

Hymes, Virginia
1992   Warm Springs Sahaptin Narrative Analysis. *In* Native American Discourse: Poetics and Rhetoric. Joel Sherzer and Anthony Woodbury, eds. Cambridge: Cambridge University Press.

Ingold, Tim
2007   Lines: A Brief History. New York: Routledge.

Jackson, Michael

1989   Paths toward a Clearing: Radical Empiricism and Ethnographic Inquiry. Bloomington: Indiana University Press.

1995   At Home in the World. Durham, NC: Duke University Press.

1996   Introduction: Phenomenology, Radical Empiricism, and Anthropological Critique. *In* Things as They Are: New Directions in Phenomenological Anthropology. Michael Jackson, ed. Pp. 1–50. Bloomington: Indiana University Press.

1998   Minima Ethnographica: Intersubjectivity and the Anthropological Project. Chicago: University of Chicago Press.

Jakobson, Roman

1960   Closing Statement: Linguistics and Poetics. *In* Style in Language. Thomas A. Sebeok. Pp. 350–377. Cambridge, MA: MIT Press.

James, William

1967   The Writings of William James: A Comprehensive Edition. John J. McDermott, ed. Chicago: University of Chicago Press.

Jumper, Elgin

2006   Nightfall: Poems by Elgin Jumper; Number Two—Native American Chapbook Series II. Sequoyah Research Center. University of Arkansas at Little Rock. http://anpa.ualr.edu/digital_library/nightfall_jumper.htm.

Karsten, Rafael

1998 [1920–1921] Entre los Indos de las Selvas del Ecuador. Quito: Abya-Yala.

Katz, Fred, and Marlene Dobkin de Rios

1971   Hallucinogenic Music: An Analysis of the Role of Whistling in Peruvian Ayahuasca Healing Sessions. Journal of American Folklore 84(333):320–327.

Kelley, José Antonio

2005   Fractality and the Exchange of Perspectives. *In* On the Order of Chaos: Social Anthropology and the Science of Chaos. Mark S. Mosko and Frederick H. Damon, eds. Pp. 108–135. New York: Berghahn Books.

Kendon, Adam

1972   Some Relationships between Body Motion and Speech: An Analysis of an Example. *In* Studies in Dyadic Communication. Aron Wolfe Siegman and Benjamin Pope, eds. Pp. 177–210. New York: Pergamon Press.

1980   Gesticulation and Speech: Two Aspects of the Process of Utterance. *In* The Relationship of Verbal and Nonverbal Communication. Mary Ritchie Key, ed. Pp. 207–227. The Hague: Mouton.

1997   Gesture. Annual Review of Anthropology 28:341–373.

2004   Gesture: Visible Action as Utterance. Cambridge: Cambridge University Press.

Kohn, Eduardo

2007   How Dogs Dream: Amazonian Natures and the Politics of Transspecies Engagement. American Ethnologist 34(1):3–24.

Latour, Bruno

1993   We Have Never Been Modern. Catherine Porter, trans. Cambridge, MA: Harvard University Press.

2005   Reassembling the Social: An Introduction to Actor-Network Theory. Oxford: Oxford University Press.

2007   The Recall of Modernity. Cultural Studies Review 13(1): 11–30.

2009   Perspectivism: "Type" or "Bomb"? Anthropology Today. 25(2): 1–2.

Laugrand, Frédéric B., and Jarich G. Oosten

2009   Shamans and Missionaries: Transitions and Transformations in the Kivalliq
        Coastal Area. *In* Native Christians: Modes and Effects of Christianity among
        Indigenous Peoples of the Americas. Aparecida Vilaça and Robin M. Wright,
        eds. Pp. 167–186. Aldershot, Hants, UK: Ashgate.

Levi-Strauss, Claude

1963   Do Dual Organizations Exist? *In* Structural Anthropology. Vol. 1. Claire
        Jacobson and Brooke Grundfest Schoepf, trans. New York: Basic Books.

1964–1971 Mythologiques. 4 vols. Paris: Plon. Trans. as Introduction to a Science of
        Mythology. New York: Harper and Row, 1969–1981.

1976   The Meaning and Use of the Notion of Model. *In* Structural Anthropology.
        Vol. 2. Claire Jacobson and Brooke Grundfest Schoepf, trans. New York:
        Basic Books.

Lord, Albert Bates

1960   The Singer of Tales. Cambridge, MA: Harvard University Press.

1968   Homer as Oral Poet. Harvard Studies in Classical Philology 72:1–46.

Mannheim, Bruce

1991   The Language of the Inkas since the European Invasion. Austin: University
        of Texas Press.

1998   "Time, Not Syllables, Must be Counted": Quechua Parallelism, Word Mean-
        ing, and Cultural Analysis. *In* Linguistic Form and Social Action. Jennifer
        Dickinson, James Herron, et al., eds. Pp. 238–281. Michigan Discussions in
        Anthropology 13. Ann Arbor: University of Michigan Press.

Manneheim, Bruce, and Krista Van Vleet

1998   The Dialogics of Southern Quechua Narrative. American Anthropologist
        100(2): 330–346.

Marcuse, Herbert

1991   One-Dimensional Man: Studies in the Ideology of Advanced Industrial
        Society. 2nd edition. New York: Beacon Press.

Martínez, Carmen

2009   Introducción. *In* Repensando los movimientos indígenas. Carmen Martínez,
        ed. Pp. 1–35. Quito, Ecuador: FLACSO.

McNeill, David

1992   Hand and Mind: What Gestures Reveal about Thought. Chicago: University
        of Chicago Press.

2000   Introduction. *In* Language and Gesture. David McNeill, ed. Pp. 1–10. Cam-
        bridge: Cambridge University Press.

2005   Gesture and Thought. Chicago: University of Chicago Press.

Mentore, George

2007   Spiritual Translucency and Pornocratic Anthropology: Waiwai and Western
        Interpretations of a Religious Experience. Anthropology and Humanism
        32(2):192–201.

2009   Interview with Edith Turner. AIBR. Revista de Antropología Iberoamericana
        4(3): i–xviii.

Merleau-Ponty, Maurice
  1962   Phenomenology of Perception. Colin Smith, trans. London: Routledge.
Morris, Brian
  1987   Anthropological Studies of Religion. Cambridge: Cambridge University Press.
Mosko, Mark S., and Frederick H. Damon, eds.
  2005   On the Order of Chaos: Social Anthropology and the Science of Chaos. New York: Berghahn Books.
Muratorio, Blanca
  1991   The Life and Times of Grandfather Alonso: Culture and History in the Upper Amazon. New Brunswick, NJ: Rutgers University Press.
Murra, John V., Nathan Watchel, and Jacques Revel, eds.
  1986   Anthropological History of Andean Polities. Cambridge: Cambridge University Press.
Muysken, Pieter
  2000   Semantic Transparency in Lowland Ecuadorian Quechua Morphosyntax. Linguistics 38(5): 973–988.
  2009   Gradual restructuring in Ecuadorian Quechua. In Gradual Creolization: Studies Celebrating Jacques Arends. Rachel Selbach, Hugo C. Cardoso, and Margot van den Berg, eds. Pp. 77–100. Philadelphia: John Benjamin.
Newson, Linda A.
  1995   Life and Death in Early Colonial Ecuador. Norman: University of Oklahoma Press.
Nuckolls, Janis B.
  1996   Sounds like Life. Sound-Symbolic Grammar, Performance, and Cognition in Pastaza Quechua. New York: Oxford University Press.
  2000   Spoken in the Spirit of Gesture. In Translating Native Latin American Verbal Art: Ethnopoetics and Ethnography of Speaking. Kay Sammons and Joel Sherzer, eds. Pp. 223–251. Washington, DC: Smithsonian Institution Press.
  2010   Lessons from a Quechua Strongwoman on Ideophony, Dialogue, and Perspective. Tucson: University of Arizona Press.
Oakdale, Suzanne
  2005   I Foresee My Life: The Ritual Performance of Autobiography in an Amazonian Community. Lincoln: University of Nebraska Press.
Oberum, Udo
  1980   Los Quijos: História de la transculturación de un grupo indígena en el Oriente Ecuatoriano. Colección Pendoneros. Otavalo, Ecuador: Instituto Otavaleño de Antropología.
Olsen, Dale
  1996   Music of the Warao of Venezuela: Song People of the Rain Forest. Gainesville: University Press of Florida.
Ong, Walter J.
  1967   The Presence of the Word: Some Prolegomena for Cultural and Religious History. New Haven, CT: Yale University Press.
  1982   Orality and Literacy: The Technologizing of the Word. London: Methuen.

Orr, Carolina, and Juan E. Hudelson

1971   Cuillurguna: Cuentos de los Quichuas del Oriente Ecuatoriano. Quito: Houser Ltda.

Orr, Carolina, and Betsy Wrisley

1981   Vocabulario Quichua del Oriente. Instituto Linguistico del Verano. Quito: Instituto Lingüístico de Verano, en cooperación con el Ministerio de Educación Pública.

Ortegón, Diego.

1989 [1577] Relación del estado en que se encuentra la Gobernación de Quijos y la Canela. *In* La Gobernación de los Quijos (1559–1621). C. Landázuri, ed. Pp. 417–437. Iquitos, Peru: IIAP/CETA.

Ospina, Pablo

1992   La Región de los Quijos: Una Tierra Despojada de Poderes (1578–1608). Procesos: Revista Ecuatoriana de Historia 3(2):3–32.

Overing, Joanna, and Alan Passes

2000   Introduction: Conviviality and the Opening Up of Amazonian Anthropology. *In* The Anthropology of Love and Anger. Joanna Overing and Alan Passes, eds. Pp. 1–30. London: Routledge.

Parker, Gary

1969   Ayacucho Quechua Grammar and Dictionary. The Hague: Mouton.

Porras, Pedro

1985   Arte Rupestre del Alto Napo, Valle del Misaguallli Ecuador. Quito: Artes Gráficas Señal.

Reeve, Mary-Elizabeth

1993   Regional Interaction in the Western Amazon: The Early Encounter and the Jesuit Years: 1538–1767. Ethnohistory 41:106–138.

Reichel-Dolmatoff, Gerardo

1975   The Shaman and the Jaguar: A Study of Narcotic Drugs among the Indians of Columbia. Philadelphia: Temple University Press.

Ricoeur, Paul

1992   Oneself as Another. Kathleen Blarney, trans. Chicago: University of Chicago Press.

Robbins, Joel

2004   Becoming Sinners: Christianity and Moral Torment in a Papua New Guinea Society. Berkeley: University of California Press.

Rothenberg, Jerome

1994   "Je Est un Autre": Ethnopoetics and the Poet as Other. American Anthropologist 96(3):523–524.

Rothenberg, Jerome, ed.

1968   Technicians of the Sacred: A Range of Poetries from Africa, America, Asia, and Oceania. Garden City, NY: Doubleday.

Rotman, Brian

2002   The Alphabetic Body. Parallax 8(1): 92–104.

2008   Becoming Beside Ourselves: The Alphabet, Ghosts, and Distributed Human Being. Durham, NC: Duke University Press.

Rubenstein, Steven Lee

2007   Circulation, Accumulation, and the Power of Shuar Shruken Heads. Cultural Anthropology 22(3):358–399.

Ruiz, Lucy M.

1993   La Infancia en Los Pueblos indígenas de la Amazonía Ecuatoriana: Una Mirada al Mundo de los Cofanes. *In* Amazonía escenarios y conflictos. Lucy Ruiz, ed. CEDIME. Quito: Abya-Yala.

Sakai, Naoki

2006   Translation. Theory, Culture and Society 23:71–78.

Salomon, Frank, and George L. Urioste

1991   The Huarochirí Manuscript: A Testament of Ancient and Colonial Andean Religion. Austin: University of Texas Press.

Santos Granero, Fernando

1986   Power, Ideology and the Ritual of Production in Lowland South America. Man, n.s., 21(4):657–679.

Seeger, Anthony

1986   Oratory Is Spoken, Myth Is Told, and Song Is Sung, but They Are All Music to My Ears. *In* Native South American Discourse. Joel Sherzer and Greg Urban, eds. Pp. 59–82. New York: Mouton de Gruyter.

1987   Why Suya Sing: A Musical Anthropology of an Amazonian People. Cambridge: Cambridge University Press.

Sherzer, Joel

1983   Kuna Ways of Speaking: An Ethnographic Perspective. Austin: University of Texas Press.

Sherzer, Joel, comp., ed., and trans.

2003   Stories, Myths, Chants, and Songs of the Kuna Indians. Austin: University of Texas Press.

Shiguango, Sharimiat

2006   Nueva Versión de la Medicina Shamánica de los Yachakuna Una Visión del Mundo Desconocido Para el Estudio de la Medicina Alternativa: Archidona, Ecuador. Quito: Imprenta Nuestra Amazonía.

Silverstein, Michael

2004   Boasian Cosmographic Anthropology and the Sociocentric Component of Mind. *In* Significant Others: Interpersonal and Professional Commitments in Anthropology. Richard Handler, ed. Pp. 131–157. Madison: University of Wisconsin Press.

Slater, Candace

2002   Entangled Edens: Visions of the Amazon. Berkeley: University of California Press.

Stark, Louisa R.

1985   Indigenous Languages of Lowland Ecuador: History and Current Status. *In* South American Indian Languages: Retrospect and Prospect. Harriet E. M. Klein and Louisa R. Stark, eds. Austin: University of Texas Press.

Steward, Julian, and Alfred Métraux

1948   Tribes of the Peruvian and Ecuadorian Montaña. *In* Handbook of South

American Indians, vol. 3. Julian Steward, ed. Pp. 535–656. Washington, DC: Smithsonian Institution Press.

Stoller, Paul
1995   Embodying Colonial Memories: Spirit Possession, Power, and Hauka in West Africa. New York: Routledge.

Sullivan, Lawrence E.
1988   Icanchu's Drum: An Orientation to Meaning in South American Religions. New York: Macmillan.

Swann, Brian, ed.
1992   On the Translation of Native American Literatures. Washington, DC: Smithsonian Institution Press.

Swanson, Tod Dillon
2009   Singing to Estranged Lovers: Quichua Relations to Plants in the Ecuadorian Amazon. Journal of Religion, Nature, and Culture 3(1): 36–65.

Taussig, Michael
1987   Shamanism, Colonialism, and the Wild Man: A Study in Terror and Healing. Chicago: University of Chicago Press.
1993   Mimesis and Alterity: A Particular History of the Senses. New York: Routledge.

Taylor, Anne Christine
1993   Remembering to Forget: Identity, Mourning, and Memory among the Jivaro. Man, n.s., 28(4):653–678.
1996   The Soul's Body and Its States: An Amazonian Perspective on the Nature of Being Human. Journal of the Royal Anthropological Institute 2(2):201–215.
1999   The Western Margins of Amazonia from the Early Sixteenth to the Early Nineteenth Century. In The Cambridge History of the Native Peoples of the Americas, vol. 3: South America, part 2. Frank Salomon and Stuart B. Schwartz, eds. Pp. 188–256. Cambridge: Cambridge University Press.

Tedlock, Barbara
1991   From Participant Observation to Observation of Participation. Journal of Anthropological Research 47(1):69–94.
2005   The Woman in the Shaman's Body: Reclaiming the Feminine in Religion and Medicine. New York: Bantam.

Tedlock, Dennis
1983   The Spoken Word and the Work of Interpretation. Philadelphia: University of Pennsylvania Press.
1985   Popol vuh: The Definitive Edition of the Mayan Book of the Dawn of Life and the Glories of Gods and Kings. Dennis Tedlock, trans. New York: Simon and Schuster.

Tedlock, Dennis, and Bruce Mannheim, editors
1995   The Dialogic Emergence of Culture. Urbana: University of Illinois Press.

Torero, Alfredo
1974   El Quechua y La Historia Social Andina. Lima: Universidad Ricardo Palma.

Trouillot, Michel-Rolph
1995   Silencing the Past: Power and the Production of History. Boston: Beacon Books.

Turner, Edith
2006   Discussion: Spiritually Merging with a Fellow Human Being's Suffering. Zygon 41(4):933–939.

Turner, Terence
1991a   "We Are Parrots, Twins Are Birds": Play of Tropes as Operational Structures. In Beyond Metaphor: The Theory of Tropes in Anthropology. James W. Fernandez, ed. Stanford, CA: Stanford University Press.
1991b   The Social Dynamics of Video Media in an Indigenous Society: The Cultural Meaning and the Personal Politics of Video-Making in Kayapo Communities. Visual Anthropology Review 7(2): 68–76.
1992   The Kayapo Appropriation of Video. Anthropology Today 8(6): 5–16.
1995   Social Body and Embodied Subject: Bodiliness, Subjectivity, and Sociality among the Kayapo. Cultural Anthropology 10(2):143–170.

Turner, Victor
1967   The Forest of Symbols: Aspects of Ndembu Ritual. Ithaca, NY: Cornell University Press.
1969   The Ritual Process: Structure and Anti-Structure. Ithaca, NY: Cornell University Press.

Urban, Greg
1991   A Discourse-Centered Approach to Culture: Native South American Myths and Rituals. Austin: University of Texas Press.

Urton, Gary
1997   The Social Life of Numbers. A Quechua Ontology of Numbers and Philosophy of Arithmetic. Austin: University of Texas Press.

Uzendoski, Michael A.
1999   Twins and Becoming Jaguars: Verse Analysis of a Napo Quichua Myth Narrative. Anthropological Linguistics 41(4):431–461.
2003   Purgatory, Protestantism, and Peonage: Napo Runa Evangelicals and the Domestication of the Masculine Will. In Millennial Ecuador: Critical Essays on Cultural Transformations and Social Dynamics. Norman Whitten, ed. Pp. 129–153. Iowa City: University of Iowa Press.
2004a   The Horizontal Archipelago: The Quijos Upper Napo Regional System. Ethnohistory 51(2):318–357.
2004b   Manioc Beer and Meat: Value, Reproduction, and Cosmic Substance among the Napo Runa of the Ecuadorian Amazon. Journal of the Royal Anthropological Institute. 10(4):883–902.
2005   The Napo Runa of Amazonian Ecuador. Urbana: University of Illinois Press.
2008   Somatic Poetry in Amazonian Ecuador. Anthropology and Humanism 33(1/2):12–29.
2009   La Textualidad Oral Napo Kichwa y Las Paradojas de la Educación Bilingüe Intercultural en la Amazonia. In Repensando los movimientos indígenas. Carmen Martínez, ed. Pp. 147–172. Quito: FLACSO.
2010a   Fractal Subjectivities: An Amazonian Inspired Critique of Globalization Theory. In Editing Eden: A Reconsideration of Identity, Politics, and Place in Amazonia. Frank Hutchins and Patrick C. Wilson, eds. Lincoln: University of Nebraska Press.

2010b   Los Napo Runa de la Amazonia Ecuatoriana. Quito: Abya-Yala.

Uzendoski, Michael A., Mark Hertica, and Edith Calapucha Tapuy
2005   The Phenomenology of Perspectivism: Aesthetics, Sound, and Power in Women's Songs from Amazonian Ecuador. Current Anthropology 46(4):656–662.

Vilaça, Aparecida
2002   Making Kin out of Others in Amazonia. Journal of the Royal Anthropological Institute, n.s., 8(2):347–365.
2005   Chronically Unstable Bodies: Reflections on Amazonian Corporalities. Journal of the Royal Anthropological Institute 11:445–464.
2009   Bodies in Perspective: A Critique of the Embodiment Paradigm from the Point of View of Amazonian Ethnography. In Social Bodies. Helen Lambert and Maryon McDonald, eds. Pp. 129–147. New York: Berghahan.

Vilaça, Aparecida, and Robin M. Wright
2009   Introduction. In Native Christians: Modes and Effects of Christianity among Indigenous Peoples of the Americas. Aparecida Vilaça and Robin M. Wright, eds. Pp. 1–20. Aldershot, Hanrs, UK: Ashgate.

Villavicencio, Manuel
1984 [1858] Geografía de la República del Ecuador. Quito: Corporación Editora Nacional.

Viveiros de Castro, Eduardo
1998   Cosmological Deixis and Amerindian Perspectivism. Journal of the Royal Anthropological Institute, n.s., 4(3):469–488.
2001   GUT Feelings about Amazonia: Potential Affinity and the Construction of Sociality. In Beyond the Visible and the Material: The Amerindianization of Society in the Work of Peter Riviere. Neil L. Whitehead and Laura M. Rival, eds. Pp. 19–44. Oxford: Oxford University Press.

Wagner, Roy
1986   Symbols That Stand for Themselves. Chicago: University of Chicago Press.

Warvin, Marqués de
1927 [1993] Leyendas tradicionales de los Indios del Oriente ecuatoriano. In Indianistas, Indianofilos, Indigenistas: Entre el enigma y la fascinación, una antología de textos sobre el "problema" indígena. Pp. 677–692. Quito: Abya-Yala.

Wesch, Michael
2009   Youtube and You: Experiences of Self-Awareness in the Context Collapse of the Recording Webcam. Explorations in Media Ecology, 8(2): 19–34.

Whitehead, Neil L.
2002   Dark Shamans: Kanaimà and the Poetics of Violent Death. Durham, NC: Duke University Press.
2003   Introduction. In Histories and Historicities in Amazonia. Neil Whitehead, ed. Pp. vii-xx. Lincoln: University of Nebraska Press.
2007   Violence and the Cultural Order. Daedalus 136(1): 40–50.

Whitehead, Neil L., and Robin Wright
2004   Introduction: Dark Shamanism. In In Darkness and Secrecy: The Anthropol-

ogy of Assault Sorcery and Witchcraft in Amazonia. Neil L. Whitehead and Robin Wright, eds. Pp. 1–20. Durham, NC: Duke University Press.

Whitten, Dorothea S., and Norman E. Whitten Jr.

1988   From Myth to Creation: Art from Amazonian Ecuador. Urbana: University of Illinois Press.

Whitten, Norman E., Jr.

1976   Sacha Runa: Ethnicity and Adaptation of Ecuadorian Jungle Quichua. Urbana: University of Illinois Press.

1985   Sicuanga Runa: The Other Side of Development in Amazonian Ecuador. Urbana: University of Illinois Press.

1988   Commentary: Historical and Mythic Evocations of Chthonic Power. *In* Rethinking History and Myth: Indigenous South American Perspectives on the Past. Jonathan D. Hill, ed. Pp. 282–306. Urbana: University of Illinois Press.

1996   The Ecuadorian Levantamiento Indígena of 1990 and the Epitomizing Symbol of 1992: Reflections on Nationalism, Ethic-Bloc Formation, and Racialist Ideologies. *In* History, Power, and Identity: Ethnogenesis in the Americas: 1492–1992. Jonathan D. Hill, ed. Pp. 193–218. Iowa City: University of Iowa Press.

2009   Interculturality and the Indigenization of Modernity: A View from Amazonian Ecuador. Tipiti, Journal of the Society for the Anthropology of Lowland South America 6(1/2):3–36.

Whitten, Norman E., Jr., and Dorothea S. Whitten

2008   Puyo Runa: Imagery and Power in Modern Amazonia. Urbana: University of Illinois Press.

Wibbelsman, Michelle

2008   Ritual Encounters: Otavalan Modern and Mythic Community. Urbana: University of Illinois Press.

Ziarek, Krzysztof

1998   Powers to Be: Art and Technology in Heidegger and Foucault. Research in Phenomenology 28(1):162–194.

Zuidema, R. Tom

1964   The Ceque System of Cuzco: The Social Organization of the Capital of the Inca. Eva M. Hooykaas, trans. Leiden: E. J. Brill.

1990   Inca Civilization in Cusco. Jean-Jacques Decoster, trans. Austin: University of Texas Press.

INDEX

Achuar, 82
alienation, 13, 203. *See also* capitalism
alphabetic writing: claimed superiority of, 4,
    8, 202–203, 205n4; differences from other
    textual systems, 40, 88; overlap with other
    forms of textuality, 10, 86–87, 217; in rela-
    tion to orality, 6, 8, 24, 206n8
Alvarado, Carlos, 72, 151, 175, 177–179, 181,
    184–185, 203; life history of, 211n6, 221
Alvarado, Patricio, 175–176, 187–188
Andi, Gerardo (Bolivar), 71–72, 215
Andi, Jacinta, 87, 88–91, 217
Andy, Anibal (El Ductur), 150–155, 219
Amazonian cultures: and the body as inter-
    connected with the world, 12–13, 21, 23–24,
    39, 81–82, 174, 201; and the body in healing,
    22, 25–26, 28–30, 38–39, 182, 207–208n10,
    209n7; and the cosmic body, 32, 37, 59,
    79–80, 97, 99, 202, 207n2; circularity in
    music among, 33, 37–49, 179; circularity
    of all things among, 22, 40, 186, 188, 198;
    circularity of stories among, 17, 112, 144;
    circularity with the land among, 5; com-
    munication philosophy of, 2–3, 5, 7–8, 10–
    12, 22, 59, 178, 200, 202–203; inversions of
    Western categories among, 32, 136, 173–174,
    185–186; poetics of, 1–5, 18–19, 30–33, 37–40,
    98–99, 137, 150, 157, 170, 178–179, 180, 202,
    205n2; storytelling among, 19, 31, 42, 58,
62, 69, 158; textuality of cultural practices
    among, 7–8, 212n7; textuality of the body
    among, 4–5, 10, 12, 21–22, 24, 44, 57, 78, 172,
    194, 198–199, 205n3; textuality of the land-
    scape among, 4, 9, 12, 14, 57, 78, 157–158,
    200, 202–203; views on nature among, 2–3,
    10–12, 56, 97–99, 103–104, 199–203
Amazonian Quichua language: history of,
    101–103, 205n1; poetics of, 1–5, 9–10, 12, 14,
    16, 19–22, 69, 78, 207n2; storytelling and
    musical patterning in, 111, 114, 182–183;
    unity of time and space in, 209n2; use of
    axis mundi concept in, 59; use of gestures
    and imagery in, 43–44; use of ideophones
    in, 109
anaconda: as figure on ceramics of Pastaza,
    185–186, 212n10; and floods, 21, 32, 42, 54,
    56–58; as killed by the Twins, 166; in rela-
    tion to the body, 32, 83; and the sun, 21,
    70–78, 171, 199, 208n4
anthropology, 8, 14–15, 18, 20, 26, 32, 98, 170,
    202, 205n2
Armstrong, Robert Plant, 83, 98, 173
Arnold, Denise, 5, 10, 24
audio technology. *See* digital technology
axis mundi: defined, 44; elicitation of,
    through gestures and ideophones, 17;
    elicitation of, through sound, 208; in flood
    stories, 186; in Iluku story, 58–61, 69; imag-

ery of, in storytelling, 21, 44, 198–199; and petroglyphs, 200; in sun origin story, 71, 77–78; and the Twin's ascent into heaven, 157, 171; in women's songs, 80, 90, 97

ayllu, 21, 31, 40, 95, 102, 158. *See also* kinship

birds: and anaconda, 32; in birds-of-prey stories, 136–142, 144, 155–156, 166, 199, 219; as defining of women's songs, 21–22, 78–79, 199, 217; in flood songs, 54–56; humanity as defined by, 60, 78, 188; in Illuku story, 68; musicality of, 179, 190; and the upper world, 59, 170; use of, in naming music groups, 175. *See also* common potoo; Iluku

blood, 1, 19, 21, 24–25, 34, 137, 177, 179, 181

body theory, 3–5, 9–13, 17, 21–25, 99, 201–203. *See also* perspectivism; *and various subentries under* Amazonian cultures

books, 13, 18–19, 197, 205n3

breast (female), 21, 84–87, 97–99, 105, 120, 199, 217

breath. See *samay* (soul/breath)

bridges: and axis mundi, 58–59; construction of, by the Twins, 105–106, 126, 128, 166; use of, as trap for mythical jaguars, 107–110, 128, 130, 143, 158, 209nn4–5, 218

Calapucha, Esteban, 35, 87, 214

Calapucha, Federico, 25, 30–32, 34, 40, 54, 87, 158, 179, 203, 214

Calapucha, Vicente, 91–97, 217

Campo-Cocha (community), 21, 53, 100, 103, 198

capitalism, 6–7, 13, 189, 193, 202–203

carelessness (*killa*), 60, 67, 78, 98, 135, 137

Casey, Edward, 13, 201

caves, 9, 59, 70, 144, 152–153, 156

Cerda, Gervacio, 84–87, 99, 203, 217

Chawamangos (Los Yumbos), 175, 190, 221

Chiuta Mountain, 11, 43–52, 54, 56–57, 197–198, 215

Choclote, Jaime, 216

Christianity, 41, 49, 66–67, 192–193, 200, 208n10, 212n11

circular relations: in shamanism, 33–40; in storytelling, 5, 17, 22, 112, 144, 179, 186, 188, 198

cities, 34, 43, 71, 141–142, 158, 210n1

Cofán, 175

common potoo (bird), 60–61, 68–69, 97–98, 208n2. *See also* Iluku

communication: Amazonian peoples' philosophy of, 2–3, 5, 7–8, 10–12, 19, 22, 59, 178, 202–203; power of culture to shape, 203; Western philosophy of, 6–10, 203

communitas: with buzzards, 137; cosmological, 174, 190–195, 201; defined, 211n4; human-jaguar, 116, 145, 151; with manioc plants, 177–179; of mountains, 42, 52, 57; with plant, animal, and other subjectivities, 2, 23; with plants used in vapor-bath healing, 26–27; with spirits, 23, 28, 33, 53, 81, 173, 207–208n10; storytelling and, 1, 22, 54, 62, 194

connectedness. *See* lines (connectedness)

context-collapse, 18–19

couplets, 37, 55, 83, 85, 92, 94, 110, 180, 182–183, 194

Cuillurguna (Twins); ascension of, 22, 163, 171, 200, 220; and the birds of prey, 22, 136–137, 155–156, 219; birth of, 118–121; cycle of narratives about, 22, 97, 99, 104, 199–200, 207n9; and the jaguars, 22, 113–114, 122–123, 130–131, 218; and the mundopuma, 22, 142–145, 150–151, 155–156, 184, 219; petroglyphs left by the, 22, 157–159, 171, 220; role of, as "world-makers" of Napo Runa civilization, 135–136

culture, 1–3, 9, 13, 18, 20, 104, 177, 181, 201

Damon, Frederick, 181, 212n9

dance: during Runa Paju gatherings, 172–178, 181, 183, 185, 190–195, 201, 221; by the Twins, 148–150, 166; during weddings, 192, 211

death: in Birds-of-Prey and Mundopuma stories, 137, 144, 156; as conceptualized by the Napo Runa, 14, 40; in Iluku story, 66–67, 77–78; presence of, in storytelling, 2, 171; as represented in flood myths and songs, 42, 49, 54; in Runa Paju music, 179, 185–190, 194–195; in Twins and Jaguars story, 112–113, 116, 210n10; in women's songs, 82, 91, 99

Derrida, Jacques, 5–10, 24

Descola, Philippe, 10, 31, 94, 104

digital technology (audio and video): context collapse caused by, 18–19; as redefining Western communication, 4; as a tool in translation, 1, 16, 197; use of, by the Napo Runa, 22, 72, 86–88, 172–176, 200, 206n12, 217

Dos Ríos (community), 103, 215–216, 218

doves, 11, 21, 87, 88–90, 97, 199, 217

dreams, 37, 39, 42, 158, 186

Ductur, El (Anibal Andy), 150–155, 219

phosis into, 11, 22, 103–104, 114; and mundopuma, 135–136, 142–145, 149–156; and music, 184–186; in Napo Runa mythology, 198–199; and petroglyphs, 158–162; Twins and, 100–102, 105–106, 116–131, 180, 209n1
Jakobson, Roman, 83, 180
James, William, 12, 78, 157, 170, 200
judgment day (*izhu*): in music, 53–57, 106, 112, 130–131, 140, 144, 144–145; in Runa Paju, 184–186, 198; in stories, 41–51, 106, 112, 130–131, 140, 144–145; Twins returning on, 167; world orders and, 21, 200

Kichwa, 102, 205n1. *See also* Amazonian Quichua language; Quichua (Ecuador)
killa (carelessness), 60, 67, 78, 98, 135, 137
killa (moon), 60, 67, 78, 98, 135, 137, 165, 167, 169. *See also* moon
kinship, 49, 54, 81, 95–97, 156, 158, 189, 200
Kohn, Eduardo, 23, 201, 207n2

ladder, 58–60, 66–68, 116, 118, 145–146, 164
language: and aesthetics, 29, 38–41, 173–174, 177, 181, 194, 201, 205–206n4; ethnopoetics and, 15–16, 18, 105; hegemony of, 8–10, 205n4; and orality, 6–7, 206n8; and other semiotic modes, 3–4; Quechua/Quichua, 101–103, 205n1, 210n9; shift to Spanish, 159, 193; and translation, 12–14, 198; views on, 1–2. *See also* communication; translation
Latour, Bruno, 6, 21, 201–202, 206nn9–10, 208n1
Levi-Strauss, Claude, 179, 210n9
linearity, 6, 17, 70, 182, 202
lines, in storytelling, identification and analysis of. *See* verse analysis
lines (connectedness), 4–5, 9, 16, 24, 30, 31–33, 37–40, 198. *See also* Amazonian cultures: circularity of all things among; linearity
Lord, Albert Bates, 69, 202, 208n3, 212n1
lugar (space), 131, 136, 167, 199

malagri supay spirit, 35
manioc: beer, 34, 87–88, 91, 103–104, 142–144, 149, 191–192; gardens, 177–179, 181, 221; as a metaphor for humans, 21, 30–32, 40, 198, 212n7, 214
Mannheim, Bruce, 2, 83, 101, 180
Marañón River (Peru), 69, 117, 137, 141
McNeil, David, 4
mimesis, 3, 60–61, 68–69, 79, 95, 97, 99, 207n5
moon: and axis mundi, 171, 208n2; gesture,

66; and Iluku song, 98, 199; man, 22, 58–65, 67–71, 98, 135, 164, 166, 168, 209n3; relation of, to other celestial bodies, 78
multimodality, 4, 18, 21–22, 39–40, 80, 172, 197–198
mundopuma: feminine figure of, 150–151; general story of, 59, 135, 156, 166–167, 184, 186; masculine figure of, 142–145; online references to, 219, 221
music: and axis mundi, 59; body and, 23, 81; features of Quichua, 83–84, 92, 98, 212n8; and history, 94; Runa Paju (modern), 172–177, 180–181, 183–186, 194–195, 211n1; semiotic complexity of, 1–3, 5, 11, 21–22, 99, 198–202; and spoken word, 15–16, 60, 79; and status, 91; *takina* (shamanic), 33–39, 81; translation of, 12; Twins and, 144, 149–150, 152–153, 156, 166; violin, 52–57, 86–87

Napo Quichua: dialect of, 101–103, 206n12; Iluku story of, 70; imagery in, 43–44; musical practices of, 53, 182, 186, 189, 190, 192, 211n1; storytelling practices of, 14, 19, 22–23, 72, 158, 171, 198–200; Twins stories of, 100, 114, 135–136, 143–144, 150, 209n1; views on shamanism, 80–81, 207–208n10, 208n11. *See also* Napo Runa
Napo River, 102–103, 105, 124, 143, 158, 218, 219
Napo Runa: aesthetic patterning of forms among, 1, 16, 180, 193–194, 202; communities threatened by petroleum extraction, 13; concept of civilization, 58, 71; concept of jaguar among, 101, 103–104, 114; healing among, 25, 28, 30; history of, 205n1; trips to salt mines of, 37; women's power among, 97, 99. *See also* Napo Quichua
nature, 10–12, 57, 206n9, 208n1
Nuckolls, Janis B., 2–3, 16, 38, 43, 80–81, 83–84, 95, 101, 109

oil: as represented in ceramics of Amazonian Quichua peoples, 185–186; as threat to Napo Runa culture, 13
Omaguas, 175, 205n1
Ong, Walter, 6–7, 206nn5–7
Ongota (community), 103, 218–219
orality, 2–3, 6–10, 14, 19, 202, 206nn6–7

pacha (time-space), 14, 30, 135–136, 173, 197, 199, 209n2
Pano (community), 34, 42, 71, 81, 86–87, 102–103, 105, 124–125; petroglyphs near, 159–162

Pano River, 103, 105, 124–125
perspectivism: as defined by experience, 96, 170, 189, 192, 202; theory of, 10–12, 23, 206n10
petroglyphs: of Napo region, 22, 32, 34, 95–96, 103, 125, 206n11; as sites of inscribed textuality, 200, 218, 220; Verna Grefa's story describing origins of, 157–162, 171
place (philosophical concept of), 12–15, 30–31, 201–202
power. See *ushay* (power)
Puma Rumi (petroglyph), 124–125, 159–162, 200, 220
Puma Yacu River, 160–161, 200, 220
puma yuyu (plant), 83, 100, 103–104, 114, 199, 218

Quechua (Peru), 14, 101–102, 180, 210n9, 210n11
Quichua (Ecuador): dialects within, 101–103; evidentials in, 38; ideophonic usage in, 109; language shift of, toward Spanish of, 159, 193. *See also* Amazonian Quichua language; Napo Quichua; Quechua (Peru)
Quijos, 205n1

Rothenberg, Jerome, 2, 24
rubber: boom, 21–22, 79, 94, 97, 189, 199, 209n2, 210n2; as used by Twins to kill birds of prey, 137–138, 156; women's songs about era of, 87, 90–91, 217

sadness, 66, 84–85, 87, 91, 140, 147, 182, 187
samay (soul/breath): aesthetics of, 28–29, 37–39, 53, 207n2; bird-human relatedness via, 97–98; as defining of music, 174–175, 194; as energy present in all things, 10, 31–33; kinship as defined by, 142, 158; and shamanism, 80–82
Sapo Rumi: community of, 49, 54, 103, 150, 157–158, 161–162; founders of, 91; online materials pertaining to, 214–215, 217, 219–221; petroglyph of, 95–96, 157–158, 161–162, 200; spiritual history of, 33–35, 37, 40; women's song about, 95–96
savage slot (concept), 6, 15
scenes, identification and analysis of. *See* verse analysis
Secoya, 175
Seeger, Anthony, 25, 79, 173, 195
Shackelford, Malcom, 213
shamanism: and *ayahuasca*, 28, 33–34, 53, 81; and blowing, 38–39, 214; and *brugmansia*,

25; and Christianity, 80, 192, 208n11; and cleansing, 26, 29, 33, 35, 38, 209n7, 214; dark forms of, 7, 29, 80–81; feminine arts of, 22, 79–99, 199; and imagination, 24, 54, 81, 83, 207n3; and mountains, 35–36, 42; music of, in myths, 140, 148–150, 152–154, 166–167; and nettles, 182; online materials pertaining to, 214; and rocks, 34, 36–37, 59, 158, 197–198, 200; in Runa Paju music, 177, 181; and storytelling, 23–28, 30–34, 80–82, 99, 103–104, 135–136, 156, 197–203; and tobacco, 28, 33–35, 164; and vapor baths, 25–30, 39, 198, 201; variation of specialists in, 80–81; and violin, 53; women's music as practice of, 80, 82, 94; and *yachak* music, 33–39. *See also* shape-shifting; *takina*; *ushay* (power); *yachak*; *yachay*
shape-shifting, 17, 22, 61, 64, 79, 99, 199. *See also* perspectivism; *and various subentries under* Amazonian cultures
Sherzer, Joel, 2, 104
Shiguango, Fermin, 21, 25–29, 43–44, 53, 103–104, 198, 203, 214–215, 218
Shiguango, Serafina, 91–97, 99, 217
Shiguango, Sharmiat, 207–208n10
Shiguango, Súnzure, 219
Shuar, 82, 175
sinzhi warmi (strongwoman), 80–81, 84, 99
Siona, 175
smell: of healing plants, 23–24, 28, 30; of humans as food to jaguars, 105, 118, 143, 146; as manifestation of spirits, 33–35
somatic poetry; concept of, 5, 10, 21, 23–25, 30–33, 39–40, 207n2; as defining of storytelling, 201, 203; relation of, to experience, 170, 172; Runa Paju as a genre of, 174, 198
soul. See *samay* (soul/breath)
sound: aesthetics of, 108–109; of the Amazonian violin, 53; and attraction, 22, 150, 199; and death, 137, 145; and ideophones, 68, 109–110, 114; as made by mountain beings, 44, 47; as manifestation of love/desire, 58; mimesis of, 60, 98–99; and multimodal complexity, 24, 29; and music, 173, 177–179, 181, 183, 191, 194, 207–208n10; and orality, 9; and perspectivism, 12; place-making and, 32; storytelling and, 42, 69; supralinguistic meanings of, 37–40; and textuality, 59; and translation, 15–17
space: Edward Casey's philosophical concept of, 12–15, 30, 32; Napo Quichua conceptualization of time and, 14, 30; and time as

video technology. *See* digital technology

Viveiros de Castro, Eduardo, 5, 10, 23, 79, 104, 206n1

volcano, 43, 46–51, 215

vultures, 137, 140–142, 156, 188, 219

Wagner, Roy, 173, 185, 211n3

Wasila Mountain, 35–37, 207, 214

website for this book, 16, 18, 42, 86, 101, 105, 144, 213

Wesch, Michael, 4, 18,

Whitehead, Neil L., 80–81, 94, 174, 191

Whitten, Dorothea S., 8, 32, 53, 69, 70, 97, 193

Whitten, Norman E., Jr.: on aesthetics of indigenous Amazonians, 53, 58, 69, 173, 193; on birds as masters of verticality, 97; on counterpower, 8, 32, 195; shamanistic recording of, 53, 181, 212n8

Wibbelsman, Michelle, 59

yachak, 21, 25, 33–34, 53–54, 80, 198–199

yachay, 25, 34, 167

Yekuana, 7–8, 158

Yumbos Chawamangos, Los, 175, 190, 221

Michael A. Uzendoski is an associate professor of modern languages and linguistics at Florida State University and the author of *The Napo Runa of Amazonian Ecuador.*

Edith Felicia Calapucha-Tapuy is a native of Napo, Ecuador, and a translator of Napo Quichua stories and songs.

The University of Illinois Press
is a founding member of the
Association of American University Presses.

———————————————————————

Designed by Jim Proefrock
Composed in 10.7/13 Dante
with Trade Gothic display
at the University of Illinois Press
Manufactured by Thomson-Shore, Inc.

University of Illinois Press
1325 South Oak Street
Champaign, IL 61820-6903
www.press.uillinois.edu